Education in Cyberspace

The use of online learning environments is now widespread in higher education, and there is a wealth of literature providing practical advice on how to teach online, develop courses and ensure effective pedagogical practice. Up until now there has, however, been relatively little work which considers the broader social and cultural contexts within which the new technologies for learning are situated.

This book provides a fresh perspective on current thinking in e-learning for higher education. It challenges orthodox assumptions about the role of technology in the teaching and learning of the future, and explores more varied and wider-reaching conceptual frameworks for learning in cyberspace.

Featuring a group of respected and experienced contributors working from a broad range of theoretical perspectives, *Education in Cyberspace* will be valued by anyone interested in the changes undergoing educational theory and practice in the digital age.

Ray Land is Professor of Higher Education Development at the University of Coventry, UK. **Siân Bayne** researches and develops e-learning at the University of Edinburgh, UK.

Education in Cyberspace

**Edited by Ray Land and
Siân Bayne**

RoutledgeFalmer
Taylor & Francis Group

LONDON AND NEW YORK

First published 2005
by RoutledgeFalmer
2 Park Square, Milton Park, Abingdon, Oxon, OX14 4RN

Simultaneously published in the USA and Canada
by RoutledgeFalmer
270 Madison Ave, New York, NY 10016

RoutledgeFalmer is an imprint of the Taylor & Francis Group

Typeset in Times by Wearset Ltd, Boldon, Tyne and Wear
Printed and bound in Great Britain by MPG Books Ltd, Bodmin

British Library Cataloguing in Publication Data
A catalogue record for this book is available from the British Library

Library of Congress Cataloging in Publication Data
A catalog record for this book has been requested.

ISBN 0-415-32882-9

Contents

Contributors   vii
Acknowledgements   viii

Introduction   1
SIÂN BAYNE AND RAY LAND

PART 1
Cultures   9

1 **New technologies, new identities: the university in the
   informational age**   11
   CAROLINE PELLETIER

2 **Deceit, desire and control: the identities of learners and
   teachers in cyberspace**   26
   SIÂN BAYNE

PART 2
Discourses   43

3 **Ambulating with mega-fauna: a scholarly reflection on
   *Walking with Beasts***   45
   BRUCE DOUGLAS INGRAHAM

4 **History in the digital domain**   55
   MARK POSTER

5 **Metadata vs educational culture: roles, power and
   standardisation**   72
   MARTIN OLIVER

PART 3
Environments 89

**6 Words, bridges and dialogue: issues of audience and
addressivity in online communication** 91
COLLEEN McKENNA

**7 Nobody knows you're a dog: what amounts to context in
networked learning?** 105
CHRISTOPHER R. JONES

8 Learning from cyberspace 117
GLYNIS COUSIN

**9 Towards highly communicative e-learning communities:
developing a socio-cultural framework for cognitive change** 130
ANDREW RAVENSCROFT

PART 4
Subjects 147

10 Embodiment and risk in cyberspace education 149
RAY LAND

**11 Screen or monitor? Issues of surveillance and disciplinary
power in online learning environments** 165
RAY LAND AND SIÂN BAYNE

Index 179

Contributors

Siân Bayne researches and develops e-learning at the University of Edinburgh.

Glynis Cousin is Academic Development Adviser at the Centre for Academic Practice, University of Warwick.

Bruce Ingraham is a Teaching Fellow at the University of Teesside.

Chris Jones is Research Lecturer in the Department of Educational Research, Lancaster University.

Ray Land is Professor of Higher Education Development at Coventry University.

Colleen McKenna is Lecturer in Academic Literacies at University College, London.

Martin Oliver is Senior Lecturer in ICT in Education at the Institute of Education, University of London.

Caroline Pelletier is a Researcher at the Institute of Education, University of London.

Mark Poster is Professor of History at the University of California, Irvine.

Andrew Ravenscroft is Deputy Director and Principal Research Fellow at the Learning Technology Research Institute (LTRI) of London Metropolitan University.

Acknowledgements

Thanks to the Oxford Centre for Staff and Learning Development for permission to publish Chapter 11, 'Screen or Monitor? Issues of surveillance and disciplinary power in online learning environments'. An earlier version of this chapter first appeared in C. Rust (ed.) (2002) *Improving Student Learning Using Learning Technologies*, Oxford: OCSLD.

Introduction

Siân Bayne and Ray Land

Education in cyberspace, more often referred to as e-learning or online learning, is an area the cultural impact of which remains substantially under-theorised. Much of the currently available literature on approaches to teaching and learning in cyberspace – and there is a great deal of it – tends to remain predominantly pragmatic, focused on technical or operational issues and evaluation research. Such approaches, focusing on the new learning environments in terms of their enhancement value and their ability – or inability – to foster effective learning as we currently understand it, are clearly valuable. Yet they often fail to step back and consider the broader social, cultural and theoretical contexts within which our technologies for learning are situated. The technological paradigm shift with which we are engaged – viewed by many as heralding a new media age – is prompting us to reconsider the very basis upon which we understand how pedagogical cultures operate within institutions of higher education.

This book represents an attempt to take this step back, in order to explore more varied, and possibly richer, ways of theorising the contexts and cultures of education in cyberspace. The essays in this volume originate from a small international gathering – the Ideas in Cyberspace Education symposium (ICE) – held in the English Lake District late in 2002, in which the possibilities for a greater diversity of theorisation in this area were explored. We have collected here a representative selection of the differing theoretical frameworks that were offered in the papers presented at the symposium. These included perspectives that drew on poststructuralist analysis, activity theory, cybercultural theory, the work of Foucault, Bakhtin, Vygotsky, McLuhan, Lacan and Derrida, to name but a few. The issues that emerged from the discussions at ICE tended to focus around the cultures, subjectivities, discourses and environments of cyberspace and we have found it helpful to use these broad areas as framing devices for this book. It is our hope that the book will begin to address the need – recognised by many who were involved in this symposium – for more fully theorised perspectives on the emergent cultures and pedagogies of education in cyberspace.

Cultures

Part 1 is concerned with the broad cultural contexts of online learning, and is introduced by Caroline Pelletier's analysis of the university in the informational age. Her chapter offers a sustained reflection on the impact of new technologies on the university, and sets a wide-reaching agenda which provides a useful context for the book as a whole. Taking account of technology as a social phenomenon, Pelletier argues that new technologies interact with other cultural forces, such as globalisation and post-modernism, to create new forms of institutional and individual identity. Her chapter considers technology's cultural and political significance for pedagogic relationships and for the university's function in society. Although much attention has been focused on the transformation of the university in recent years, the role played by technology in such transformation has, according to Pelletier, not been theorised significantly. As a result, our perception of the role of technologies within educational contexts has tended to lack sophistication.

Pelletier acknowledges that there is a need for the practical guidance that constitutes much of the currently available literature on education in cyberspace, but argues that too specific a focus on technical capability runs the risk of undermining the potential for the transformation of educational practices through technology. That networked technologies do not merely channel the same information differently but also work to constitute new forms of action and interaction is a theme taken up by Pelletier and revisited from different perspectives elsewhere in the volume. Choices about how the university engages in technological change are, Pelletier argues, driven by the ideological positions it holds. Its engagement with new media must therefore involve the university in the development of a *political* consciousness. This opening chapter thus identifies questions which are key to the book as a whole. How are new technologies interacting with other cultural forces, such as globalisation and postmodernism, to reconstitute both the university and its subjects? In what ways can new technologies help the university thrive in a social context undergoing radical transformation? And – Pelletier's key point – what *ideological* choices does the university make when it decides on the mode of its engagement with the new technologies for learning?

Siân Bayne's chapter works from a perspective similar to that of Pelletier, in that it considers some of the ways in which identity is reconfigured through the mediations of technology. However, where Pelletier takes a broad view of the place and nature of the academy in the digital age, Bayne rather explores the modes of identity formation of individual learners and teachers within computer-mediated learning environments. Her approach combines discussion of learners' and teachers' accounts of identity formation online with an over-arching metaphor drawn from classical mythology, seeing in the myth of Arachne drawn from Ovid's

Metamorphoses a useful allegory of the clash of online and embodied modes of identity formation. This chapter describes the online environment as forging fundamental change in the ways in which identities are formed, seeing the new modes as creating significant unease among learners and teachers engaged with online spaces. Learning to work with these new modes of identity formation is, Bayne argues, key in beginning to come to terms with the new cultures, and the new pedagogies, of the digital age.

Discourses

Part 2 of the book, concerned with the discourses of cyberspace, opens with Bruce Ingraham's ironically titled 'Ambulating with megafauna'. Ingraham's chapter builds on his earlier studies of scholarly rhetoric in digital media, and explores the possibility of a scholarly discourse conducted within terms other than those normalised through the mediation of print. By analysing the BBC's interactive television series *Walking with Beasts*, he considers one model for an alternative scholarly form – the interactive multimedia documentary. Is it possible for argument conducted using a media mix similar to that of the *Walking with Beasts* series to be considered as 'scholarly'? What is the relation between the form of scholarly argument and its legitimation? And what critical and presentational skills will we need to nurture in ourselves and our students if we are to engage in scholarly discourse mediated by non-print technologies?

A different perspective is brought to bear on the question of scholarly discourse and practice within the digital domain by Mark Poster. Considering cyberspace from the perspective of a practising historian, Poster considers to what extent the shift from print to the digital affects academic disciplines – his primary example is that of history – which depend upon stable symbolic records. Poster considers a point which is key in many of the essays offered here when he asks, 'Is digitisation simply a more efficient means of reproduction, storage and transmission of documents, whose availability in space and time is enhanced for the application by historians of research techniques and methods? Or does digitisation cause an alteration for historians in the constitution of truth?'. In pursuing these questions he raises a complex set of issues which historians urgently need to address as their discipline encounters the new discursive forms and practices. As history web sites proliferate, constructed by a wide range of individuals, with equally wide degrees of qualification, how do we establish the academic legitimacy and authenticity of the texts they contain? Indeed, how do we decide who 'counts' as a bona fide historian? What is more, the differences between the relatively stable print archive and networked, digital data is prompting profound change in the way historical data is perceived, constructed and used. The latter, Poster argues, is fluid, accessible, open to alteration, transformation and re-distribution by a potentially global collective of consumer-producers. In such circumstances, how we understand the 'integrity' of a text, and the way in which historical 'truth' is inscribed in it, become matters open to urgent question.

In his overview of the changes undergoing his own subject area, Poster presents a compelling review of the way in which the new media age might work to affect every aspect of a discipline, encompassing not only a transformative effect on text, subject, method and pedagogy, but presenting a profound challenge to its fundamental epistemological assumptions. He raises issues which are key not just to historians but to academics, teachers and students of all disciplines who are finding aspects of their traditional practice migrating into cyberspace.

Martin Oliver is also concerned with the ways in which shifts in technology might impact on the practices of academics working in cyberspace. His chapter takes a sustained and detailed look at one particular aspect of digitisation – the role of metadata within higher education. Metadata is the 'tagging' for searchability of digitised 'learning objects' which can then be shared across programmes and institutions – an apparently straightforward and unproblematically useful instance of technological enhancement which, as Oliver demonstrates, actually has profound implications for the construction of academic roles and power relations within the academy. While acknowledging its potential benefits in terms of the management of digitised information, Oliver sees metadata as having a tendency to move us towards an instrumental, performative view of educational processes. In proposing metadata and the sharing of learning objects as the 'saviours' of higher education, there is a tendency to deny the culturally specific, tacit, responsive elements of teaching in favour of a move which sees learning as being largely about access to information, irrespective of the particular, situated contexts within which learning takes place. Metadata, Oliver argues, imposes a reductive terminology on the complexity of the language we use to talk about learning and learning materials, and has the potential to contribute towards a view of education in which the role of the academic is marginalised and educational diversity is denied. Despite the tendency of its proponents to construct metadata as a natural path for progress in the electronic 'delivery' of learning it rather, as Oliver suggests, represents a problematic move which has far-reaching implications for the way in which we understand the role of the academic and the project of education itself.

Environments

Part 3 of the book begins with Colleen McKenna's chapter exploring issues of audience and addressivity in online communication. Whereas much of the theoretical work on online communication has focused on how people read and interpret digital information, this chapter considers the other side of the bridge and interrogates the virtual audience and its impact on online utterance. In doing this McKenna draws on theories of dialogic discourse, specifically the notion of language as a territory shared by both addressor and addressee. More particularly, her chapter considers the complexity of audience online, and the impact of this on communication and identity construction in email, virtual learning environments and web-based hypertext documents. She draws on Bakhtin's argument that both speaking subject *and* addressee determine the content of what is uttered. If we apply such thinking to online communication, she suggests, we can begin to explore the significance of the ways in which audience is constructed via the new technologies. The writer of an email, for example, controls and imposes a certain hierarchy on his or her audience by using the 'To', 'Cc' and 'Bcc' fields, but the fluidity and distributability of email text means that it is at the same time removed from the control of its writer through its capacity to be cut, pasted and forwarded to multiple, unknown individuals and groups. In learning to use email, we also learn to negotiate this unknowability of audience. McKenna applies a similar analysis to the texts generated in virtual learning environments and to the writing and publication of hypertext documents on the web. Throughout her chapter, she examines issues of addressivity with reference to online education and the specificities of online text to which students must be alert in order to engage meaningfully in electronic communication. In particular she raises the question of how student writers manage the complex nature of audience online, and to what extent multiple audience determines the content of discourse. As she points out, the act of writing an essay for a familiar tutor is distinctly different from that of 'publishing a web document to an unknowable audience'.

The unknowability of internet audiences is a theme which is continued by Chris Jones in his chapter on context in networked learning. Much as the writer of an email exercises only limited control over the dissemination of his or her text, so the designer of the networked learning environment, Jones suggests, confronts limits in the extent to which he or she is able to exercise control over the context within which his or her online classroom is used. If face to face learning convention has evolved in such a way that it allows teachers considerable control over the learning experiences of their students, the 'fluidity' of the online environment and the contexts within which it is deployed tends, according to Jones, to undermine this capacity to control. Working within this theme of the increased unknowability of students' learning contexts online, and stressing throughout the importance of socially situated theories of learning, Jones' discussion is broad-ranging. He discusses the problem of technological determinism within UK policy initiatives, provides a thoughtful critique of relational approaches to learning, and anchors his discussion in an analysis of students' own experiences of the evolving contexts within which networked learning takes place.

Jones' contention is that policy initiatives relating to learning and the internet are deterministic to the extent that they are driven by a belief in the ability of technology to transform education, rather than an interest in the pedagogical principles which might drive the adoption of technology. Glynis Cousin, however, takes a contrasting view in her contribution, which argues against the over-simplistic adoption of truisms such as 'the pedagogy must lead the technology'. For Cousin, such a perspective draws on an unhelpful division between pedagogy and environment, and between human subject and technological artefact. Cousin argues rather that any new communication technology works towards the partial reconstruction of the subjectivities of its users and their understanding and agency within the world, creating new opportunities and new problems for the ways in which they think, feel and act. Her argument is that technologies are constitutive of our identities and for this reason we cannot afford to regard them as 'mere instruments'. Discussion about how to address questions of student engagement with learning technologies must take place within an understanding that their adoption involves us in a shift into a new media paradigm in which learner, teacher and the task of education itself are at least partially re-formed. Cousin's chapter ends with a consideration of the ways in which Deleuze and Guattari's rhizome might help us to conceptualise such new modes of engagement.

Part 3 ends with Andrew Ravenscroft's chapter and his attempt to move away from case-based accounts of dialogue within online learning environments towards an analysis capable of embracing more theorised accounts of learning and communication online. By considering dialogical theories of learning, discourse analysis and dialogue modelling techniques, the chapter investigates the cognitive features and socio-cultural conditions that would characterise more naturalistic e-learning environments and communities. Such environments would need to foster and support the forms and patterns of dialogue interaction, or 'dialogue games', that would hopefully lead to the adaptive cognitive changes desired. Ravenscroft's chapter is informed by an expansive assessment of social theory and its application to e-learning, and ends with an attempt to formulate a framework for learning which is capable of embracing the specificities of the virtual community.

Subjects

The first chapter in Part 4 is Ray Land's investigation of the theme of embodiment within virtual learning spaces. The 'screening' of the body and the textual formation of identity within such spaces introduces a fluidity to the process of subjectivity construction which many find disquieting. Learning subjects within such spaces often appear to find the experience of communicating online to be 'cold' and inauthentic in comparison to face to face learning. Through a critique of Dreyfus' preoccupation with the pedagogically valuable 'riskiness' that (according to Dreyfus) only embodied learning contexts can bring, Land works towards an alternative perspective which places more value for learners on the reconfigured embodiment experienced in cyberspace.

The theme of the constitution of the subject in online learning spaces is continued in the final chapter by Ray Land and Siân Bayne. This considers the implications of the surveillance or 'student tracking' capabilities of virtual learning environments (VLEs). Alongside their tools for communication, assessment and so on, VLEs tend to integrate sophisticated, very easy-to-use methods of generating detailed data about individual students' use of the learning environment. Drawing on Foucault's writing on panoptic power, and on Poster's extension of this into the idea of the 'super-panopticon', Land and Bayne explore the implications of this kind of surveillance for learners and teachers.

The ideas presented in this volume are diverse, and they emerge from a range of rather different theoretical perspectives, yet they share an openness to the idea that, in cyberspace, education needs – or tends – somehow to be conducted *differently*. The nature of this difference, and the extent to which pedagogical transformation ought to be driven by technological change, are issues which are very much open to debate. There are, however, shared areas of concern: the effect on learners and teachers of the fluidity and unknowability of online text and subject; the need to devise pedagogies and learning opportunities which work with the specificities of the digital environment; the importance of maintaining a view of the situatedness of the learning subject; issues relating to the exercise of power within online environments, particularly managerial power, and the urgent need to look beyond the preoccupation with instrumentality and performativity which still dominates much discussion of the role of technology within higher education.

The diversity of the volume is in a sense an indication of the dynamism and interdisciplinarity of this area of study, an area which we hope will gain in influence and scope, while maintaining its richness and variety.

Part 1
Cultures

1 New technologies, new identities

The university in the informational age

Caroline Pelletier

Introduction

For the last fifteen years, the university has been suffering from an identity crisis. Under the impact of globalization and postmodernism, the university has been undermined sociologically and epistemologically (Barnett 2003). In a globalized, knowledge economy, universities have been co-opted as instruments of economic growth and social inclusivity whilst competing not only among themselves but also with scores of new knowledge producers, such as corporations, consultancies, research centres and think tanks. Just as universities have moved centre stage economically, the value of their basic resources – knowledge, truth and reason – has been deflated by postmodernism, with its emphasis on language, power and local narratives. A debate has ensued about the positive and negative implications for the university and, more fundamentally, about whether the university retains credibility either as a functioning institution or as a concept embodying certain ideals.

These transformations have been analysed from different perspectives. Scott emphasizes the impact of the shift from an elite to a mass higher education system, linking massification to the closer subordination of higher education to national political purposes (1998a, 1998b, 1995). Gibbons *et al.* focus on the transformation of knowledge production, with the new mode characterized by social accountability, reflexivity and problem solving in a practical rather than a cognitive context (1994). Delanty tackles the university's cultural agenda, noting higher education's role in supporting a more cosmopolitan version of citizenship (2001). Barnett places emphasis on the complexity of institutional management, examining how it has addressed competing ideological projects, such as quality, entrepreneurialism and competition (2003, 2000).

In most of these accounts, however, there has been little theorization of the role played by technology, despite widespread recognition of its importance. This omission has hampered a critique of the implications of technology within the university, and produced a plethora of crude ideas about its potential.

The literature on educational technology has not always proved helpful. In discussing the significance of new media for universities, it refers largely to their technical capabilities: how virtual learning environments enhance the experience of distance learning students, how electronically available resources aid research. Technology is understood largely in terms of the content it supports and the learning experience it stimulates. Such approaches are clearly useful and necessary, but they can often neglect to analyse the social, historical and institutional contexts within which technology is situated and used.

According to Cuban (1986) it is precisely this failure to appreciate the social context within which teachers and learners operate which has historically undermined the effort to transform educational practices through technology. Educational technologies, as Cuban emphasizes, are not simply the outcome of technological advance but the result of social and institutional demands which technology helps to fulfil. In this sense, technologies are systems of cultural transmission, creating new contexts within which existing social interests express themselves.

In the case of new media, these contexts are characterized by a shift in the flow of information. Networked technologies bring to an end the era of traditional mass communication that instituted a fundamental break between producers and receivers of information (Slevin 2000). In one-way mass communication – for example, printed books – the reciprocity and interdependency between providers and receivers is relatively straightforward; the reader reflects on the book in isolation from the author who wrote it; the book's authority is established by its published status, that is, by its fixity; the user is separate from the knowledge production process. Current pedagogies and organizational structures within the university are heavily dependent on this pattern of information flow. The two-way nature of new media challenges these practices by allowing users and producers to interact. One-way communication gives way to dialogue, shifting the focus of interaction from the transmission of knowledge to its negotiation.

The consequences of these technical characteristics are not pre-determined. Interactivity can introduce new voices into the university, enabling perhaps more collaborative patterns of knowledge development, and more poststructuralist forms of subjectivity which Poster (1995, 1990) describes in terms of the mode of information. But they can also facilitate automated and repetitive testing, objectifying the student's intellectual development, reinstating the figure of the autonomous rational learner in order better to submit them to an instrumental performative agenda (Lyotard 1984).

New media's potential is realized at a particular time and place. In the university, technology is compounding the institution's identity crisis. The various power brokers – such as the state, the academic community, corporations, civic organizations – enlist the help of technology to advance their own arguments and marginalize competing conceptions. They do so by presenting over-determined perspectives on the implications of technology for the university. New media are seen as having inherent consequences for the university's practices and beliefs. To use Barnett's term, technology is an ideology, similar in nature to other ideological projects within the university such as managerialism, entrepreneurialism or access (2003).

My aim in this chapter is to challenge deterministic conceptions of technology by emphasizing that it offers the university a set of choices. Those choices are not unlimited but bounded within our historical situation. New media, alongside globalization and postmodernism, are entering the university and the university will need to respond.

My argument has three parts. In the first, I pick out some central arguments from the globalization literature and highlight the context within which new media are deployed in the university. My aim is to emphasize that globalization combines contradictory, competing forces and that its consequences, therefore, are not determined. I go on to examine the options which new media hold for the university in terms of pedagogy and, in the third part, in terms of its future as an institution. My argument is that in order to identify and distinguish between the choices which new media present, the university requires a political consciousness – 'political' with a small 'p', as I am not rallying support for any particular form of politics. The university will inevitably make choices in the way it uses technology. The danger is that it will view these choices as purely technical matters, rather than ideological battles that have ramifications for the politics of globalization as they are played out in the university.

Globalization and the university

Many theorists adopt a deterministic view of globalization. In Castells' work on the network society (2000, 1997), networked technology, free capital flows and technocratic capitalism are inseparably bound together. This determinism stems from a failure to distinguish between globalization as a sociological phenomenon (the spread of global communication networks, the consequent reordering of time and space, etc.) and globalization as a political project (the movement for free capital flows). As a result, sociological causes of globalization, such as information networks among other elements, are seen as having an inherent political identity. This obscures an analysis of the significance of globalization for the university and unnecessarily restricts the options available to it.

Two themes from the globalization literature can illustrate this point: the decline of the nation state and the reconstitution of space.

The decline of the nation state

The decline of the nation state has transformed the body politic. Once national citizens, we now assume significance as consumers and global citizens. Cast within the image of the nation state, the university's identity undergoes a similar transformation, ceasing to be an institution of national culture, justified by the meta-narrative of emancipation, and instead providing the knowledge, skills and beliefs necessary to a globalized economy and governance system.

Some theorists, such as Barnett, have explored the creative opportunities opened up as a consequence (2000). The university is liberated from its duty to indoctrinate a parochial national culture and is intellectually rejuvenated by embracing the multiplicity of discourses in society. It no longer replicates elitist traditions, and instead assumes a more democratic role, experimenting with the different cognitive frameworks given voice by cultural fragmentation. As knowledge is less important than attitude in the fast-paced globalized economy, the university need no longer objectify students as vessels of knowledge, but can focus instead on enabling them to determine their own subjectivities and cultivate their ability to respond to change. Uncertainty and complexity here are a universal cultural conditions, affecting all social agents alike.

Other theorists, such as Sennett (1998), argue that globalization has not led to creative, multicultural possibilities but to a more exploitative form of capitalism. The function of education, according to this scenario, becomes the aversion of risk. By generating technical skills for employability, the university seeks to deliver a new but fragile version of security, one based on human capital. From this perspective, the university becomes the ally of a ruthless economic system, reskilling individuals without giving them a stable sense of security, be it material or ontological. Risk, complexity, the fragmentation of identity, may be cultural phenomena but they can be deployed as political strategies. Uncertainty is not politically innocent. Whilst liberating for some, it is debilitating for others.

The problem with Barnett's perspective is that it focuses on globalization's sociological attributes and overlooks its political context. Sennett, however, does not examine how globalization opens up new avenues for changing the situation it describes.

A third perspective is possible. One could argue that the university would be failing its learners if it simply despaired of political action or took it as given, as a cultural inevitability. As the university helped create, and continues to sustain, globalization's social conditions, supplying the system with the raw material of growth – knowledge – it seems reasonable to argue that it has a duty to intervene in the resulting social politics. It could be expected to educate in a way that enables individuals to create their own subjectivities, whilst enabling them to resist becoming marginalized labour, prime-tuned for exploitation, as portrayed in Sennett's work.

This requires a political consciousness about the uneven, unequal way globalization affects individuals, and a belief that something positive can be done about it.

In practice, the university has not proved adept at resisting powerful interests, particularly the state. It has maintained a policy of non-interference in society to protect its own academic autonomy. Yet it is precisely this attempt to remain apolitical that is so clamorously partisan. The values which the university is adopting in a globalized world – performativity, the mercantilization of knowledge, the extension of property rights to intellectual matters – are those which have shrunk the measure of what is valuable in the university to what is productive economically.

The reconstitution of space

A second theme within the globalization literature is the reconstitution of space. In the analysis of this phenomenon, the same confusion often arises between the sociological and the political. The argument runs as follows: by allowing interaction to take place in physically disjointed places, new technologies re-define space-specific notions such as 'community' or the 'university' as processes rather than places. For example, the identity of the UK Open University, which uses technology extensively, is not based on location but in terms of information flows between displaced students, tutors and researchers. Process, rather than space, holds the academic community together.

Some theorists go on to argue that these changes in conceptions of space lead to the creation of new elites. Castells (2000, 1997) argues that elites are no longer tied to places but become unified around the globe through networks, producing an internet culture whose identity is not linked to any specific society but to membership of the managerial circles of the informational economy. Castells' argument suggests that those universities historically focused on creating elites would as a result become institutions of ahistorical, acultural learning, detached from specific locales. On the other hand, those universities that define their mission mainly in terms of widening participation would remain rooted in the culture of their locality. This would make higher education a site of structural schizophrenia, between two spatial logics: the space of network flows and space of real places. The disjuncture could worsen social divisions resulting from social groups constructing their identity around either physical, or virtual, time and place. Some might say that this has already happened in higher education, pointing to the division between universities adopting a local mission aimed at widening participation, and those that maintain their exclusivity to target high-flying, high fee-paying audiences.

However, by collapsing the consequences of technology into fears about political globalization, Castells overlooks the possibility that networks might foster cultural dialogue rather than tribalism, exchange rather than schizophrenia. This more optimistic interpretation necessitates a wider understanding of information, encompassing information as culture as well as instrumental data (Delanty 2001). This conception roots information flows in the historical and cultural circumstances of participating actors. The university, in this scenario, would broker cultural knowledge across time and space, promoting inter-cultural exchange rather than tribalism.

My contention is therefore that, in interpreting globalization, maintaining a distinction between the sociological and the political is crucial. Globalization, and the new technologies which enable it, do not inherently express a political ideology. Though bounded by context, social agents do not simply incarnate network logic, be it neoliberal or poststructuralist. Globalization and technology present individuals with a series of choices, not a given horizon.

New media theory and pedagogy

There are many options also in the way the university can deploy educational technologies. To date, however, much of the literature on higher education and new media examines pedagogy in abstract, outside of the institutional setting in which it is to be enacted. For this reason, one often encounters similar problems to those found in the literature on globalization. Theorists such as Castells force a political identity onto sociological phenomena, overlooking the range of political options made available by these phenomena. New media literature is frequently equally deterministic, but its determinism applies to the communicative structure of new technologies and its cultural and pedagogical significance. In focusing on technical aspects, it overlooks the political context within which new media are used.

This can be illustrated by examining two aspects of electronic communication which are particularly prominent in the literature: hypertext and non-linearity; and the social distribution of knowledge and consequent challenge to authority (see, for example, Poster 1995, 1990; Turkle 1997).

Hypertext

What is compelling about hypertext is the way its structure is amenable to deconstruction. By breaking up the linearity of the narrative, special attention is drawn to its constitutive structures. When learners are referred to a website rather than a book, there is no end to the associations they might follow up. Meaning and closure are infinitely deferred (McKie 2000). This changes the educational experience by foregrounding richness of associations and literary modes of interpretation rather than a search for propositional truth. Composition and creativity replace knowledge at the top of the educational agenda. This echoes Barnett's argument regarding the impact of risk and uncertainty (2000).

In practice, however, computers have often been used in education to stifle creativity. As Dutton (1999) and Laurillard (2000) point out, instructional software has tended to emphasize drill and practice rather than composition. In the bureaucratized university, the potential for free exploration is perceived as a sign of disorganization rather than an opportunity for creativity. Like distance learning before it, internet-based learning has more often than not been conceived in terms of systematic progression, with clearly stated learning objectives, regular summaries and limited bibliographies.

The atomization of knowledge on the web page and unitization of learning which it necessitates has encouraged this further. The very potential for disorganization has fostered a radical counter-attack, as seen in the e-University, which conceives of learning as units bolted together rather than in terms of less clearly defined flows of meaning (HEFCE 2000). The rationale is that students need systematic organization and predictable outcomes to exercise consumer choices.

Two-way, decentred communication has not led, in the case of the e-University, to an acceptance of jointly constructed knowledge but rather to an emphasis on product guarantees. The fluidity of the internet, which media theorists proclaim as the condition for its creativity, has in fact fostered a pathological dislike of non-linearity. The reasons for this relate to globalization's social conditions. As Sennett points out, uncertainty has more often led to an aversion of risk rather than creativity.

The social distribution of knowledge

The second argument within the new educational media literature is that, by enabling dialogue between time and place defined groups, electronic communication demystifies hierarchy and promotes solidarity between disadvantaged groups who can share information horizontally. Within the context of the university, the internet is welcomed as a tool for widening access and making the curriculum more democratic, by including voices within it which have not been heard before, such as the post-colonial world, women, part-time workers – voices which have emerged out of globalization's cultural fragmentation. McKie describes the internet as 'an agora, a space for democratic global exchange' (2000: 127). For Laurel, it is a 'manifestation of a huge new wave of narrative vigour and joyous cultural polyphony' (1993: 213).

The optimism of this argument is somewhat defeated by the political context within which new media are used in the university. Participation in higher education is widening, but the values that the university is adopting – performativity, the mercantilization of knowledge, the extension of property rights to intellectual matters – are going unchallenged. With its rhetoric of just-in-time learning, the internet enshrines the notion of productivity in education, and undermines claims for non-instrumental intellectual exchange.

Most educational technology theorists have a positive view of technology, yet they frequently overestimate its autonomy. A two-way decentred system of communication could indeed lead to greater critical questioning of the *status quo*; interactive knowledge formation, which puts dialogue rather than brute facts at the centre of the education process, could prove liberating in its existential focus or at least intellectually stimulating. However, one cannot acknowledge the opportunity for new pedagogies if the focus is primarily on the attributes of the technical medium while ignoring the contexts within which knowledge is produced and received. Given its potential, it is not enough to document how the internet can oppress or liberate. The focus should rather be on the particular kinds of internet participation which perpetuate the oppressive forces within globalization or which release its creative potential.

New media can serve many ends. Their communicative structure cannot be analysed without regard to their potential impact on the university's identity. If, for example, the university defines its mission in terms of intellectual experimentation and democratic politics, new technologies' challenge to modernity's epistemology opens up real opportunities. The interdependence created between producer and user of knowledge, the splintering of disciplinary traditions and the social hierarchies they sustained, and the decline of positivism make for a more dynamic institution. However, these phenomena are all reversible. Should the university focus on technical skills, the decline of the author's authority further legitimates an instrumental and consumerist form of education that entrenches the performative agenda. These are not technical issues but competing ideologies.

This leaves the university steering a difficult course. New technologies, under conditions of globalization, reinforce the drift towards reductive functionalism. However, their communicative structure could serve as a powerful antidote. New technologies therefore do not supply the university with an identity by virtue of their communicative structure; they do not lead it inevitably towards a more poststructuralist future. They do, however, heighten the stakes and complicate the choices, for their creative potential to democratize knowledge can only be realized by taking the risk that they may achieve the exact opposite. The issue is not so much about whether to use technology, but how.

The role of new technologies in definitions of the university

In the wake of globalization, a body of literature has emerged on the identity of the university, suggesting how the institution can be re-engineered to survive the challenges posed by social and economic change, massification and new technology. It is perhaps a measure of the crisis within the sector that many of these blueprints actually leave the university with less scope to exercise the choices created by globalization and new technology, rather than more.

I will examine three of these blueprints, to identify what kind of identity they project for the networked university.

Daniel's mega-university – the panopticon of the modern age?

In his book on the technology-driven mega-university, former vice-chancellor of the Open University John Daniel (1998) defines the university's mission in terms of responding to student needs: the university's survival is dependent on its ability to adapt itself to the demands of its customer base. Educational technology makes this possible by enhancing flexibility and reducing unit costs. The university has little authority to decide how it should be used since 'student needs' dictate the pedagogy. Helpfully, Daniel also knows what those needs are: 'mass training for work and employability [and] the framework of ethics and values that allow them to become self-regulating' (5). Daniel is explicit in arguing that these values are imposed: 'modern communications make it increasingly difficult to impose such frameworks by authority. Education and training are a primary route to responsible citizenship' (5). In the mega-university, student-centred, technology-enabled learning seems to be a euphemism for updated forms of social control.

Daniel's argument expresses some of the hopes that higher education policy makers pin on e-learning, which is that it will open access to education and offer equality of opportunity. E-learning, from this perspective, is a socially progressive solution in a capitalist society, providing skilled employees to the economy and equalizing opportunities across society. In promising to marry social justice with globalized capitalism, it is no coincidence that new technologies have played a key role in the education policies of the Third Way, in the US and the UK. The emphasis on new technologies also bears witness to a shift in definitions of citizenship, with productive employment, or contribution to the economy, as its predominant indicator.

Despite its good intentions, this vision of the technology-enabled university is unpalatable, and has done much to give new technologies a bad name among those in higher education who want a more open, less instrumental role for the university than just disciplining workers. In the way it deploys new technologies, the mega-university sets itself up as a modern-day panopticon (Foucault 1977; see also Chapter 11 of this book). In its version of online learning, the sovereign power of the tutor is replaced with the impersonal and invisible gaze of the facilitator. Student-centred pedagogy, which obscures the facilitator's authority and thus makes it less challengeable, expedites the disciplining of multiple individuals. Precise measurements of progress, which online learning facilitates well, can be provided on an uninterrupted basis, heightening the disciplinary effect that Foucault assigns to examinations. Non-reciprocal surveillance is facilitated through the monitoring of every activity, every contribution to a discussion. Laurillard (2000) says that students can thereby look back over missed discussions or previous students' work. However, such a facility can also be used to set standards for what is normal, identify more quickly what is abnormal, and take measures to rectify it by customizing learning to what are termed 'students' needs' – although the needs of other parties, such as the state or the economy, may be confused with these. Authority is more diffused, but knowledge remains centralized.

Delanty's cosmopolitan project

Other theorists have come forward with less instrumentalist agendas, which seek to preserve for the university a wider role beyond economic growth. Delanty (2001) in his work on the cosmopolitan university emphasizes the multiplicity of cultures and discourses given voice by globalization. In Delanty's vision, the university becomes a site for communication and connectivity. It is not so much an institution as a space for the channelling of discourses created by cultural fragmentation. Delanty locates this space in the collective, public sphere and sees virtual universities as a threat to this vision: 'the virtual university is a privatized institution in that it links the private world of the home with the equally private world of the market' (127). His argument is rooted not so much in the fact that virtual universities are often set up by private corporations, but that technology itself threatens the idea of publicness, in so far as it fragments the public sphere into individual multiplicities. Technology extracts the needs of students from their social context by individualizing them. To have a public sphere, one needs a 'sense of place', a real physical space, 'a communal, residential place beyond the private sphere' (127). Deterritorialization undermines the public domain, which the university is dedicated to serving.

Delanty does not explain why the public domain needs a sense of place. His argument appears rather technophobic, echoing those who believe technology, especially television but now also the internet, inherently undermines community. One objection to his argument might be that put forward by Meyrowitz (1985), that it is only when a 'sense of place' is undermined that the oppressive tendencies of community can be challenged; by enabling communication between groups normally kept separate, political solidarity and thus democracy becomes possible.

A second objection could be that the public domain has become endangered by forces far greater than technology. Delanty also points the finger of blame at multinational corporations, but these would not be so powerful were it not for the support of governments. The public sphere is threatened not so much by market forces as by the democratic state, which has spent much of the last few decades subsuming notions of collectivity to individual wealth creation. The argument that the public sphere is opposed to and overwhelmed by capitalist companies, with new technologies in their train, is a simplification of the situation. Rather, the question is: what does the public domain and the idea of citizenship represent in a democratic society which is gradually emptying out these terms of their meaning? Is it still possible to use such collective and political concepts when the very value of politics is being denied? Delanty identifies a real problem but mistakes its cause.

Protecting the public domain requires more than an effort 'to humanize technology'; it calls for the relegitimation of the public sphere. The doubters to be convinced are not technology users but a disbelieving society, unclear about the alternatives to marketization and privatization and uncertain about what is involved in citizenship at a time of cultural fragmentation.

Delanty interprets the trend towards technology-enhanced learning as an intensification of the West's global-brand, high-technology culture. However, he overlooks how it could equally help realize his democratic cosmopolitan project. With technology, universities can go deeper and wider: deeper in the sense of meeting the needs of social and ethnic groups underrepresented in elite systems and impatient with the old academic culture; wider in the sense that they must take account not only of non-Western intellectual traditions but also of pluralism within the Western tradition. Such plurality makes possible a relatively non-institutional space, as emphasis is placed on communicational interaction rather than on tradition and authority. This is not sufficient to revive a belief in the public sphere, but it can provide a channel for discussing why a public sphere is desirable.

Readings' university of dissensus

Readings' (1996) argument about the ways forward for the university does not focus specifically on the role of technology. However, his vision of the university of dissensus echoes well with much of the new media literature on the impact of new technologies on communication and learning. The philosophy of online education, as developed by McKie (2000) and Sandbothe (2000) among others, resonates well with what Readings advocates.

One of Readings' prime concerns is to be rid of the idea of autonomy in education; teaching needs to be understood as other than the inculcation of an inherent human autonomy, for the notion of the sovereign subject underpins attempts to separate education from the creation of the social bond and enables a purely technical version of learning. Readings rejects what he calls the Sausurrean pedagogical model: 'Such a model tends to emphasize in the classroom situation either the addressee (the student as free subject), the sender (the professor as authority) or the referent (the subject matter as inviolable corpus of knowledge)' (Peterson 1999: 38). Instead, Readings proposes the Bakhtinian model of dialogism. This has many resonances with new media theory on the nature of electronic communication. The main function of the university, Readings' model proposes, is to hold judgement open as a question. Teaching and learning would be rephrased as sites of communicational obligation, but without the goal of arriving at a consensus: 'I am evoking the dialogue form in order to refuse the modernist privileging of the sender over the addressee' (Readings 1996: 155).

It is commonly argued in some new media literature, for example in Poster (1990, 1995), that new technologies challenge such hierarchies that make the professor an absolute authority and students receptacles for the transmission of knowledge. This chimes well with Readings' thesis. The emphasis which electronic communication puts on dialogue, on continuing conversation, defies efforts to put an end to questioning and could thus help realize Readings' recommendations.

The problem with Readings' argument, however, is that whilst resisting the notion of individual autonomy, it enshrines institutional autonomy; that is, it rests on a belief that the university can and should extract itself from the pressures and conditions of the world around it, that it should keep the question of judgement open when, according to its own analysis, capitalist consensus in society more broadly is successfully closing it. It thus disqualifies the university from intervening in society.

Readings' argument is contradictory. Keeping the question of judgement open is dependent on a political belief that is not open to question and that, more importantly, cannot be isolated from the world around it. His argument represents an unrealistic effort to carve out an institutional space for the university outside of society, not a form of social resistance to dominate politics.

Furthermore the university of dissensus can hardly compete as a material force with globalization as a political project, the one with too little identity, the other with too much. Despite the resonance of Readings' argument with the claims of new media theorists, therefore, his is not a credible model for the networked university.

Politics in the university

A weakness in all these blueprints is that they tend to view the university as a blank space, a framework with little identity of its own. Daniel's mega-university is the vacant space of the marketplace, a commercial version of Delanty's open but empty public forum. Readings' university of dissensus is the blank framework that allows others to interact without interference. The university is nothing in its own right; it does not intrude into society but only responds to it. It cannot contribute to the debates in wider society, only serve as a channel for their expression.

In so doing, all three proposals seek to depoliticize the university, or rather multiply its politics, and thus turn it into an institution of culture, of multiculturalism. Such an effort addresses the realities of cultural fragmentation in a globalized world. However, it does not adequately address the realities of conflict in society or the dominance of powerful discourses, such as performativity. As a result, these visions of the university seem poorly equipped to deal with the pedagogical choices called for by new technologies within the context of globalization.

In its deployment of new technologies, the networked university can support efforts to democratize knowledge, challenge disciplinary boundaries and enable a more participative, innovative curriculum. However, it can also use technology to support a world view in which the student is the servant of the economy, whose needs are defined in terms of technical skills and whose inclusion in society is justified largely by the acquisition of those skills.

New technologies raise political problems for the university, problems which reflect wider struggles in a globalized society. The political colours of globalization are not inherent. Similarly, the way new media reshape education and the university is subject to debate. That debate cannot be resolved by appealing to the inherently liberating effect of new media's communicative structure. Nor should it be allowed to end when the needs of the economy are put forward at the expense of other value frameworks, such as citizenship. This is not to deny the university's important responsibility in providing education and training for jobs. But it does emphasize that the university requires certain conditions in society to flourish, such as the opportunity for non-instrumental exchange, dialogue and critique. These are crucial if the university is to foster an education which enables its learners to deal with radical, and socially discriminating, levels of uncertainty and risk in an age of globalization.

Perhaps the most workable proposal for the networked university in an age of globalization is Barnett's ideological institution (2003). Barnett notes that the university has traditionally not declared itself for or against any particular set of values. It sees itself as a ring-master, encouraging debate between contestants taking up different value positions whilst censuring itself on its own values. This is a disingenuous stance as freedom of speech, engagement and criticality are themselves value orientations. Barnett suggests that the university should acknowledge its own ideological commitments, which call for a certain kind of tolerant and generous communicative process. Knowledge and ideology are not opposites, but inseparable partners. Denying this is not only naïve but dangerous, in so far as it leaves the process of knowledge formation to those who cloak their ideologies in technical clothing.

Barnett's argument chimes well with the one made in this chapter. To exercise the choices which new media present, the university needs a political identity, as the learning and knowledge generated through new media are political issues. Feminism formulated a similar argument decades ago in relation to gender studies. New media, like feminism, call for a political consciousness in so far as their origin and use in the university are deeply connected to the political struggles in contemporary society. The way the university deploys new technologies is not a technical issue. Political consciousness is necessary to resist those who would foreclose the argument about the university's use of new media by pointing to the 'realities' of globalization, be they multicultural or economic. Globalization is not an expression of a single ideology but the context within which competing versions of society and the university are currently being debated.

Poster's work on the mode of information indicates that new media spell the end of individual autonomy. One can extend this argument to say that they also spell the end of academic autonomy. The notion of academic autonomy is based on the belief that the university as an institution can and should remain independent of ideological conflicts. Yet the pedagogical opportunities created by new technologies, their capacity to favour performativity as well as more sophisticated, potentially more interesting definitions of education, require the university to implicate itself in the political debates animating society. In its choice of pedagogical approaches with respect to new media, the university will also be choosing its political values and ideological identity.

References

Barnett, R. (2003) *Beyond all Reason: Living with Ideology in the University*, Buckingham: Open University Press.

Barnett, R. (2000) *Realising the University in an Age of Supercomplexity*, Buckingham: Open University Press.

Castells, M. (2000) *The Rise of the Network Society*, vol. 1 of *The Informational Age: Economy, Society and Culture* (2nd edn), Oxford: Blackwell.

Castells, M. (1997) *The Power of Identity*, vol. 2 of *The Informational Age: Economy, Society and Culture*, Oxford: Blackwell.

Cuban, L. (1986) *Teachers and Machines: The Classroom Use of Technology Since 1920*, New York: Teachers College Press.

Daniel, J.S. (1998) *Mega-Universities and Knowledge Media: Technology Strategies for Higher Education*, London: Kogan Page.

Delanty, G. (2001) *Challenging Knowledge: The University in the Knowledge Society*, Buckingham: Open University Press.

Dutton, W.H. (1999) *Society on the Line: Information Politics in the Digital Age*, Oxford: Oxford University Press.

Foucault, M. (1977) *Discipline and Punish: The Birth of the Prison*, London: Allen Lane.

Gibbons, M., Limoges, C., Nowotny, H., Schwartzman, S., Scott, P. and Trow, M. (1994) *The New Production of Knowledge*, London: Sage.

HEFCE (2000) *Business Model for the e-University: Report to the HEFCE by*

PricewaterhouseCoopers, Bristol: Higher Education Funding Council for England.

Laurel, B. (1993) *Computers as Theatre*, Reading, MA: Addison-Wesley.

Laurillard, D. (2000) 'New technologies, students and the curriculum: the impact of communications and information technology on higher education', in Scott, P. (ed.) *Higher Education Reformed*, London: Falmer Press, pp. 133–153.

Lyotard, J.F. (1984) *The Postmodern Condition: A Report on Knowledge*, Manchester: Manchester University Press.

McKie, J. (2000) 'Conjuring notions of place', in Blake, N. and Standish, P. (eds) *Enquiries at the Interface: Philosophical Problems of Online Education*, Oxford: Blackwell, pp. 123–133.

Meyrowitz, J. (1985) *No Sense of Place: the Impact of Electronic Media on Social Behaviour*, New York: Oxford University Press.

Peterson, T.E. (1999) 'Whitehead, Bateson and Readings and the predicates of education', *Educational Philosophy and Theory*, 31(1): 27–41.

Poster, M. (1995) *The Second Media Age*, Cambridge: Polity Press.

Poster, M. (1990) *The Mode of Information*, Chicago: The University of Chicago Press.

Readings, B. (1996) *The University in Ruins*, Cambridge, MA: Harvard University Press.

Sandbothe, M. (2000) 'Media philosophy and media education in the age of the internet', in Blake, N. and Standish, P. (eds) *Enquiries at the Interface: Philosophical Problems of Online Education*, Oxford: Blackwell, pp. 59–77.

Scott, P. (1998a) *The Globalization of Higher Education*, Buckingham: Open University Press.

Scott, P. (1998b) 'Massification, internationalization and globalization', in Scott, P. (ed.) *The Globalization of Higher Education*, Buckingham: Open University Press, pp. 108–129.

Scott, P. (1995) *The Meanings of Mass Higher Education*, Buckingham: Open University Press.

Sennett, R. (1998) *The Corrosion of Character*, New York: WW Norton.

Slevin, J. (2000) *The Internet and Society*, Cambridge: Polity Press.

Turkle, S. (1997) *Life on the Screen: Identity in the Age of the Internet*, London: Phoenix.

2 Deceit, desire and control

The identities of learners and teachers in cyberspace

Siân Bayne

Introduction

How do students and teachers experience the construction of identity online? How do such identities relate to those they inhabit in embodied 'real life'? Employing an over-arching metaphor drawn from Ovid's myth of Arachne, this chapter weaves together theories of the constitution of the subject in cyberspace with the accounts of students and tutors, in order to explore the themes of mutability, deceit and metamorphosis in identity construction online. In particular, it will consider the common perspective emerging from students' accounts in which online modes of identity formation are viewed negatively, as a dangerous deceit or deviance from the 'natural'. These perspectives will be compared with the narratives of tutors for whom, surprisingly, the online space becomes a place in which traditional hierarchies can be re-asserted, and conventionally teacherly identities re-cast.

The myth of Arachne

Ovid tells the story of the metamorphosis of Arachne:

Arachne, the motherless daughter of a cloth dyer, was famous for her skill as a spinner, weaver and clothmaker. Her talent was so renowned that the nymphs would gather around just to watch her working. Everyone knew that she had been taught this skill by Athene, goddess of reason and law, and inventor and teacher of women's arts. Arachne, however, persisted in denying that she owed anything to Athene's teachings, and to prove it she challenged the goddess to a weaving competition. Athene, affronted, agreed, and each began her competing tapestry.

Athene wove a cloth with a central panel showing her victory over Neptune on the Acropolis of Athens, in which, by causing an olive tree to grow from the rock, she laid claim to the city. The corners of her tapestry showed scenes of mortals whose violation of the laws of the gods had caused them to be punished by metamorphosis – Haemon and Rhodope becoming mountains, the queen of the Pygmies becoming a crane, Antigone becoming a stork.

Arachne wove a tapestry showing the metamorphoses undertaken by the gods in order to have intercourse with mortal women. Jupiter is shown as the white bull carrying off Europa, as the swan pinning down Leda, as a satyr, an eagle, a shower of gold, a flame, a shepherd and a snake. Neptune is shown as a bull, a ram, a horse, a dolphin and a bird. Apollo appears as a peasant, a hawk, a lion and a shepherd. Bacchus is a bunch of grapes, and Saturn is shown as in the shape of a horse, siring the centaur Cheiron – half horse, half man.

Athene sees that Arachne's tapestry is flawless. Infuriated by her rival's success, she hits her over the head four times with her weaving shuttle. Arachne, terrified, puts a noose around her neck as if to hang herself. Athene relents and allows her to go on living, but for punishment turns her into a spider hanging from her web, destined forever to spin. (paraphrase of Ovid 1986: 134–138 (book IV, lines 1–147))

Mythical themes

For me, this story represents a mythical encapsulation of a paradigm shift taking place as learning moves into the digital realm. The clearest analogy – that of the mastery of the medium of the web, the woven tapestry – is only part of its richness. This is a story about the power relationship between a teacher and a student; about different, literally competing, ways of creating, or weaving, the world. It is also about mutability, deceit, mutation and metamorphosis – these are to be the central themes of this chapter.

In Athene and Arachne we see represented, respectively, the figures of teacher and student. Athene's tapestry places herself as teacher at the centre – the miracle of her own creativity is celebrated in the representation of the creation of the olive tree. This firm centre anchors the rest of the tapestry, consisting of images of mortals transmuted into animals and objects as punishment by the gods for their pride. In this vision, metamorphosis is a punishment for transgression of the laws of the gods; stability and the rule of law are its key themes, with the stable embodiment of the mortal as the natural state and mutation as a mark of deviance. Athene represents the cartesian subject, the acting subject firmly at the centre of a world ordered by reason.

By contrast, Arachne's tapestry is centreless. No one image holds down and fills with meaning or moral the images which crowd the woven space. In this decentred world metamorphosis becomes a motif of desire, a marker of the union between the mortal and the immortal, an event constitutive of edgily erotic pleasure rather than a punishment for transgression. In challenging the hierarchy of teacher and student, Arachne illustrates other, more fundamental boundary transgressions – those between the mortals and gods, and between the animal and the human. In this sense, it is a cyborg tapestry. Haraway famously constructs the cyborg as a potentially dangerous yet celebrated figure, which

> appears in myth precisely where the boundary between human and animal is transgressed. Far from signalling a walling off of people from other living beings, cyborgs signal disturbingly and pleasurably tight coupling.
>
> (Haraway 1991: 152)

Most closely associated with another boundary transgression – that between human and machine – the cyborg, cybernetic organism, represents an Arachne-like celebration of fluidity:

> a cyborg world might be about lived social and bodily realities in which people are not afraid of their joint kinship with animals and machines, not afraid of permanently partial identities and contradictory standpoints.
>
> (Haraway 1991: 154)

As Hayles has explained:

> Mingling erotically charged violations with potent new fusions, the cyborg becomes the stage on which are performed contestations about the body boundaries that have often marked class, ethnic, and cultural differences. Especially when it operates in the realm of the Imaginary rather than through actual physical operations (which act as a reality check on fantasies about cyborgism), cybernetics intimates that body boundaries are up for grabs.
>
> (Hayles 1999: 84–85)

The two tapestries thus represent competing world views which operate within the various contexts of learning and teaching online. Athene's world of modernity – centred (either on teacher or learner), stable (as far as regards both textuality and the rules governing identity formation and body boundaries), and unambiguous as to hierarchical relations – is challenged by Arachne's vision of a decentred world of creative pleasure in boundary transgression, cyborg identities, 'potent fusions and dangerous possibilities' (Haraway 1991: 154) – the celebration of the fluidity of metamorphosis. The metaphor extends into the arena of learning online in that here pedagogical methods and intentions rooted in principles of textual stability and the dissemination of knowledge among stable, autonomous subjects are often at odds with a medium in which both text and subject are liable to metamorphosis, to the shape-shifting which is so much a feature of our lives in the digital realm.

If Athene represents modernity, reason and law, Arachne perhaps shows us a vision of postmodernity, of the embrace of shape-shifting and the operation of the impulses of desire. Desire, which emerges in Lacanian thought as a consequence of our immersion in language is, as Belsey has described it, an inarticulable desire 'for an imagined originary presence, a half-remembered "oceanic" pleasure in the lost real, a completeness which is desire's final, unattainable object' (Belsey 1994: 5). The relevance of this vision of desire to the concerns of this chapter rests not only in its status as the restless, unknowable opposite of reason – an opposition represented in the two tapestries – but also in the critique of 'oneness' which emerges from Lacanian thought. As Sarup points out, for Lacan the principles of singleness, unity and indivisibility in the human subject have become an 'ideology' attempting to 'close off the gap of human desire' (Sarup 1992: 127). In Lacanian theory the subject is not unified, knowing and knowable; instead it is multiple, diffuse and fragmented, a process rather than a stable entity.

The theme of the subject in process, of the possibility of transformation, of the idea that we as subjects are never complete, never 'finished', will be important in the following sections. These will discuss the transformation or metamorphosis of the subject online, first in general terms, and then by focusing in on narratives of identity formation among online learners and teachers.

The mutable subject online

The internet as a realm in which the potential for metamorphosis of the self is almost limitless has been celebrated since the early days of the medium. The invisibility of the physical body and the opportunities for the linguistic construction of identity in online communication is seen by some to 'literalize Lacan's notion of the self as textual' (Monroe 1999: 70). Turkle's well-known study of internet identities sees online self-creation and expression of multiplicity as part of the broader movement towards the postmodern, flexible self:

> The Internet is another element of the computer culture that has con-
> tributed to thinking about identity as multiplicity. On it, people are
> able to build a self by cycling through many selves ... In its virtual
> reality, we self-fashion and self-create.
>
> (Turkle 1996: 178–180)

Within the classroom context, while giving voice to the multiplicity of the subject is rarely an explicit pedagogical aim, the anonymising and apparently equalising characteristics of computer-mediated communication are often seen to offer benefits to learners beyond the pragmatic ones of freedom from some of the temporal and spatial constraints of 'traditional', on-campus education. Findings which report increased contributions in online discussion of disadvantaged, 'shy' and female students (Alexander 1997; McConnell 1997; Belcher 1999; Kimbrough 1999), the success of the online environment in increasing collaboration among students (Hiltz 2000), and the tendency for online student groups to become less focused on their tutors (Dubrovsky *et al.* 1991; Eldred and Hawisher 1995) all imply, however obliquely, that something shifts at the level of the subject when online learning takes place.

There are grounds, however, for being circumspect about the extent to which Turkle's ideas about the self-creating, self-fashioning internet subject can be applied to the online classroom. First and most obviously, Turkle's study is for the most part of individuals involved in MOOs – real-time, wholly anonymous virtual worlds in which the game of persona creation can be played with few immediate consequences for embodied 'real life'. In the pedagogical context, this is not usually the case. As Monroe points out, 'Anonymity in a networked classroom is a short-lived possibility; before long, an online persona will be fitted with a Real Life body' (Monroe 1999: 76).

Second, the whole concept of self-fashioning and self-creating paradoxically assumes a secure, stable subject somewhere in the background who does the fashioning and creating. It is an image which would sit more neatly in Athene's tapestry, one of a secure subject acting on a world where identity creation has knowable rules, rather than a vision of the subject undergoing the possibly exciting but also deeply risky metamorphosis which takes place at the prompting of desire.

Third, in celebrating the challenge to the liberal subject posed by disembodied communication, there can be a tendency to under-recognise the significance of embodiment (Shapiro 1994; McWilliam and Taylor 1997; Whitley 1997; Hayles 1999; see also Chapter 10 of this book). Even were communication to take place in a wholly anonymous, wholly online context, we cannot simply throw off the ways in which who or what we can be online is informed by our existence as subjects with bodies. Shannon Wilson sums up this point within the context of learning online:

> Although bodies 'disappear' when academic work moves online, the ways gender, race, class, and academic position (to name the obvious) shape discursive exchange cannot simply be overcome or put aside. The ways we speak/write and hear/read are thoroughly shaped by our experiences as embodied subjects.
>
> (Wilson 1999: 137)

This does not mean that we have to take an essentialist view of the body as an end point to the free play of identity formation, indeed it would make no sense to do so when the body is itself so mutable, its form so socially determined and its surface so much the locus of our demonstrations of identity. It does, however, mean that we do not start completely anew when we work online.

Despite the reservations outlined here, however, it seems reasonable to approach the issue of identity formation online with a working assumption that within cyberspace identities are more freely transformable, boundaries less firmly drawn, and possibilities for metamorphosis of the self more open. Stone, even while keeping a firm grip on the principle of embodiment, sees a propensity to metamorphosis as a particular quality of the human in cyberspace:

> There is ... a protean quality about cybernetic interaction, a sense of physical as well as conceptual mutability that is implied in the sense of exciting, dizzying physical movement within purely conceptual space.
>
> (Stone 1991)

My approach to exploring these themes with learners and teachers was to work with them in generating accounts of the ways in which they perceived of the issue of identity construction online.[1] What emerged in these accounts was a series of tensions between the possibilities and temptations of multiplicity and the sense of the unity of the self as the desired, normal state. Dividing the individuals I spoke to into two groups – students and tutors – reveals two quite different perspectives on the possibilities of metamorphosis of the self in cyberspace.

Out of control: tales of metamorphosis among students

A series of negative perspectives emerged among students relating to the idea that the self online might be anything other than a direct representation of the single, embodied identity presented in the face to face classroom. There was a tension in the narratives of many of the students between the idea that they might, consciously or otherwise, have presented multiple personas online, and the sense that to do so was in some way deviant. In fact, 'negative perspective' is rather too light a term for the range of antipathies and anxieties voiced in the students' accounts.

A unifying theme in all of these accounts is the fear of *loss of control* through the modes in which identities are expressed online, a fear which, as I will show in the next section, is directly at odds with the experience of the online teachers I spoke to. Within this theme, particular aversions emerged which I have grouped under three headings: danger, personality split, and deceit and perversion.

Danger

In some accounts, what theorists might call an expression of multiplicity seemed, to the student, to be more like an act of self-betrayal.

If you do do it, and try and create a picture of yourself then you begin to believe it yourself probably. I didn't do any of that! [laughs] ... but there is a danger if you do that. You can develop this persona for yourself and get a bit carried away with it, and then it blends, because you've done it when you describe yourself and then it makes you change what you say, you get further and further and further away from the truth. So there is a danger I think, that you develop a picture of yourself and if you carry it to extremes you can't ever retract from it. I can see that there's a big danger there with online learning, you get yourself into a vicious spiral.

Sue

The fear of loss of control is expressed here in a series of spatial metaphors, almost as though the true self, grounded in reality, is potentially distanced ('further and further') by the constructed persona. This movement is cast as dangerous in the sense that the persona can gain a separateness which makes the re-establishment of unity ultimately impossible. The constructed persona is seen almost as gaining an autonomous power over the true self ('it makes you change what you say'). This is seen as purely negative, an 'extreme', 'vicious' movement away from 'the truth'. There is no joy here in the free-play of identity, rather a feeling of threat, of danger to the self.

I'm not, I couldn't do it! I don't know 'cos I feel like I'm not being honest, or I don't feel comfortable in doing it or something, or I feel like I'm going in a dangerous path.
    Why is it dangerous?
    Maybe dangerous because you may start thinking that 'Whoa that might be true!', that would be, then you start believing it, when it's not really, so it's not even useful for yourself I think, you know. It's just that I think that [pause] it's like you know being an actor, sometimes it may be dangerous if you get, I'm not an actor or anything but you know, I think I could get too much into a character which is not yourself, and you kind of lose the division between the character and yourself. That is dangerous, because you may lose your balance, you know, in yourself.

Paulina

Again, there is danger in the threat to the 'real' self by the online, constructed self, as though the real self is something fragile, protected by a boundary which is too easily transgressed, too vulnerable to a loss of 'division'. In constructing an online persona we again risk a dangerous loss of control. In Paulina's account, maintaining a coherent self is a balancing act – there is a possibility that, without the safety net of our commitment to a truthful, unitary identity, we might fall permanently into another (somehow untrue) version of ourselves. Identity formation online becomes a performance here, with the risk of the role taking control of the player, of the actor becoming the acted upon.

Personality split

In Charlie's account, loss of control takes the form almost of a Jekyll and Hyde type metamorphosis online.

> Sometimes in a tutorial you think 'O, I don't think that should be said' 'cos you're like, like you'll get shot down, whereas [online] you just type it in anyway, and press the button, 'cos it's not like you're actually saying it at all, so it's not you, it's like you're just a name, people won't attach it to, like, who you are. You can kinda say what you want and by the time you've hit send it's there, you can't take it back. I mean I've written things I've regretted before and and [the tutor's] said y'know 'Careful now!' and I've thought 'I wish I hadn't said that now'! [laughs] I don't know why I did it. I think people do generally just say things that they wouldn't normally say, they behave differently, even have opinions they wouldn't have in reality kind of thing. I mean it's not something I consciously do, like I'm 'Yes! I can be a totally different person and you'll never know', it's not something you'd consciously do but maybe it's something which after I've written something I'd think 'O, would I actually say that in a tutorial', and more often than not the answer would be no.
>
> Charlie

There is a tension here between Charlie's construction of himself as a careful, thoughtful student in the face to face classroom, and his expression of an online identity which seems almost wholly adrift from his other, bodily present self ('it's not like you're actually saying it at all, so it's not you'). Again, the online self is described almost as having a kind of autonomy, making comments, expressing opinions and exhibiting behaviours which are at odds with the identity Charlie expresses in reflecting on them. Charlie's narrating voice is interspersed by opposing voices – the warning voice of his tutor ('Careful now!'), the Jekyll voice of 'normal' Charlie ('O, I don't think that should be said', 'I wish I hadn't said that now', 'O, would I actually say that in a tutorial') and the out-of-control, Hyde version of himself which is described as emerging online whether he will or not ('Yes! I can be a totally different person and you'll never know!').

Deceit and perversion

In Claudia's account, the expression of an online persona is associated with deceit.

Do you think, when you're talking in your online classroom, d'you think that you're the same *you* that you are when you're talking face to face?

Well, I think so but, that's a difficult question. I don't know if you can ever tell when you're being really yourself or when you're kind of lying a bit. Or it's not only lying, I mean I pretty much always try, I always try to be like myself. I'm the kind of person that believes I want to be myself all the time, or at least know what I'm doing, you know. But I think sometimes maybe the message comes across differently, you know I'm trying to say something and then the other person understands something else or thinks I'm a different person or something.

Claudia

The extract first constructs only two ways of being online – 'being really yourself' or 'lying a bit' – as though in articulating an identity Claudia as an individual might have access to a simple choice between truth and deceit. This response to the question is then qualified to acknowledge that the issue might not be so clear cut. Being herself might be more a case of 'at least knowing what I'm doing', of being able to maintain conscious awareness of how or who she is. Moving even further away from her original conceptualisation, Claudia's account ends with the suggestion that, ultimately, her online identity is something which is not unilaterally formed, it's constructed socially, multilaterally, alongside those with whom she is communicating, to whom she is likely to appear as 'a different person'. Her account concludes with the idea that the construction of her online identity is not simply a matter of choice between truth to herself and a decision to deceive, it is something which lies outside her individual control.

A similar sense of the social formation of identity comes through in Richard's narrative, though here the sense of deceit is far more strongly formed and the online persona – in this case quite consciously constructed – is described as deviant to the extent of perversion.

I didn't switch gender, but I made myself about 20-odd-years younger, and I was surprised by the ease with which you could kind of get away with that. It was also slightly disturbing as well, y'know well it felt very manipulative. I mean I remember there was, there was a Canadian girl started talking to me, and by that time I'd kind of toyed with this identity and what it'd become, it very rapidly got established and other people started talking to me in that identity, and I just felt very uneasy about maintaining that identity 'cos I just felt it was very deceptive and it felt manipulative and I thought, 'I just want to get out of this'. But what I did learn from it is how easy it would be to construct and get away with those identities, well get away with it, live within them if you like. In that case it felt uneasy kind of morally.

In what respect?

I dunno, it just felt a bit pervy I suppose.

Richard [2]

What comes through most strongly from the accounts summarised here is that there is a tension in students' narratives between the ideal of an embodied, authentic, anchoring self, the self that goes along to tutorial classes on a Tuesday afternoon, and the possibility of other, deviant, less authentic selves which emerge online and which threaten the anchoring subject with the possibility of their autonomy. The possibility of the cyber-space classroom as a space where resistance and play can take place in the form of experimentation and protean interaction does not appear. Instead, in these accounts, it is a place where identity formation is fraught with anxiety.

Clearly it is not just online that we are troubled by the contradictions of multiple identities – this is a condition of our subjectivity. As Stuart Hall comments:

> Within us are contradictory identities, pulling in different directions, so that our identifications are continually being shifted about. If we feel that we have a unified identity from birth to death, it is only because we construct a comforting story or 'narrative of the self' about ourselves.
>
> (Hall 1992: 170)

However, it does seem as though, for these students, the medium disrupts the ease with which their narratives of the self are maintained. When shifted online, the 'comforting story' seems to gain a disquieting edge. To return to Lacan, we might see the feeling of unease which students experience when considering the possibility of their own multiplicity in terms of the ego's search for unity, the 'illusory ideal of completeness' (Sarup 1992: 66).

To bring to bear the over-arching metaphor I am using in this chapter – the two tapestries – it seems that when working online these students are caught between the two worlds of Athene and Arachne. On the one hand, they are engaged in a medium which seems to offer looser boundaries, more space in which alternative subject positions might be articulated, somewhere where 'the restless movement of desire' (Usher and Edwards 1994: 73) perhaps has a freer rein. On the other hand, they are immersed in Athene's cartesian world in which 'normal' is the centred, observing self and metamorphosis is a mark of deviance. In Arachne's world, 'desire, which is absolute, knows no law' (Lacan 1977: 311). In Athene's, mutability is the punishment meted out to the lawless.

Constructing 'the teacher': tutors' accounts

Perhaps not surprisingly, tutors' narratives described a more 'knowing' perspective on online identity than the students' tended to, one which was more focused on the conscious control of their online persona.

So what's this persona like then, that you think you projected?

O I don't know. I think reasonably kind of [pause] yeah reasonably kind of formal teacher trying to kind of initiate dialogue, trying to kind of be supportive, trying to challenge them, [pause] trying to kind of point them in certain directions. Trying to kind of share experiences, but experiences related to the subject. [pause] Yeah very much as the kind of [gestures] 'tutor'.

Tom

In his account of the identity he constructed online, Tom takes almost a textbook list of the characteristics of a 'good teacher' – stimulating, supportive, challenging, guiding, informed – and describes himself as, quite consciously, stepping into them. The image is almost of the formal teacherly identity being strapped on like a suit of armour and, in fact, the metaphor of teaching as a conflict does come up later in Tom's narrative.

Would you say you felt more comfortable teaching online than teaching face to face?

Comfortable. [pause] Comfortable in the sense that I felt more in control, or I feel more in control of my contributions. You know, you can think, there's a bit more space to think. I mean the classroom situation can be quite intense, it can be quite, you know, you're up there in the centre of things, and they immediately assume that you have more knowledge than they do in a particular area, which is probably not necessarily the case. You're very much up there and yeah that can be quite stressful, it's the stressful part of teaching. And if you're not feeling too great or there are other things on your mind, so that you know, to give a really good teaching performance is I think an art in itself. And I think in the online situation, I think there's a bit more control, a bit more space.

So when you say you feel like you're in the centre in a face to face classroom, is that...

Well you are! You are! It's like, us against them! [laughs]

Is that different online though, are you not in the centre online?

[pause] Yeah, but I've got more control, I've got more control with what I say.

Tom

The key word for Tom here, used repeatedly, is 'control'. Where the student narratives stressed a feeling of lack of control over an almost threateningly autonomous online self, the virtual learning environment provides for Tom the space and time to construct an identity which can provide a more effective, more thoughtful, more controlled 'teaching performance'. While the teacherly identity Tom described himself as stepping into (stimulating, supportive, guiding and so on) tends towards the student-centred model, the teacherly persona he describes acts very much as the centre of the classroom (the knowledgeable expert, 'up there in the centre of things'), both in its physical and virtual manifestations. In the 'us against them' conflict, Tom stands at the centre of the demanding, expectant mob of students. In the online classroom he is much less vulnerable, more in control, having had time to don his teacherly armour before entering the fray.

Delia's account describes a similar, 'teacherly' construction of herself:

> I think I'm more confident about being stern online than I am in face to face environments. I think I can sometimes project a much more confidently authoritarian self, or authoritative self as well, if I feel that students are missing the point, or that they are mis-reading what's being said. Then I think I do tend to be a little bit more forceful in the way in which I say, 'Yes but you should be talking about *this*' or, 'Yes, I realise that but I do *know*' sort of tone. 'You should listen to me a bit more carefully', that kind of thing.
>
> Delia

For Delia the online classroom provides a space in which she can take up the subject position of the teacher as authority figure (both 'authoritative' and 'authoritarian'). In this extract her narrative voice is permeated by her 'teacherly' voices prescribing students' activities ('You should be talking about this') and asserting her own position as authority figure ('I do *know*'; 'You should listen to me').

Delia's account seems to hint that the authority wielded by her online self is an improvement on her face to face teaching self, which is less confidently demanding of respect. Interestingly, her students' perceptions are almost completely opposite to her own:

> I don't think you have respect for tutors on line, as you would in the tutorial groups. Y'know, they're just other students, that are contributing. You don't really pay attention to what they say.
>
> Charlie

> Face to face I think there's more respect given to her because she's there, you know? She's a lecturer and we do respect her. [Online] it's like it's a different person almost, because it's just a woman checking our comments and what we say.
>
> Megan

It could be that Delia's voicing of herself as 'more confidently authoritarian' online is a response to the 'equalization phenomenon' experienced widely in computer-mediated communication (Eldred 1995; Dubrovsky *et al.* 1991) and referred to by her students. It is possible that the flattening of the teacher–student hierarchy which is taking place online causes Delia, in this account, to take up a more authoritative, 'teacherly' subject position in an attempt, conscious or otherwise, to reinstate a hierarchy which the medium tends to undermine.

Neither Delia's nor Tom's accounts suggest the anxiety expressed in students' narratives of the online persona getting out of control, threatening the 'real' self with its autonomy. On the contrary, in the tutors' accounts the online classroom provides a space in which a controlled and controlling teacherly identity can be constructed. Mark's narrative tells a similar story, though there is here more unease about the way in which he constructed an authoritarian identity online:

> Well certain emails like I remember looking at them and thinking 'Good God, I sound like a boring, stuffy old prig, "Now classroom, please behave! Pay attention! Stop doing this"'. There's some of that, sometimes you know there were emails I sent out which, having thought about them, I was trying to present this, 'I am the teacher and you must listen to this because there are important issues here', which were very different from the way I would've presented if I was in class. So yeah there were two, there were different faces that were being presented.
>
> Mark

This account is reminiscent of Charlie's 'Jekyll and Hyde' narrative – Mark's 'reflecting' voice looks back in dismay at the identity presented online, that of the 'boring, stuffy old prig' issuing prescriptive instruction to his online class in a way which is at odds with the approach taken by his face to face teacherly self.

Despite this, what emerges most strongly from these accounts is the sense of tutors using the online space to construct themselves as authority figures, and of this construction being far less problematic, far less a cause of anxiety than the descriptions in identity narratives provided by students. There may be a certain amount of disquietude, but there is no sense of guilt, danger or deceit in these tales of metamorphosis.

Conclusion

Online environments may create a space where the narratives of the self maintained face to face are more readily disrupted, but there is nothing deterministic about this. If the students' accounts revealed an edgy anxiety about their subjective multiplicity online which is at odds with tutors' more controlled construction of teacherly selves, it could be for a variety of pragmatic reasons: longer experience of online learning environments and the modes of selfhood involved in them among tutors; more familiarity with theories of multiple identity formation online among tutors; a less guarded approach in interview among students which increased the extent to which they were willing to give accounts of more anxiety-making identity issues.

I think, however, that above all these identity issues are an important strand in a tapestry which spreads further, one which incorporates all the contradictions and difficulties involved in the shift into the digital realm. Within the learning context, the metaphors we use (virtual classrooms, virtual campuses, desktops, tutorial rooms), and the practices we engage with (online seminars, lecture note delivery, online group work) are to a large extent carried over from practices developed in very different, face to face learning situations. In looking to the internet as a new, faster way of delivering old, familiar goods we perhaps create tensions like the ones described in this chapter. Poster refers to this as the 'culture of instrumentality', and what he says about the state and the economy could apply equally to education online:

> In their approach to the Internet, the state and the economy frame it as something that is useful to them, something that may improve their pre-existing practices, make things go faster or more smoothly. Or not.
>
> (Poster 2001: 2)

The problem with such an approach is that:

> As long as we remain within an instrumental framework we cannot question it, define its limits, or look to new media in relation to how it might generate new cultures. In this way, the culture of instrumentality obstructs research on the Internet, research that might open up the question of culture.
>
> (Poster 2001: 3)

The nature of the new learning cultures that might be fostered online is still, like Haraway's body boundaries, 'up for grabs'. However, if we see an instrumental culture operating in the delivery of online learning, it is perhaps less surprising that the online space becomes for teachers, however unwittingly, a place in which old hierarchies can be re-asserted and traditional, 'teacherly', authoritarian identities re-cast. The tensions described here perhaps result from new, online learning cultures emerging from within existing, hierarchical pedagogical frameworks, from the contest between the stable, ordered world of Athene and the decentred, cyborg world of Arachne.

My intention is not, in concluding, to tie the loose ends of the myth up with those of the narrative tensions generated by my interviews to create a tidy parcel. The tensions in the students' and teachers' narratives are, I think, reflected in rather than resolved by the allegorical framework I have used. However, I would like to return to the end of the story of Arachne, to consider its conclusion.

It appears at the end of this story that Athene, while losing the battle, wins the war. Arachne's tapestry is more finely crafted, but Athene's world view wins the day as Arachne herself suffers metamorphosis as punishment by being turned into a spider. However, the ending, for me, is not quite so clear cut. What is apparently Arachne's punishment could also be seen as her reward in that by subjecting her to metamorphosis the goddess gives the mortal woman the gift of true mastery of her medium – the web, which now becomes her home. The spider is the weaver *par excellence*, and perhaps it is within these terms that we should consider our own inhabitation of the web, the digital realm. In our potential for mutability online perhaps lies the key to our comfort with – if not mastery of – the medium. Arachne's ending involves the embrace of shape-shifting, the taking up of a cyborg state. It gives for me a new resonance to Haraway's famous assertion of her preferred way of being – 'I would rather be a cyborg than a goddess' (Haraway 1991: 181).

Notes

1 The interview extracts given here were generated as part of a larger research project exploring themes of conflict within online learning environments. Unfortunately, space does not allow here for important contextual information about interviewees. Details of research method are, however, available from the author.
2 This learner – unlike the others – is describing his experience in an internet chat room, not in an online classroom. I suspect learning contexts in which it would be possible for students to consciously self construct to this extent are rare. Students may be aware of this, but still the popular image of the middle-aged man self-presenting as a child or a woman for deviant purposes can colour their perception of the identities of their online peers:

> just not knowing who you're talking to, because you don't know who you're talking to. They could've said they're a girl but they could be a 50-year-old man sort of thing. Y'know, that's not going to happen in a university setting cos they've all got their university matric numbers and stuff, but the whole not knowing who you're speaking to thing, I can be really wary about that.
>
> Alison

References

Alexander, J. (1997) 'Out of the closet and into the network: sexual orientation and the computerized classroom', *Computers and Composition*, 14(2): 207–216.
Belcher, D.D. (1999) 'Authentic interaction in a virtual classroom: leveling the playing field in a graduate seminar 1 – the future of work and power', *Computers and Composition*, 16(2): 253–267.

Belsey, C. (1994) *Desire: Love Stories in Western Culture*, Oxford: Blackwell.

Dubrovsky, B.J., Kiesler, S. and Sethna, B. (1991) 'The equalization phenomenon: status effects in computer-mediated and face-to-face decision-making groups', *Human–Computer Interaction*, 6: 119–136.

Eldred, J. and Hawisher, G. (1995) 'Researching electronic networks', *Written Communication*, 12(3): 330–359.

Hall, S. (1992) 'The question of cultural identity', in Hall, S., Held, D. and McGrew, T. (eds) *Modernity and its Futures*, Cambridge: Polity Press.

Haraway, D. (1991) 'A cyborg manifesto: science, technology and socialist feminism in the late twentieth century', in *Simians, Cyborgs, and Women: The Reinvention of Nature*, London: Free Association Books, pp. 149–181.

Hayles, N.K. (1999) *How We Became Posthuman: Virtual Bodies in Cybernetics, Literature and Informatics*, Chicago: University of Chicago Press.

Hiltz, S.R. (2000) 'Measuring the importance of collaborative learning for the effectiveness of ALN: a multi-measure, multi-method approach', *Journal of Asynchronous Learning Networks*, 4(2).

Kimbrough, D.R. (1999) 'On-line "chat room" tutorials: an unusual gender bias in computer use', *Journal of Science Education and Technology*, 8(3): 227–234.

Lacan, J. (1977) *Ecrits: A Selection* (trans. Sheridan, A.), London: Tavistock.

McConnell, D. (1997) 'Interaction patterns of mixed sex groups in educational computer conferences: part I – empirical findings', *Gender and Education*, 9(3): 345–363.

McWilliam, E. and Taylor, P. (1997) *Teacher Im/material: Challenging the New Pedagogies of Instructional Design*, web page, http://www.aare.edu.au/97pap/mcwie526.htm (date of access: 19 February 2004).

Monroe, B. (1999) 'Re-membering mama: the female body in embodied and dis-embodied communication', in Blair, K. and Takayoshi, P. (eds) *Feminist Cyber-scapes: Mapping Gendered Academic Spaces*, Stamford, Connecticut: Ablex Publishing, pp. 63–82.

Ovid (1986) *Metamorphoses* (trans. Innes, M.M.), Harmondsworth: Penguin.

Poster, M. (2001) *What's the Matter with the Internet?*, Minneapolis: University of Minnesota Press.

Sarup, M. (1992) *Jacques Lacan*, London: Harvester Wheatsheaf.

Shapiro, S. (1994) 'Re-membering the body in critical pedagogy', *Education and Society*, 12(1): 61–79.

Stone, A.R. (1991) 'Will the real body please stand up?', in Benedikt, M. (ed.) *Cyberspace: First Steps*, Cambridge, Massachusetts: MIT Press, pp. 81–118.

Turkle, S. (1996) *Life on the Screen: Identity in the Age of the Internet*, London: Phoenix.

Usher, R. and Edwards, R. (1994) *Postmodernism and Education*, London: Routledge.

Whitley, E. (1997) 'In cyberspace all they see is your words: a review of the relationship between body, behavior and identity drawn from the sociology of knowledge', *OCLC Systems and Services*, 13(4): 152–163.

Wilson, S. (1999) 'Pedagogy, emotion and the protocol of care', in Blair, K. and Takayoshi, P. (eds) *Feminist Cyberscapes: Mapping Gendered Academic Spaces*, Stamford, Connecticut: Ablex Publishing, pp. 113–151.

Part 2

Discourses

3　Ambulating with mega-fauna

A scholarly reflection on *Walking with Beasts*

Bruce Douglas Ingraham

Introduction

What follows is perhaps best understood as a reflection on the scholarly use of interactive media/multimedia inspired by the BBC's recent series *Walking with Beasts* (BBC 2002). However, it is important to say at the outset that, while much of what follows might appear to be critical of these programmes, that is not the intention. It would be entirely inappropriate to criticise the programme makers for not doing things they never intended to do. Rather they are to be praised for the steps that they have taken in what is potentially a very interesting area of development for academic discourse. The question is not, so to speak, 'Why is this programme *not* scholarly?'. Rather it is, 'What can scholars learn from such a programme about which models may be most appropriate for the conduct of academic discourse in an emerging, highly mediated culture of ubiquitous, multimedia computing, where the advantages of both the internet and broadcast television have become fully integrated?'

This chapter follows on from a previously published paper (Ingraham 2000), which explored a range of issues concerning the impact of contemporary information and communication technologies on the conduct of scholarly argument through non-print mediated discourse. Here the critique of *Walking with Beasts* seeks to further explore these issues by examining one model of such discourse – scholarly interactive multimedia documentary.

The argument presented here rests on the hypothesis that PCs, the Internet, and broadcast television *as we currently understand them* will all disappear in the next 10 years and be replaced with flat-screen, interactive, voice-controlled, media access and display systems capable of accessing any or all media. These will be of variable sizes depending on their locus (e.g. domestic or office) and portability.

There is a significant corollary to this hypothesis which is that it is also true for print-based media – especially newsprint, pulp fiction and very probably the various forms of print-based scholarly discourse. The focus of this chapter will be on a consideration of the implications for the conduct of scholarly argument, and educational discourse more widely, if it is presented in a medium such as that suggested by the hypothesis.

Using the 'interactive' broadcast television series *Walking with Beasts* and its associated website as an example of a rudimentary interactive multimedia documentary, the chapter will seek to elaborate some of the criteria that such a production would need to meet in order to satisfy the academic community of its 'scholarly' *bona fides*. In so doing the chapter touches upon the question of what constitutes a 'valid' scholarly argument and to what degree the rhetorical affordances and constraints of its mediation play a role in that valorisation. For example what role, if any, should narrative or montage play in structuring an interactive scholarly documentary? What skills, both critical and presentational, will scholars and students need to master in order to conduct scholarly discourse outside the medium of print? We might even ask whether properly valorised scholarly argument can be conducted in media other than print.

The argument

The argument being pursued here is that in a world of ubiquitous multimedia computing, there will clearly be new opportunities for the conduct of scholarly discourse (Ingraham 2000). Moreover television documentary, especially if conceived of as interactive, provides a potential model for the future of scholarly discourse in a highly mediated culture. While the underlying hypothesis – namely that PCs, the Internet and broadcast television in their current forms will all be displaced in the next 10 years by newer systems – may be something of an over-simplification, this would appear to be a reasonable prognostication for the developed world (Techlearn 2002). It is the desktop PC that will most obviously change. It is likely literally to disappear from domestic use and, even where it persists for office functions (in both business and domestic environments), it will probably consist of no more than a mouse, flat screen and keyboard to which a palm top computer can be connected.

Of course, the Internet won't go away, but the desktop PC will cease to be the primary interface with it. Palmtop computers/mobile phones and televisions will. Similarly, televisions won't disappear, but it seems likely that they will become wall-mounted, flat screen devices and television programming will become increasingly interactive. Video on demand will become readily available and, at least domestically, these devices will be the primary interface with a more media-rich Internet, an interface that will probably be voice activated and controlled.

Much of this development already exists and it is really only the final integration of the systems that we await. Certainly, there is an increasing number of examples of things that represent elements of this new interactive cyber world. Existing Internet news 'channels' that include streaming media represent the potential of video on demand, and we can see the shift towards user control of information flow in news agencies like *MyWashingtonPost.com*. These allow users to determine the contents of their news 'paper' which can, in turn, be downloaded to a handheld or other device. Similarly, the capacity to select the camera from which to view some sporting events on satellite and cable television reflects the increasing shift of control from producer to consumer. Finally, the increasing use of email and telephone to interact in real time with radio and television talk shows is doubtless a harbinger of things to come, as are telesales programmes and Internet marketing and the growing number of Internet games communities.

A corollary

There is a corollary to this hypothesis that is also of considerable significance to academic discourse, and that is that such development is also true for paper-based media. A very interesting series of articles on the future of text in a digital world can be found at the *Text-e* website, http://www.text-e.org/. Of course, books won't disappear, but it is reasonable to suppose that the portable paper medium through which they are currently disseminated will be replaced by the even more flexible and portable medium of the palmtop computer or text reader. Why buy tons of newsprint or pulp fiction, when you can download comfortably readable electronic versions of the same? An examination of the full implications of this corollary must lie outside this chapter but it is perhaps relevant to note that research by myself and colleagues at the University of Teesside (Bradburn and Ingraham 2003), and that of others (List 2001), suggests that the principal obstacles to reading text from screens are not technical limitations, but are to do with ergonomics and poor text design. As such, there would seem to be little reason why we should not access text from the media access devices that we use to access information in more complex media formats.

Scholarly rhetoric in digital media

Of course, the fact that a technological opportunity exists doesn't necessarily mean that academia must exploit it. There is, however, one reasonably convincing argument as to why academics should do so. All academics have an obligation to consider all the evidence available concerning whatever the object of their study is, irrespective of the medium in which that evidence is contained. However, the implications of this argument are perhaps more complex than is commonly recognised.

Emerging digital communication technologies offer, among other things, two opportunities for the conduct of scholarly discourse. First, they provide the opportunity to include information in non-print(able) formats within scholarly discourse and, second, they provide the opportunity to conduct scholarly discourse in non-print(able) formats. In both cases, the conduct of the discourse is problematised. It is problematised because scholarly argument is fundamentally rooted in print. This simply means that as academics we have 500 years of experience in articulating our arguments through print. We have well developed and well understood conventions in which we have been trained and into which we induct our students. This is not true for the emerging electronic media.

From a semiotic perspective, this can be viewed as a problem of rhetoric. That is, the effectiveness of an academic argument is a matter partly of the quality of the evidence, partly of the robustness of the reasoning, and partly of the representational conventions through which the argument is mediated, namely, its rhetoric. It is these conventions that, as a general rule, we do not well understand for media other than print. Take television news, for example. It is both an object for scholarly examination and a source of evidence for other scholarly arguments. However, the evidence contained in a news broadcast is not a transparent record of facts. Its significance is mediated by a whole range of broadcast conventions that need themselves to be interpreted if the meaning and importance of the evidence is to be fully comprehended.

This is true for any and all media. Each medium may be understood to have its own conventions, its own rhetoric, which contribute to the generation of its significance. Scholars wishing to include such evidence in their discourse will need to learn to evaluate the impact of these rhetorics in order to fully understand the significance of particular pieces of evidence in the context of wider arguments. Still further, it is likely that these rhetorics will again be modified by their interaction with one another in complex multimedia objects. In short, using multimedia evidence within scholarly discourse requires academics to acquire new sets of evaluatory skills and techniques if they are to ensure the reliability of their evidence.

Ambulating with mega-fauna

How much more important, then, will be the rhetorics of the media with which we engage if we take advantage of the second of the opportunities and begin to produce scholarly discourse in media that are not printable. In my earlier paper (Ingraham 2000), I suggested that documentary television, especially if conceived interactively, could provide a viable model for such discourse. The scope of an hour or half hour documentary programme is often not dissimilar to that of a lecture or scholarly article and, very frequently, they are equally well researched and convincingly argued. Ironically, what conventional documentaries are not is, by scholarly standards, well documented. Although experts are commonly interviewed, there is none of the panoply of references through which academics normally both test the legitimacy of evidence and opinion, and through which a particular argument is located in the wider context of an area of scholarly debate. However, this lacuna can easily be filled in an interactive documentary where hyper-information structures can be used to position the broadcast documentary within the wider area of discourse.

The other obvious way in which documentary often differs from conventional scholarly discourse is in the use of narrative. Documentary programmes are much more likely to use narrative as a strategy to maintain and direct an audience's attention than are scholarly articles or books. There is nothing intrinsically wrong with using narrative within the context of scholarly discourse. Many historical and biographical studies almost inevitably involve narrative. A particularly interesting example of academically sound historical narrative is Garret Mattingly's *The Armada* (1959). Although now perhaps overtaken by more recent research, in its time it was perhaps the definitive academic study of the Armada and yet its narrative style pushes the distinction between novel and monograph almost to breaking point. More recently, Laurillard *et al.* (2000) very interestingly argue that a greater use of narrative may be essential to the development of scholarly discourse in a digital world.

Walking with Beasts

The BBC's recent series *Walking with Beasts* is an example of an interactive, multimedia documentary. To the best of my knowledge, it is the first educationally oriented, interactive documentary to be broadcast in the UK during prime time. However, it is not as yet what most academics would recognise as scholarly discourse. Indeed, I am only aware of one formally published interactive work of scholarship in which print is not the primary medium of communication. That is Hardy and Portelli's (1999) 'I can almost see the lights of home – a field trip to Harlan County, Kentucky'. The model employed in that essay is really that of the radio documentary. There are, of course, innumerable examples of media-rich scholarly resources available on the Internet (for example, *The Citysites Electronic Book*, Balshaw *et al.* 2000), but none for which text is not the primary medium of communication. Similarly, there are many examples of educational films and television programmes, but again they often lack clear scholarly documentation and may also be difficult to interrupt for purposes of reflection.

As indicated at the outset of this chapter, the primary reason that *Walking with Beasts* is not a work of scholarship is that it never had any pretensions of being one. Having said that, it does provide an excellent image of what such an interactive scholarly article might look like, not least because it is eminently well researched and scientifically very robust. Because it is an interactive documentary, it does to a great degree overcome the problem of not being well documented. When viewing the programme, it was possible to call up a range of additional 'Fact Files' in order to gain details about particular issues raised during the broadcast. This is not possible when the programme is not being broadcast, but if one goes to the Fact Files on the *Walking with Beasts* website and click on the image of the mammoth one can see an image similar to that which could be seen during the broadcast when viewing additional information. Just as on this page, during broadcast the 'video stream' was reduced in size and placed in the upper right hand corner of the screen while the rest of the screen was given over to the additional information. The additional information available during broadcast was further enhanced by this large information and media-rich website. It continues to be available, as is some further information for digital satellite television viewers.

In a fully integrated interactive digital documentary such as that envisaged in the hypothesis underlying this chapter, all of these resources would be readily available at the time of viewing. As it stands, even if fully integrated this information wouldn't quite constitute scholarship, but it does constitute an educational resource. The issue here is the target audiences. On the one hand, *Walking with Beasts* is targeted at a reasonably educated prime time audience and, on the other, it is targeted at secondary school teachers and pupils. Consequently, the level of the discourse is appropriate to that level of education, but there is no reason why it couldn't have been targeted at an academic audience.

However, *Walking with Beasts* also falls short of being a fully featured example of interactive documentary, because it is not actually very interactive. Most importantly, the broadcast video was broadcast video, not video on demand. Consequently, the viewer had no control over the flow of the programme and its narrative. If you called up the additional information the programme just continued, and you might well have missed something important while you were seeking further enlightenment on some point that was already past. Clearly in a fully interactive scenario that would not be true. One would pause the video presentation while exploring other information in various media including other video streams. Interestingly, even in the DVD version of *Walking with Beasts*, where one might have supposed there would be a greater degree of control, the extra information is on a separate disc and consequently even less readily available. Nonetheless, it is possible to imagine a number of different ways in which the full range of information and media could be displayed and consulted at will. Indeed, the issue of how best to design access to multi-channel information resources is itself a complex and interesting area for further research (cf. Boyle 2002).

Usefully, *Walking with Beasts* is also an example of a documentary in which narrative plays a significant rhetorical function. As such, an analysis of elements of the first few minutes of the sixth programme in the series, 'Mammoth Journey', will perhaps serve as an indication of how the rhetoric serves to shape and support its argument without necessarily betraying its essential scientificity. Overall, the programme 'argues' the case for a particular view of what ice age life was like for a variety of species including humans and mammoths. This 'argument' is presented via a narrative of a migratory journey of a herd of mammoths.

The opening images set the narrative in the last ice age and focus on the perils of the migration forced upon the herd by the coming winter. These images and accompanying voiceover end when one of the mammoths falls through the ice and is unable to extricate itself. Over the images of the herd and the trapped mammoth, the voiceover continues, 'Such are the bonds between mammoths that the herd does not leave their stranded sister. They stay nearby. Distressed but powerless to comfort her.'

The images continue while the sound track is composed of the noise of apparently distressed elephants (mammoths) and the howling of a wolf. At this point the voiceover continues, 'Before long the scavengers have started to gather.' An image of a human observing the scene appears, followed by an image of a wolf. The rhetorical force of this passage, which is setting the scene for the whole programme, is to humanise the mammoths and bestialise the humans.

In some respects, this is typical of the genre of natural history to which *Walking with Beasts* belongs. Much wildlife documentary anthropomorphises its subjects in order to sustain interest in the narrative. Such techniques can, as in this case, be a little cloying. However, they needn't (and don't in this case) necessarily vitiate the acceptability of the argument. For example, there is sound evidence to indicate that elephants frequently behave in ways that are highly suggestive of emotions like grief and it is not unreasonable to suppose that mammoths may have behaved similarly. There is also plenty of available evidence to suggest that early humans were both predators and scavengers. Indeed, some of the evidence to support both these arguments is made available via the interactive 'Fact Files' available during the broadcast and on the website.

The narrative goes on to introduce the cast of characters – a herd of five female mammoths with a young male and a baby male calf led by a 'matriarch' (sic), and a group of humans. The humans are introduced less as predators and more as tool users who benefit from living in close proximity to the mammoths. This is significant because another set of cast members, a group of Neanderthals, are later introduced as 'supreme hunters' in possession of a 'secret weapon' – fire – by means of which they kill the matriarch.

Of course, the story has a happy ending. Even though the matriarch is lost, the baby survives and mammoths as a species may be said to have their revenge over the Neanderthals, because they outlive them by 22,000 years. *And*, even more importantly, the humans outlive all the others and come to build museums and interactive documentaries through which they tell this tale, even though the explicitly stated moral of the tale is that 'no species lasts forever'.

Clearly, this slightly tongue in cheek analysis is rather crude and the production is susceptible and deserving of much more sophisticated analyses. However, the point is that the function performed by the narrative in sustaining the interest of the audience in the argument, and persuading them of its legitimacy, is susceptible to analysis and interpretation. We can understand the role that it plays and as such understand how to use such tools to support the presentation of such arguments. If approached with an appropriately critical eye, the narrative in no way undermines the quality of the research or the credibility of the argument. It merely engages the learner with it.

Costs

However desirable the notion of developing such modes of discourse may be, in the end the question of the cost of doing so cannot be ignored. The production values of a series like *Walking with Beasts* are very high, both in terms of quality and cost, and this may suggest that such an approach to academic discourse will forever be prohibitively expensive. This is not the place to undertake a thorough examination of the financial implications of developing interactive multimedia scholarship on the sort of scale envisaged here, but there are a number of points that perhaps suggest that in reality the costs may be less prohibitive than one might at first suppose.

The first of these points is that for many disciplines there already exist huge quantities of multimedia resources that are available, or can be made available, for study and inclusion in media-rich discourse. For example, there are archives of film, television and photographic material that go back almost two hundred years and many of these are held by academic institutions (e.g. the British University Film and Video Council – http://www.bufvc.ac.uk/). There may nevertheless be significant IPR issues to be resolved, but there is self-evidently no profit to be made by rights holders in making access to materials prohibitively expensive. Ultimately, it is in their financial interests to evolve pricing strategies that will empower the sort of academic discourse envisaged in this chapter.

Second, the question of the cost of producing such discourse is not dissimilar to the question of where the money has come from to put PCs on the desks of every academic in the developed world. Since 1985 the UK has spent about £500,000,000 encouraging the use and development of computers in higher education and that does not include the cost of hardware, software or infrastructure. It is continuing to invest very large sums every year through the Learning and Teaching Support Network (http://www.ltsn.ac.uk/) and similar initiatives. In short, it would appear that where there is a will…

The third point is that 'hardware' costs of producing broadcast quality materials are falling very rapidly. For example, digital cameras and editing suites that would have cost tens of thousands only three or four years ago are now available at prices that put them easily within the reach of academic departments (Puttnam 2002). The cost of production skills and time still remains at a premium, but more and more young people are training in these areas. As Laurillard predicted in her keynote address at the UK Association of Learning Technologies Annual Conference (1996), it seems likely that education managers will gradually recognise that significant numbers of skilled support staff will be as crucial to twenty-first-century higher education as the academics themselves. Nonetheless, there remains an unresolved issue with respect to the level of media literacy that will be required by academics, not only as interpreters, but also as producers.

Fourth, there is a useful distinction to be made about levels of publication that is akin to the distinction that is already made with respect to print-based materials and publication via lectures and lecture notes. Academics regularly publish printed, or print-oriented materials to their students in formats that are far less refined than formal publication via journals or books (see Ingraham 2000). The same can be true with respect to multimedia publication. Using tools like PowerPoint or Boxmind, academics can produce multimedia objects with lower quality production values that can, rather like some lectures, serve as drafts of formal quality multimedia productions. Again, there are issues concerning media literacy implicit here, as there are in relation to the evolution of a new style of academic publishing industry.

Finally, underlying all this is the increasingly global market that is being created by contemporary developments in communications. Academic publication today is to some degree in a state of crisis because of the small size of some of its markets. The capacity to conduct academic discourse online, any time, any where, is likely to impact significantly on the unit cost of producing high-quality interactive discourse. In the 1960s the economist John Kenneth Galbraith's lectures were so popular that close circuit-television was used to deliver them to multiple lecture theatres at Harvard. Stephen Hawking is now an international celebrity whose work, if globalised through something like the proposed UK eUniversity, would doubtless recover its costs.

Accordingly, I see no reason to suppose that academia will be unable to exploit the opportunities becoming available in our emerging cyber culture. Rather it is up to academia to determine how best to embrace this new culture without undermining the seriousness of its endeavours.

References

Balshaw, M., Notaro, A., Kennedy, L. and Tallack, D. (2000) *The Citysites Electronic Book*, http://artsweb.bham.ac.uk/citysites/ (date of access: 20 February 2004).

BBC (2002) *Walking with Beasts*, http://www.bbc.co.uk/beasts (date of access: 20 February 2004).

Boyle, T. (2002) 'Towards a theoretical base for educational multimedia design', *Journal of Interactive Media in Education* (2), http://www-jime.open.ac.uk/2002/2/boyle-02-2-t.html (date of access: 20 February 2004).

Bradburn, E. and Ingraham, B. (2003) *Sit Back and Relax*, http://readability. tees.ac.uk (date of access: 20 February 2004).

BUFVC, *British Universities Film and Video Council*, http://www.bufvc.ac.uk/ (date of access: 20 February 2004).

Hardy, C. and Portelli, A. (1999) 'I can almost see the lights of home – a field trip to Harlan County, Kentucky', *Journal of Multimedia History*, Vol. 2, http://www.albany.edu/jmmh/ (date of access: 20 February 2004).

Ingraham, B. (2000) 'Scholarly rhetoric in digital media', *Journal of Interactive Media in Education*, http://www-jime.open.ac.uk/00/ingraham/ingraham-t.html (date of access: 20 February 2004).

Laurillard, D. (1996) 'Closing speech at the Association of Learning Technologies Annual Conference', *ALT-N 15*, The Association of Learning Technologies, Oxford, UK.

Laurillard, D., Stratfold, M., Luckin, R., Plowman, L. and Taylor, J. (2000) 'Affordances for learning in a non-linear narrative medium', *Journal of Interactive Media in Education*, http://www-jime.open.ac.uk/00/2/laurillard-00-2-t.html (date of access: 20 February 2004).

List, D. (2001) *Screenreading*, http://www.dennislist.net/scread.html (date of access: 20 February 2004).

Lord Puttnam of Queensgate (2002) 'Closing speech at the Association of Learning Technologies Annual Conference', The Association of Learning Technologies, Oxford, UK, http://www.alt-c2002.org.uk/puttnam_keynote.pdf (date of access: 20 February 2004).

Mattingly, G. (1959) *The Armada*, Boston: Houghton Mifflin Company.

My Washington Post, http://www.mywashingtonpost.com (date of access: 20 February 2004).

Techlearn (2002) *Educational Computing for the 21st Century*, http://www. techlearn.ac.uk (date of access: 20 February 2004).

Text-e, Bibliothèque Centre Pompidou, Paris, http://www.text-e.org/ (date of access: 20 February 2004).

4   History in the digital domain

Mark Poster

Introduction

What is at stake in the alteration of the material structure of cultural objects from the paper forms of manuscript and print to the digital form of computer files? In particular, how is the change affecting academic disciplines which rely upon stable forms of symbolic records? More specifically still, how is the discipline of history affected by the digitization of writing? Is digitization simply a more efficient means of reproduction, storage and transmission of documents, whose availability in space and time is enhanced for the application by historians of research techniques and methods? Or does digitization cause an alteration for historians in the constitution of truth?

Digital disciplines

Katherine Hayles suggests that digital culture introduces into the epistemological procedures of the Humanities and Social Sciences a logic of pattern and noise, one that contrasts with an older logic of presence and absence (Hayles 1993). In the digital domain of zeros and ones (Plant 1997), everything is in principle immediately present and at the same time always distant, mediated by information machines. Digital information is on the server, in cyberspace, on the hard disk, in RAM, never palpable to beings ensconced in a Newtonian universe. By contrast, in the world of atoms, an epistemology of presence and absence prevailed at least since Plato introduced a hierarchy in which voice receives privilege over writing. In the domain of atoms – let us call it for convenience, the analogue world – truth consists in a certain relation to presence, either presence in the consciousness of an embodied speaker, or in the representation of that consciousness in voice, or, finally, in the representation of that voice in a printed or handwritten text. The epistemology of the analogue, or its ideology if you prefer, is that of an original that is defined as subsisting in consciousness; truth exists in consciousness in the first instance. Voice, handwriting and print sustain that epistemology through the supplement of representation. Derrida's critique of this epistemology inserts deferrals in time and space within the ideology of presence, revealing its repressed underside as the position of absence. Deconstruction remains within the epistemology of presence/absence, complicating its intentions, reversing its priorities, unsettling its metaphysic of the origin without, however, discarding its terms.

If digital culture constitutes an epistemology of randomness/pattern, it inserts a new logic of truth within a cultural world caught up in an older binary of presence/absence. One might say that now, in the era of information machines, in an age when cultural objects reside within such machines, the strategy of interpretation shifts to the question of the pattern within the noise. Truth cannot find its origin in consciousness but in the interpretive process that sifts patterns from a background of noise. One might then also go along with Neal Stephenson in *Cryptonomicon* (Stephenson 1999) and give priority in the question of truth to the decoding of messages, to the extraction of patterns from the devised noise of encrypted signs. In this case, one knows that a pattern exists, but the agent that formed the pattern is so removed from the presence of the signs – through the machinic mediation, through the encoding process, etc. – that decoding must look to the pure text, to the array of signs, and apply methods like statistics and other algorithms that do not suppose an originating consciousness but only a pattern related to a language. Encrypted messages constitute a heaven of structuralist linguistics, one where meaning pertains solely to the string of symbols.

Epistemology is, then, complicated first by the deconstructive move to reverse the binary of presence/absence, then by the addition of the binary pattern/randomness. At issue is not the displacement of analogue truth systems by digital truth systems but the establishment of a field where both are at play, independently and in mixed forms. We have then a very messy situation confronting us.

Disciplining the discipline

In this messy situation, with so much in the Humanities appearing up for grabs, uncertain and in turmoil, the ability of the discipline of history to respond to the challenge and opportunities of new media depend in part on how tightly the boundaries of the discipline are guarded, or how open historians are to new developments affecting their methods and assumptions. From the 1970s to the 1990s, the discipline of history shifted interest toward the social and the everyday, away from grand politics and intellectual history. Although many of these younger historians were Marxist in orientation, the empiricist epistemology that characterized political history changed very little in the shift to social history. Social historians, like their forebears, searched the record for conscious acts of agents (Poster 1997). Despite the shift of field to the social, historians, clinging to established methodologies, defensively rejected the theoretical innovations that coursed through the disciplines of the Humanities in the last third of the century. Borders of the discipline were closed to any hint of 'fiction,' of questioning the objectivity of the past, of introducing critically oriented theories, and self-reflection on assumptions. Those who insisted upon doing so, like Hayden White, generally found themselves shunned or marginalized. Remarkably the same conclusion may be drawn concerning another shift of emphasis in the discipline: the turn in the 1990s to cultural history and global history. Although the field of inquiry is now radically different from what it was in the 1950s and 1960s, the epistemological rules remain the same.

A question that follows from this summary of the state of the discipline is who qualifies as a bona fide historian? As new media challenge many of the habits of the discipline, it is urgent to inquire about the readiness of the discipline to face what might be perceived as strange new procedures of inquiry. In this vein, most often academics in history departments will respond to the question of membership in the guild, 'Only those who have a PhD from a history department.' But at least in three quite prominent recent cases, Edward P. Thompson in British social history, Arthur M. Schlesinger in the political history of the United States, and Philippe Ariès in the cultural history of France, that criterion would not suffice: none earned a PhD in history.[1] In another criterion of qualification, many scholars from disciplines other than history write books which are taught in history courses at universities. These important exceptions to conventional judgment – and there are many more examples like them such as Herodotus and Thucydides – encourage us not to slough off the question with statistical probabilities but to open it to fresh inquiry.

If it is not possible to guarantee with certainty the historian's identity, perhaps an easier question might be, what qualifies as a work of history, as historical knowledge or truth? A simple answer might be those works which are accepted as such by historians. But then we are in an awkward logical circle, as the reader/listener might have noticed. In my experience, faculty in history departments that offer PhDs in history often utter, in relation to papers by students and even published works, the phrase 'that is not history.' This comment pertains not to the question of the coherence of the students' texts or the quality of their research effort but rather to the theoretical aspect of their work. Historians habitually draw a boundary around their discipline, excluding from it scholarly works which at least on the surface are historical in the simple-minded sense that they are about the past. In fact one might, with Foucault, designate the phrase 'that is not history' as a discursive 'rule of formation' of the discipline (Foucault 1972). Students are often told in no uncertain terms that their work is 'not history' when they deploy in their texts theories from poststructuralists, for example.

Here are some instances of the problem from my own experience. In a

job talk at my university a young historian presented a paper on the historical conditions of Lacanian psychoanalysis in the 1920s, the relation of the
emergence of French psychoanalysis with legal institutions. Distinguished
members of the department voted against hiring her, using the argument
that Lacan 'is not history.' In another instance, a graduate student at the
University of Toronto told me that her adviser urged her not to include
Foucault's name in her dissertation, not even in a footnote, because 'that is
not history.' Or again, some years ago I presented to my department the
proposal of a distinguished colleague from the French literature department at my campus who wanted to give a course in the history department
on the relation of history to literature in the eighteenth century, an age
when the demarcations between the two discourses was murky at best.
This was an easy one; many colleagues demurred with the phrase 'this is
not history.' And one more example: while attempting to qualify with
enough undergraduate credits for entry into a graduate program in
history, I took a course in 1963 on European history at St. Johns University in Queens, New York from an instructor who was also a priest in the
Catholic Church. He announced to the class, much to my naive surprise,
that prominent historians of the day (he mentioned the most distinguished
American historian of France of the day, R.R. Palmer of Princeton University), regarded two categories of scholars as automatically 'not historians': Communists and Catholics. Although such judgments are not often
aired in official journals and at panels of the convention of the American
Historical Association, they are commonplace in the practice and
decisions, in the institutional activity, of history departments. Keeping the
boundary of history defended against fiction, theory, non-Protestants and
non-liberals is the difficult work of the gatekeeper. These personal
examples illustrate, I hope, not that gate-keeping ought to be abolished
but that historians have an overly narrow sense of what may be included
within their safe boundary. So today, when digital culture introduces its
new conditions of truth, the discipline of history may need to rethink the
location of its Maginot Line. It may behove historians to redefine who and
what are included in their club.

Historical data

The digitization of texts, images and sounds presents several levels of
problems for defining the nature of historical truth. The first concern in
the minds of most historians is the fate of data that originally existed in
print or manuscript forms. That data may now be located in digital files on
the Internet. Roy Rosenzweig has shown how quickly historians have con-
verted documents into digital files and posted them on the Internet
(Rosenzweig 2001). One major archive, 'American Memory,' the online
resource of the Library of Congress's National Digital Library Program
(NDLP), contains over five million records. Full text digital versions of

countless academic journals are available online for historians especially from JSTOR (the Scholarly Journal Archive) and Project Muse. Thousands of sites have been constructed on the web by teachers of history and history enthusiasts, by Civil War re-enactors, family genealogists, and other groups achieving high numbers. These sites are constructed by a combination of professional historians and amateurs, raising the question of verifiability of documents to a new level of urgency. It is often not clear if documents on the web have been put there by those holding PhDs in history. The pedigree of web sites is notoriously uncertain. Nonetheless these sites, which are sometimes very popular, contain a rich trove of text, images, and sounds.

In addition to worries about authenticity, another troubling aspect of history-on-the-web is the increasing privatization of document collections and, even worse, the increasing concentration of media companies owning these databases. In a sense, access to historical documents has always presented difficulties for the scholar. Collections are often controlled by governments, corporations, and private individuals who may be reluctant for various reasons to open them to researchers. One skill not taught in graduate school but that remains essential for historians is that of identifying strategies for overcoming obstacles to such collections. Legal hurdles are often most burdensome; copyright law, in one stroke, prevents access to vast classes of documents. Yet digitization changes the nature and extent of the difficulties. Since it renders distribution and copying cost free, the Internet lightens the burden of many research chores. From home one can access countless documents and locate information with great ease. Yet the great advantages of digital culture put in question many of the established systems of control. In response, the music and film industries lobbied hard to undermine the best features of the Internet with the passage in 1998 of the Digital Millennium Copyright law which significantly expanded corporate control of culture and, for historians, reduced access to data collections.[2] Digital culture thus opens a new political dimension to access, one that seriously affects historians, although I am not aware of any response to the DMC by the American Historical Association. In the first instance, then, digitization changes the nature of historical documents by rendering them easily available, introducing new questions of certification, and opening the issue of access to direct and controversial political questions.

A second aspect of the digitization of data is that it renders all documents potentially fluid, changeable at the whim of the reader/viewer/listener. At present many digital document formats are closed. Certain hypertext novels, for example, can be read and the reader can add 'links' but the nodes of the story cannot be changed. Also, Adobe's pdf format forbids alteration of the document and additionally prevents cutting and pasting of passages. Many of the books and articles that have been digitized and are available online come to the reader in pdf format. JSTOR articles and Netlibrary books are in pdf. Using such closed formats perhaps promotes the widespread distribution of documents but preserves their original forms – some would say, their integrity. Inured to print media and paper formats, modern culture has for centuries abided closed formats. But digital culture lends itself more readily than print and broadcast media to open cultural objects, to the simultaneous reading and rewriting of texts, to viewing and re-imaging of pictures, and to listening and transforming of auditory items. Word processing, image viewing and audio programs all allow and encourage the position of audience to become, at the same time, the position of author, artist and composer. Furthermore, the network of digital objects encourages these figures to become distributors. Functions that were separate in the print and broadcast ages of media, are now merged or at least have their boundaries blurred. Digital culture introduces principles of reception that echo the era before mechanical reproduction: the traditions of oral story-telling and folk music in which each reception was also a transformation. In the digital mode, these practices, once limited to the proximity of voice, now may disseminate globally. As a result, historical documents face a danger of losing their 'integrity' and becoming open to continual transformation, surely a nightmare for historians.

Digital archives

The archive has been central to the epistemology of history from its inception. For historians, travel to archives in the nineteenth century was analogous to fieldwork for anthropologists, a sine qua non of professionalization. Archives gained new importance beginning in the 1970s with the trend toward social history. If nineteenth-century historians, given the salience of the history of the nation state, consulted the collections of governments, late twentieth-century historians, more concerned with previously ignored groups (the working class, women) and institutions (the family, the labour union) investigated legal documents, church registries, and land-holding records. Both political and social historians regarded the visit to the archive as a prerequisite of scholarship, investing in it great emotional energy.

In a pioneering study of the gendered nature of historical practices, Bonnie Smith demonstrates the emotional fascination of historians for archival work. She distinguishes the graduate seminar, characterized by a mood of civic rationality, from the journey to the archive where historians found 'love, melodrama, and even obsession' (Smith 1998: 116). The trip to the archive was most arduous, especially in the nineteenth century. Historians viewed themselves in heroic terms, overcoming dangers, costs, and inconveniences to access ill-sorted records and the authentic traces of the past. In this context, emotions were easily incited. Even the legendary founder of modern history, Leopold von Ranke, was affected. He described his experience in the archive thus: 'Yesterday I had a sweet, magnificent fling with the object of my love, a beautiful Italian, and I hope that we produce a beautiful Roman-German prodigy. I rose at noon, completely exhausted' (119). The archive was the occasion for a most masculine flurry of emotion. Smith concludes her analysis by indicating the imbrication of archives with truth and feeling: 'archives became the richly imagined repositories of knowledge and the guarantors of truth' (128). One can also conclude that social historians from the 1970s onward, including many women, continue to associate truth with feeling, albeit in a more complex mixture of gendered experience.

The physical form of documents as print and manuscript papers conditions the architecture of the archive. Papers require an enclosure safe from the elements of nature, and papers that are rarely consulted, such as those in archives, likely will be housed in an obscure location and given little attention in their arrangement. By their nature archives of paper are off-putting, remote, inaccessible, and poorly organized. Digital archives, by contrast, require no journey at all, only 'surfing' with 'navigator' or 'explorer,' metaphors that conceal the absence of travel in space. Such repositories may be 'searched' with the ease of database algorithms, with a tap on the keyboard or a movement of a mouse. Information can be extracted from them with simple cut and paste operations of the word processor, not the arduous copying by hand or even machine. The new archive far less likely elicits feelings of heroic conquest in men or analogous emotions in women. Perhaps the digital context will reduce the intensity historians invest in the archive and perhaps they will less likely fall under the illusion, characteristic of earlier generations, that archives contain the truth of the past, that the reassembly of their documents constitutes by itself, to quote Ranke, 'the past as it actually was' (Novick 1988). Perhaps digital archives will lessen the false objectivism of historians and afford a turn to a more self-reflective and constructivist understanding of the historical text.

In other disciplines, such as anthropology, literary criticism and art history, scholars have begun to investigate the media that contain cultural objects. Museums have attracted much attention in these fields as important constituents of the epistemological practice of the discipline. The way cultural objects are stored and are available for reception thus is understood to influence the kind of knowledge produced about them. Jacques Derrida muses about the influence of an email archive on the early psychoanalytic association (Derrida 1995). His use of the term 'archive' is more general or metaphorical than the historians', including in the category any stored collection of information. In this sense, museums and public libraries would also qualify as archives. Using Derrida's definition, an archive denotes a material collection of data and is distinguished from memory, although the brain is certainly a material being and memory changes its chemistry however minutely. If other disciplines than history have been most interested in the functioning of the archive, historians have focused attention on memory. In recent years, they have explored oral history and testimony as a continuation of the trend toward social history but also in new directions such as the question of historical trauma (La Capra 1998, 2001). While historians have wrestled with questions of the epistemology of memory, and addressed the comparison of written/print records with oral evidence, they have paid much less attention to the archive and its potential transformation into digital forms.

Curious about the recognition by historians of the importance of the archive to their disciplinary truth, I did some searches of online journals, using the latest technology of the California Digital Library. I searched for the word 'archive' in the texts and titles of articles in some of the leading journals of the field: the *American Historical Review*, *History and Theory*, the *Journal of Modern History*, *French Historical Studies* and the *Journal of Interdisciplinary History*. In the *AHR* going back to the 1960s, there were 119 instances of the word 'archive'; in *History and Theory* (which went back only to 1998) and the *Journal of Modern History* combined there were 120. A search of the other two journals yielded not one result. Of the 239 mentions, only one raised questions about the archive in general in relation to historical truth. One may conclude that, compared to the great interest of historians in the question of memory and its relation to more permanent traces in paper, the media change of the archive has not aroused much concern.

But an older technology yielded slightly better results: an email to a friend asking about the question of digitization of archives resulted in a reference that proved suggestive.[3] A German scholar, Wolfgang Ernst, compares digital archives with historical narratives in relation to archaeological evidence. He argues that inscriptions on stones from Roman antiquity confront the historian with bits of data, forming a kind of archive, which can only be absorbed in historical narratives by seriously violating the limits of the evidence at hand. He contrasts the mute, modular, partial, highly ambiguous shards of script that constitute a good deal of the 'archive' of ancient history, with the pleasingly unified fullness of meaning in historical narratives, underlining 'the dissonance between analytical archaeology and synthetical history' (Ernst 1999: 61). Ernst speculates on a new history that would take its point of departure from hyper-text databases where modules of documents reside in heterogeneous juxtaposition. 'Maybe the computer has the better memory of the past,' he snidely suggests (62). His polemic against narrative history, however, rejoins the profession's objectivist leanings. A synthetic model of archaeology and digital archives, in his mind, is closer to some form of facticity than the elaborated stories of conventional historiography. Digital archives for him return history to a grounded methodology of fidelity to the documents, the old empiricist saw.

Ernst remains within the binary history/fiction. Perhaps digitization permits a move outside this opposition. Computerized databases suggest the inseparability of the discursive need for narrativizing (introducing 'fiction') and the insistence to heed the material form of the information. Digital documents, for instance, require aesthetic choices about the display of the data, even in the matter of keyword indexing that greatly affects access to information. At the same time, digital documents remind the researcher of their inauthenticity, that they are not relics from the past but transcodings of a recent vintage (Manovich 2001). In these ways, digital archives obey epistemological canons that depart from the familiar rules of usage associated with more conventional sources.

Historians online

In addition to the digitization of historical documents, writings by historians are also migrating to computer formats and appearing online. Historians are publishing their work in online journals, print journals are available online, and even monographs and other larger works are being posted to web sites. There are also a number of centers for historical research that treat directly the question of the new media, such as the Center for History and New Media at George Mason University. In all of these ways the writing of historians is increasingly present on the global computer network. One question persists from our earlier discussion of digital data: how does the user authenticate web sites that contain historical writing? It is easy enough for someone to copy a piece from my web site and place it on their own, under their own name, perhaps with alterations of their design. Such acts that were called plagiarism in the age of print (and which instructors are quite familiar with) will likely increase with digitization and the new principle of the variable cultural object.

Digital culture also facilitates new kinds of texts by historians, texts that combine audio and visual components.[4] Multimedia documents are as easy to create as linguistic texts. Ted Nelson's vision of 'Xanadu,' a global, hypertext library, put forth in the mid-1960s (Nelson 1965) anticipated what has become the reality of the World Wide Web. Some scholars, as in the William Blake Archive edited by Morris Eaves, Robert Essig, and Joseph Viscomi (http://www.blakearchive.org/) put online the poetry of William Blake whose printed texts included drawings that were integral to the reading. They have utilized the web to transfer, as faithfully as possible to the original print versions, work that appeared first in rudimentary multimedia forms. This form of transcoding, however, ignores the difference between print and digital media, taking advantage only of the propinquity of the web as a means of dissemination. Gregory Crane's Perseus Digital Library (http://perseus.mpiwg-berlin.mpg.de/), covering ancient Greek and Latin writing, and others like George Landow whose databases concern the work of Charles Dickens, deploy greater features of digital culture. Landow built multimedia databases including literary works, historical works that relate to the same period, and images from the period (Landow 1997). As many have argued, the transfer of texts to the web, even limited to the juxtaposition of multiple media and cultural objects in a single database, introduces an associational logic of web space that runs counter to the more linear logic of print. Hypertext promotes jumping from one site to another, with no hierarchical, tree-like structures, such as numbered pages or library catalogue files to control the narrative of discovery or research. It remains unclear how these features of digital culture – hypermedia and associational links – will affect the construction of historical narratives.

If the material form of the web presents a challenge to the bookish discipline of history, it also poses a threat to the institutional procedures of certification. Anyone, even an undergraduate history major, can publish their work on a web site for all to see. In one respect, Carl Becker's phrase becomes a literal reality: 'everyman his own historian' (Becker 1935). No obstacle stands in the way of publicly displaying historical scholarship. The practice of expert readers and referees in publishing houses and journals is bypassed by digital culture. Ease of publication poses an enormous problem for all the disciplines, including of course history. For the student or layperson, the web offers exciting possibilities for distributing historical scholarship; for those in the discipline, the issue is more complex. To what extent will departments and campus review committees accept publication online for credit toward promotions and tenure? As economies of publishing discourage the printing of narrow monographs and revised dissertations, presses are beginning to issue 'books' exclusively in digital formats. Will these publications earn the status of paper books? And as print journals are appearing in digital form, the lines are blurring between paper and online distribution. Again digital culture destabilizes established traditions of scholarly evaluation and review.

Life online

Digital culture presents further difficulties for historians. Not only are archives online and historical writings online but social life itself in part occurs on the web and the Internet more broadly. Historical experience itself is in part digital. Personal letters take the form of email. A great variety of chat rooms, bulletin boards, electronic cafes and public meeting rooms proliferate on the Internet. Guest workers in foreign lands and diasporic peoples in general utilize the Internet to maintain daily contact with family and friends back home. Young people expand their social contacts through instant messaging. Online games are a major activity for countless thousands. Wireless telephony is becoming digital. In some places, bandwidth is great enough to afford video conferencing. Millions exchange music files in digital form on the Internet. In fact, digital culture is designed for and characterized by remote intimacy, communication mediated by machines, in short, by virtual reality. Interlaced with RL (real life), VR obeys rules that are significantly different from familiar forms of society. Most saliently, the historian's assumption about individual and group agency is sharply challenged by social encounters heavily mediated by networked computing, by information machines. The interface of the Net, where no one ever knows for sure who you are, presents an enormous problem of theory and methodology. How will historians write the history of life on the screen when it is uncertain who is acting and to what extent the actor is a human being, a machine, or some combination of the two?

An example from ethnography

One of the richest and most nuanced studies of social experience on the Internet is Don Slater and Daniel Miller's ethnography of Internet use in Trinidad, *The Internet: An Anthropological Approach*. Based on interviews with Trinis (as Trinidadians prefer to be called) in the late 1990s, the book contains numerous surprises. In Trinidad, the Internet is not understood as an extension of American imperialism, but as a facility completely adaptable to local conditions. Trinidad, as a Third World nation, nonetheless has very high Internet usage. The only social category left out of Internet culture is the older population, a demographic trait that cuts across all nations. Trinis do not see the Internet as an intimidating, arcane technology but as easily assimilable to their existing cultural patterns. At the time of the study fully one-third of Trinis had Internet access at home and Internet cafes were ubiquitous in the urban landscape (Miller and Slater 2000).

Miller and Slater provide a comprehensive overview of Internet use in Trinidad: which groups use it and how, which aspects of the Internet are most heavily used, how the political economy of Trinidad relates to the Internet, and, above all, how the history and culture of Trinidad link up with Internet use. They argue that the long history of Trini diaspora creates conditions ripe for Internet use; since Trinis are unusually dispersed around the globe they have a need for a cheap means of communication such as the Internet. The Internet, they claim, enables a solidification of the ethnicity of Trinidad. Further, they show how Trinis represent themselves to the world by web pages and other features of the Internet, another way that the Internet strengthens local identity. Finally they contend that Trinis received the Internet as matching and enhancing local cultural practices. They practise 'liming': 'filling one's time with skilled banter, dancing and drifting onwards to other places (a street corner, a club, someone's house, another island). . . . [It] was regularly cited as the Trini pleasure they most wanted to recover on or through the Internet' (89). And they did so in emailing and in chat rooms. The Internet for Trinis was not a strange technology that was learned with difficulty and seen as altering their behavior. Use of the Internet flowed directly from pre-existing cultural habits.

This very sketchy outline of Miller and Slater's surprising findings indicates the importance of empirical studies of Internet use. Their results contradict most assumptions about new media. However, their work points to a problem with such inquiry: they proceeded from the assumption 'that we need to treat Internet media as continuous with and embedded in other social spaces' (5). In other words, they assume that the distinction between the virtual and the real presents no epistemological hurdle to their investigation. Continuing from there, they simply interviewed Trinis about their use of the Internet. They inserted into their study the figure of the rational agent, one who deploys technologies, engages in practices, expresses cultural forms, and has full self-understanding of those experiences. Historians will find this agent convincing since it is the chief narrative conceit of historical writing. Yet it begs the very question that needs to be asked when humans engage with information machines and digital culture, to whit, what are the alterations in the cultural construction of the subject under such conditions? This question might not be answerable by historical agents who appear to have every motive to disavow it. If cultural practices generally tend to work at the unconscious level, then profound changes in cultural modes are even more likely to go deliberately unrecognized, if I can use that oxymoronic phrase. In the present case, Trinis know that they are Trinis but as *agents* cannot recognize that they became that way and are sustained in that identity through discursive practices embedded in fields consisting of relations of force. How likely would it be then, for Trinis – or any other group – to ask how, when I am chatting on the Net, do I know that my conversant is a Trini and how, under those conditions, can I represent my true Trininess?

The historical and social science study of the media often concentrates on 'effects,' such as whether a certain TV show, which depicts violence, is likely to lead to violent acts by viewers, or even whether the reporting in the media of actual violence in society increases its incidence, as in copycat violence. These studies contain a dubious epistemological assumption of a sensationalist theory of action – sense data from outside is internalized by the subject leading, in some cases, to its reproduction. This epistemological principle becomes even more questionable, I contend, in relation to the Internet. Sensationalist theories of truth presuppose a pre-media agent who is affected by information as an external force. Cultural and social practices are far more complex than that. In any case the image of the subject presumed by such research is contravened by the multiple marriages of human and machine in digital cultures. We need instead to study the links and assemblages of humans with various media. Our categories are profoundly humanist and need to be modified to account for such mediated social experience.

Finally, there is a still more difficult question: digital culture mixes into other media cultures, and into face-to-face relations, situations where humans are proximate and deploy primarily language as a medium.

Humans are now going in and out of various different configurations of media situations. Questions then arise about how these transitions are managed and how each medium experience affects the others. One study that approaches this multimedia condition is Nancy Baym's work on soap operas. Her text is noteworthy especially for its comparison of television viewing with Usenet participation – a broadcast and a digital medium – along with telephone conversation and proximate, voice dialogue. The book provides a model of how to approach the dense mediascape of the current conjuncture (Baym 2000).

One last issue that I would like to call to the attention of historians and social scientists is the following: when you study the archive of a chat room in the effort to comprehend life online, all you have is the digital script, a script that does not represent a social act, but rather *is* that social act. True enough, reading a chat room archive misses the flow of text on the screen, which often combines several conversations in fast-moving and inter-twined complexity. But in any case such a text is quite different from say a transcript of a courtroom trial. The latter is a record of spoken dialogue by co-present agents concerning prior actions. The former – the chat room or archive – has no external referent; the archive is the entirety of the encounter or exchange. The agents in the chat room exist, while they are there, solely by their textual interventions. Language in the chat room, mediated by networked computers and software programs, constitutes the agent in the act of enunciation and only thereby. What analytic categories, one might ask, are required to render intelligible such a human/machine interface? What ontology of subject and object are capable of rendering coherent these bizarre, monstrous engagements?

Teaching history with digital technology

Digital culture upsets standards of the teaching of history in every way imaginable. Steeply rising anxiety over web plagiarism, the intrusive emailing of questions to professors, posting of student work on web pages, online evaluation and testing of students, online research and submission of work in the form of new media, distance learning – in these and many other ways, digital culture offers innovations in higher education at every level. Some of these innovations are relatively innocuous, like download-ing online research or the use of email or listservs to facilitate the adminis-tration of the class. Other changes, on the contrary, promise to transform basic aspects of the disciplines. The ease of students' exchanging and posting their own work introduces potentially fundamental alterations of educational experience. More cogently still, research on the web intro-duces a logic of association, a horizontal epistemology of a 'flat' discursive regime in which every site is equal, depending on the protocols of the search engine rather than on intrinsic quality or financial support. This replaces the hierarchical or vertical search logic of the card catalogue, the layout of the library, the linear material organization of the book, or the judgment of the professoriate and the discipline. In addition to the leveling effect of web architecture, digital culture promotes an epistemology of the link and module. What becomes interesting in digital text is not so much the string of symbols but the connections made most often between preexisting cultural objects, be they text, sound, or image. In the analogue world, higher education promoted truth regimes of argument, rhetoric, comprehensiveness of research, and the like. How will teachers inured to these epistemological habits evaluate a link between a picture and a module of text taken from some document? Will such a link even be considered an accomplishment of learning?

Historians are probably no better or worse than faculty in other disciplines in adapting to the classroom of the digital age. One aspect of the new circumstances that has achieved some attention is the creation of online learning tools. There are many examples of highly successful web pages designed by faculty and graduate students to promote historical education. One thinks immediately of the University of Virginia Center for Digital History, with its projects on 'the Valley of the Shadow' (concerning the civil war), 'Virtual Jamestown' (an online tour of the colonial city), various digital databases such as 'Virginia Runaways Project' (on escaped slaves) and 'the Dolly Madison project' (a multimedia database about the President's wife). Countless historians have produced excellent teaching tools that, generally speaking, are open to all teachers in the field. One can only applaud these experiments in digital historical culture.

Other aspects of the application of digital culture to higher education may be less worthy of praise. In the field of distance learning there are many important experiments, but here there are also serious dangers. Pecuniary impulses, so unconstrained in American culture, combine with digital technology to produce software packages for distance learning that undermine the basic principles of education: critical inquiry and academic freedom. The advent of digital culture has encouraged some entrepreneurial types to view higher education as little more than a potential market. Heedless of educational culture, these companies imagine they can improve on the efficiency with which information is transmitted from the mind of the teacher to the mind of the student. They need only capture the mind of the teacher in a digital recording system and transfer it to a software system by which it can be commodified and sold. This perversion of education is facilitated by digital culture and must be resisted by faculty in all disciplines.

History as media history

The drastic novelties of digital culture suggest, at the very least, that the history of the media must become a major topic for historians. This apparently harmless innovation in the epistemological repertoire of the discipline ought to incite far less resistance than some of the other suggestions offered in this chapter. Students of media from other disciplines would benefit greatly from comparative historical work. Too many studies of the Internet, for example, are flawed by a lack of perspective on the topic, becoming lost in the dazzling novelty of the new technology. Some important work has already been done on topics ranging from print (Johns 1998), to the telegraph (Carey 1989), photography, panoramas, and other visual technologies of the nineteenth century (Crary 1992), the telephone (Fischer 1992), film (Charney and Schwartz 1995), radio (Douglas 1987), television (Spigel 1992), and others too numerous to mention. Not all these histories, it might be noted, are by historians.

Despite the appearance of many noteworthy studies in media history, the constitution of the field of the history of the media will be no easy task. One issue concerns the relation of media to one another and the relation of new media to old media. Bolter and Grusin have put forward an interesting hypothesis they call 'remediation' (Bolter and Grusin 1996), the complex way new media attempt to disavow their novelty and assert it at the same time. More than this, the question of the history of information machines, culminating so far in digital media, concerns issues of the materiality of the media, the relation of media to agents, the interface of subjects to objects, the question of humans to machines, the alteration of space/time configurations, the issue of artificial life and the changing boundary between life and non-life, and a plethora of other problems that fundamentally reconfigure the objects of historical analysis, the figure of the historian as subject of history, and the status of history as a truth regime. Media history raises no less a question than the history of the human and the non-human (Guattari 1993). Digital culture, after all, imposes the question of information machines as agents, placing agency itself in question, a hard nut for historians to crack. Finally, the rapid pace of the introduction of digital culture suggests another kind of problem, one that I do not believe historians until now have dealt with: rapid change of media implies a rapid change of analytic categories, leading to the recognition of the tentative nature of all such epistemological tools. We are thus well outside the binary certainty/relativism, and in a new age of conditional truth regimes, a far cry from history 'as it actually was.'

Notes

1 Of the three, only Schesinger held a post in a history department.
2 Benedict (1986) discusses these issues regarding the revision of the Copyright Law of 1976.
3 The person in question is Dominick La Capra who I thank for the reference.
4 For an interesting discussion of the impact of digital culture on historians see Schwartz (2001). Schwartz argues that digital culture presents in a new way visual material in relation to textual material. She takes Benjamin's notion of the image as 'flash' as an important reconceptualization of history.

References

Baym, N.K. (2000) *Tune In, Log On: Soaps, Fandom, and Online Community*, Thousand Oaks: Sage.

Becker, C. (1935) *Everyman His Own Historian*, New York: Crofts.

Benedict, M.L. (1986) 'Historians and the continuing controversy over fair use of unpublished manuscript materials,' *American Historical Review*, 91(4): 859–881.

Bolter, J. and Grusin, R. (1996) 'Remediation,' *Configurations*, 4(3): 311–358.

Carey, J. (1989) *Communication as Culture: Essays on Media and Society*, New York: Routledge.

Charney, L. and Schwartz, V. (eds) (1995) *Cinema and the Invention of Modern Life*, Berkeley: University of California Press.

Crary, J. (1992) *Techniques of the Observer: On Vision and Modernity in the Nineteenth Century*, Cambridge: MIT Press.

Derrida, J. (1995) 'Archive fever: a Freudian impression,' *Diacritics*, 25(2): 9–63.

Douglas, S. (1987) *Inventing American Broadcasting: 1912–1922*, Baltimore: Johns Hopkins University Press.

Ernst, W. (1999) 'Modular readings (writing the monument): the case of *Lapis Satricanus*,' *Rethinking History*, 3(1): 53–73.

Fischer, C. (1992) *America Calling: A Social History of the Telephone to 1940*, Berkeley: University of California Press.

Foucault, M. (1972) *The Archaeology of Knowledge*, New York: Pantheon.

Guattari, F. (1993) 'Machinic heterogenesis,' *Rethinking Technologies*, V. Conley, Minneapolis: University of Minnesota Press.

Hayles, K. (1993) 'Virtual bodies and flickering signifiers,' *October*, 66 (Fall): 69–91.

Johns, A. (1998) *The Nature of the Book: Print and Knowledge in the Making*, Chicago: University of Chicago Press.

La Capra, D. (1988) *History and Memory after Auschwitz*, Ithaca: Cornell University Press.

La Capra, D. (2001) *Writing History, Writing Trauma*, Baltimore: Johns Hopkins University Press.

Landow, G.P. (1997) *Hypertext 2.0*, Baltimore: Johns Hopkins University Press.

Manovich, L. (2001) *The Language of New Media*, Cambridge: MIT Press.

Miller, D. and Slater, D. (2000) *The Internet: An Ethnographic Approach*, New York: Berg.

Nelson, T. (1965) 'A file structure for the complex, the changing and the indeterminate,' *Proceedings of the ACM National Conference*, 84–100.

Novick, P. (1988) *That Noble Dream: The 'Objectivity Question' and the American Historical Profession*, New York: Cambridge University Press.

Plant, S. (1997) *Zeroes + Ones: Digital Women + the New Technoculture*, New York: Doubleday.

Poster, M. (1997) *Cultural History and Postmodernity: Disciplinary Readings and Challenges*, New York: Columbia University Press.

Rosenzweig, R. (2001) 'The road to Xanadu: public and private pathways on the history web,' *Journal of American History*, 88(2): 548–579.

Schwartz, V. (2001) 'Walter Benjamin for historians,' *American Historical Review*, 106(5): 1721–1743.

Smith, B. (1998) *The Gender of History: Men, Women, and Historical Practice*, Cambridge: Harvard University Press.

Spigel, L. (1992) *Make Room for TV: Television and the Family Ideal in Postwar America*, Chicago: University of Chicago Press.

Stephenson, N. (1999) *Cryptonomicon*, New York: HarperCollins.

5   Metadata vs educational culture
Roles, power and standardisation

Martin Oliver

Introduction

Metadata is widely heralded as the necessary means to a worthwhile end: the re-use of information (Downes 2001). However, re-using materials remains highly problematic within higher education (Beetham 2002). In this chapter, some alternative readings of the roles and functions of metadata will be explored. Tensions attendant on the introduction of metadata will then be outlined, raising questions about its impact on educational culture. This will include examining the contestation of academic roles and responsibilities, the relationship between learning and 'learning objects', evidence of the processes through which resources are re-used and the semantic implications of standardising terminology. These themes will then be interpreted in terms of the way in which power is used to control or redefine academic practices. Several implications for the future of work with metadata arise from this analysis. Specifically, it will be argued that if metadata is to achieve its advocated role in transforming higher education, either metadata standards or educational diversity will have to 'give'.

Background

What is metadata?

The most frequently cited definition of metadata is that it is 'data about data' (Wiley 2000: 10), a role explained through analogy to library card files or the label on a can of soup. In electronic documents, such descriptions are typically stored within the file itself (e.g., the 'head' section of HTML pages) or in a related file, and may contain a title, description, a unique identifier, the sources this particular resource was derived from, etc., in accordance with commonly-adopted cataloguing schemes (Beckett 2002).

Thus far, metadata seems straightforward but unexciting. Metadata becomes educationally interesting with the notion of 'learning objects' – 'elements of a new type of computer-based instruction grounded in the object-oriented paradigm of computer science' (Wiley 2000). Others claim this definition is unnecessarily narrow; 'learning objects' should include any educational content (Quinn and Hobbs 2000). Irrespective of debates about scope, learning objects are considered to be educational resources accompanied by metadata, usually conforming to an internationally recognised scheme (for example, the Instructional Management Systems Learning Design Specification or the Institute of Electrical and Electronics Engineers Learning Technology Standards).

This approach is based upon several assumptions best illustrated by the work of Merrill (2001). Merrill adopts an engineering paradigm and is explicitly reductionist, searching for unambiguous definitions of the components of instruction. He argues that instruction can be split into knowledge components (things, actions or properties) and strategy components (showing, telling, asking and doing). To do this, several assumptions are made: that teaching and understanding are facilitated by an unambiguous vocabulary for describing phenomena; that what to teach is a separate question from how to teach; that there are various kinds of learning outcomes; and that the goal of descriptive systems is to be accurate and efficient.

This 'Instructional Design Theory' is argued to be enough to allow 'student's effective and efficient acquisition of the desired knowledge and skill' (291). The descriptive theory involved is explained in terms of knowledge objects, defined using criteria synonymous with those of learning objects. However, Merrill goes further by requiring relationships between knowledge objects to be described (e.g., whether they are part of, a step of or an event of another process, and whether they are instances or subclasses of some parent entity).

What is claimed for metadata?

Metadata is portrayed as a means of transforming higher education and enabling lifelong learning, by:

> meeting users' expectations of flexibility and ease of use ... [and] facilitating access to information, so that their efforts may be concentrated on achieving individual objectives, rather than merely searching for the objects to achieve them.
>
> (Foster-Jones and Beazleigh 2002: 54)

Some authors go further, arguing that metadata enables the development of automated systems that can create customised pathways through pre-prepared learning materials on the basis of a user model (e.g., Wiley 2000). There are clear parallels between this vision and the idea of Intelligent Tutoring Systems. Moreover, it echoes existing policy agendas such as that expounded in the Dearing Report for UK Higher Education.

It is clear from [Appendix 2] that continued expansion will require a radical shift in the way university teaching is carried out. The implications of the 'Future' model are far-reaching. To achieve that kind of cost curve, while preserving staff–student contact, it was necessary to increase RBL [Resource-Based Learning] to cover the majority of student learning time.

(NCIHE 1997: Appendix 2)

This economic argument assumes that common material is taught in a range of institutions and that consortia could be formed to develop and share high-quality resource-based learning materials. This assumption is echoed on an international scale by Downes:

The world does not need thousands of similar descriptions of sine wave functions available online. Rather, what the world needs is one, or maybe a dozen at most.

(Downes 2001: 1)

Downes recognises the complexity of sharing course materials but concludes, 'the current system will have to change'. Meanwhile, he argues, the way forward involves institutions sharing smaller units of material. In common with Foster-Jones and Beazleigh (2002), Downes frames the central issue as facilitating learners' discovery of, access to and selection of information resources – a role in which educators may (but do not always) act as intermediaries.

Discussion

The reconstruction of roles

Within the descriptions of the functions of metadata are claims about roles, many of which involve changing patterns of work. Downes (2001) advocates that educational systems should change to accommodate the potential of metadata. More modestly, Foster-Jones and Beazley (2002) concluded that systematic tagging of resources would prove overwhelming unless it was automated or made the responsibility of academics. Similarly, in the Dearing Report (NCIHE 1997) it is suggested, 'many staff would seek to spend some of their time on development of learning materials, because these will enshrine the core of their teaching' (NCIHE 1997: Appendix 2).

These examples illustrate a recurrent thread in which the role of lecturers is reconstructed. Analysis of such accounts is telling. For example, in the Dearing Report, lecturers are not described as having a teaching role in any section where technology is mentioned; instead, they are described as materials developers (Smith and Oliver 2002). Foster-Jones and

Beazley (2002) argue that they should have responsibility also for adding metadata. Merrill goes further:

> Too often instructional designers leave these important what-to-teach decisions to so-called subject-matter-experts (SMEs). Often a SME knows how to perform the task that is the goal of instruction but is unaware of the knowledge components that are required to acquire this knowledge and skill. A primary role of the instructional designer is to determine these granular knowledge components and their sequence.
>
> (Merrill 2001: 293)

Here, lecturers are dismissed as 'so-called' experts, are subsumed into 'people who know how to do things', and the role of designing educational experiences is given to instructional designers. It is hard to read such accounts without recalling the alarmist predictions of Noble (1997) in which academics are systematically marginalised in the interests of economic efficiency.

Changes to roles do not begin and end with lecturers, however. In the Dearing Report, for example, learners are rarely talked about at all in the context of technology. Where mentioned, they have needs, receive learning and – the sole time they are described as active – make informed choices about courses in relation to costs and potential employment opportunities (Smith and Oliver 2002). Lecturers are, at least, still portrayed as active producers in most accounts; students are swiftly rendered as needy consumers of information.

The relationship between learning and learning objects

The repositioning of roles, described above, presupposes a particular view of learning, framing the relationship between learning objects and education as simple and unproblematic. Learning becomes a process of selecting and receiving information; curricula are simply ordered content (Downes 2001). Such conceptions represent the simplest possible way of understanding courses – one most academics hold, but only as one amongst other, more sophisticated alternatives, including consideration of interactions with students and pedagogic style (Oliver 2002). Moreover, in the examples used to advocate metadata, students choose materials based solely on their own beliefs about what they need; in contrast, academics design curricula by reference to existing practice, logical pre-requisites, departmental, institutional and/or personal values, and so on. There is a gulf between the simplistic conceptions of curriculum design described in metadata texts and the cultural, historical and inter-personal practices of academics.

In many papers, it is simply assumed that provision of easily accessible educational resources is equivalent to learning (for example Anido-Rifón *et al.* 2002). This may be because the central concern of metadata researchers is access to resources. However, problems are inevitable if this is treated as being the whole of the educational process. This assumption of equivalence between resources and learning may reflect a naïve view of the pedagogic process. Although more sophisticated models do exist (such as the IMS Learning Design Specification), these still elide the differences between instruction and learning. Whatever the cause, the epistemological implication is acute. The value of the kinds of wisdom and virtue associated with traditional academic forms of knowing is diminished in favour of commodified forms of knowledge whose value is demonstrated through economic application (Barnett 1994).

This trend reflects and exemplifies wider social developments that emphasise performativity and the commodification of knowledge:

> We may thus expect a thorough exteriorisation of knowledge with respect to the 'knower', at whatever point he or she may occupy in the knowledge process. The old principle that the acquisition of knowledge is indissociable from the training (*Bildung*) of minds, or even of individuals, is becoming obsolete and will become ever more so. The relationships of the suppliers and users of knowledge to the knowledge they supply and use is now tending, and will increasingly tend, to assume the form already taken by the relationship of commodity producers and consumers to the commodities they produce and consume – that is, the form of value. Knowledge is and will be produced in order to be sold, it is and will be consumed in order to be valorised in a new production: in both cases, the goal is exchange.
>
> (Lyotard 1979: 5)

This phenomenon is not new, but is particularly acute where computers are involved. In Lyotard's analysis, the spread of computers leads inexorably to the privileging of certain types of knowledge – i.e. those that can be translated into an electronic format. This poses a particular threat for professional knowledge, much of which is tacit, and hence difficult to capture in any form at all (McMahon 2000). This would imply that any representation of knowledge (including an electronic representation) as held by a professional community must, of necessity, be impoverished. To draw on Wenger's concepts (1998), such representations would be reifications alone, rather than the combination of reification and participation that are essential for learning. They also rely upon pre-specification – a marked contrast to the emergent qualities of learning Wenger discusses and which academics treasure and protect (Oliver 2002).

Moreover, as Thorpe has pointed out (Thorpe 2002), the view of learning as an individual process has been superseded during the last twenty years, replaced by the idea that learning is an inherently social phenomenon. Metadata's claimed potential rests in its ability to locate or customise resources for individuals; although group activities are supported by the IMS Learning Design Specification, attention to the social nature of knowledge remains absent.

Metadata's claims to support learning thus appear credible because texts advocating this approach remain silent on any problems metadata cannot deal with. Whether this is deliberate or not, framing learning solely as a problem of accessing relevant (quality) information resources (or instructions for activities) presents it as solvable by ignoring the complexity of curriculum design, knowledge representation and the social aspects of learning.

The feasibility of re-use

While texts may describe metadata as a way of facilitating re-use, there is more to this problem than simply accessing existing materials. How should a teacher re-use such resources when the original expertise, let alone professional wisdom (Rowland 2000) that contextualised them – in other words, all the kinds of tacit knowledge that electronic resources have been argued to be poor at capturing – is missing? For example, the IEEE's Learning Technology Support Architecture document claims:

> This Standard is pedagogically neutral, content-neutral, culturally neutral and platform-neutral.
>
> (IEEE 2001)

Such claims are thoroughly critiqued in Earle's account of courseware description and re-use (2002). Here, she identifies

> the fallacy that unless a pedagogical position is made explicit (whether in terms of an individual's beliefs or the functionality of a system), it does not exist. In effect, what is usually touted as pedagogical neutrality by software vendors is merely pedagogical naivety.
>
> (Earle 2002: 6)

Thus assumed neutrality belies the hidden influences – the tacit professional knowledge referred to above – that guides how the creator believes the resource *ought* to be used. Lack of awareness of these taken-for-granted cultural cues will profoundly affect the way in which a resource is used (Kuutti 1996). Thus, educators may select a resource that (according to the metadata) is appropriate and of a high quality, only to find out at the point of use that their beliefs and those of the designer are in conflict.

The very idea of re-use is an over-simplification. Instead of being a problem of access to existing resources, it involves a process of appropriation. To appropriate a resource the new user must imagine how the designers intended it to be used and adapt their practice accordingly, or else must conceive of some new use for the materials (Wenger 1998). Thus appropriation may be easy across related contexts but can involve considerable creativity in other situations.

This goes some way towards explaining why re-use remains such an intractable problem in higher education. Viewing re-use as a social process portrays it very differently from its description within the metadata literature. The problems here are not confined to finding resources, nor even to selecting them. Instead, they are as much cultural as technical, since a potential new user must be able to 'read' the intended pedagogy from the artefact or else envisage new ways of adopting it.

Standardisation vs diversity

Having argued that cultural context is important in understanding re-use, it seems reasonable to ask how metadata copes with cultural diversity. Traditionally, it has not. The IEEE standards (2001), for example, talk of being 'culturally neutral' – and are thus open to the same critique that Earle provided for their claim of being pedagogically neutral. The Learning Design Specification now recognises 'culturally relevant content' but still fails to recognise that it, too, must be culturally interpreted. Why has this situation arisen? Metadata presupposes open standards – 'a language understood and used by everyone' (Downes 2001: 11). By assuming that declarative descriptions can adequately define the semantics of this shared language, Downes describes how Extensible Markup Language (XML) can provide a common syntax so that 'a piece of learning material, no matter where it is located, may be seamlessly integrated into an online course, provided that the XML tags are employed consistently, that is, provided the semantics are the same' (17).

This approach is philosophically problematic. Traditional texts on semantics focus on the sense-reference debate, wherein the link between a word and its referent (typically understood to be its meaning) is shown to be complex and ambiguous. Classic problems of this type illustrate the difference between what a word refers to and what people understand the word to mean – in other words, the difference between a positivist relational philosophy ('the meaning of the word is this object') and a subjective, phenomenological position ('peoples' understandings of the meaning of this word are personal and varied').

> At this point, following the linguistic understandings of semiotic and language processing theory, it would seem that to identify meaning, relevance and purpose through the interpretive act of metadata creation would largely be a question of clear and unambiguous definition. And the issue of semantics itself would seem to be reducible to a question of clearly associating a word, sign or token with a definition.
>
> (Friesen 2002: section 3)

However, more recent thinking proposes a more radical reinterpretation (Whitson 1997), involving chains of meanings where each word is understood in relation to other words (or comparable signifiers), so that the idea of something being signified disappears entirely. This 'discursive shift' involves the construction of meaning through the use of language.

> It may be useful to recall that the words and taxonomies being used in any metadata specification are not simply raw data. Contrary to what the word 'metadata' might imply, the use of terms to describe a learning resource type – or any other aspect of a document or object – is a reflection of the knowledge, interpretation and judgment of the indexer. [...] Meaning, in other words, is perhaps not a matter of definitional or analytical rigour, but of doing and of using words. [...] Emphasizing that interoperability is a matter of degree, rather than an all or nothing proposition, [...] suggests that interoperability varies with the degree of commonality between communities.
>
> (Friesen 2002: section 5)

This epistemological difference is illustrated by related research. In a study of academics' use of a toolkit for curriculum design, Oliver and Conole (2002) examined how the meaning of specific teaching terms varied depending on their context. The term 'lecturing' provides a rich example of this; the practices associated with this term varied not only between disciplines and people (even within course teams), but also *for* each person depending on the year of students being taught, the number in the class, their expectations and so on. It was impossible to provide a precise definition; its meaning was determined in relation to other terms (such as 'tutorial', 'seminar', etc.), a taken-for-granted context and ambiguous, tacit practices. By contrast, Downes (2001: 8) uses the example of 'the meanings of such terms as *Paris, the capital of France*, and *European* [as] understood by almost all speakers of English'. In contemporary British society, the political aspects of being able to label students as European (rather than, say, English or Welsh) are obvious: the meaning of the term is *not* understood in the same way by all who use it, but is powerfully influenced by individuals' political perspectives.

Thus requiring academics to produce metadata becomes an interesting exercise of power. This might be interpreted as a beneficent act, empowering lecturers to describe their own practice without reliance on information specialists such as librarians. However, the way in which academics are allowed to describe their materials is telling; it must follow set rules and use a controlled vocabulary, which (by virtue of being 'generic') cannot precisely reflect their practice. Foucault (1977) describes how those who are constantly watched come to internalise the rules of those who observe them, and Freire (1970) likewise describes how those who are oppressed may internalise the likeness of their oppressors. Requiring academics to describe their world using language developed by others clearly follows such patterns of oppression.

The implications are clear: metadata represents a unitary, definitive narrative, legitimated by conformance to pre-specified standards. This approach fails to capture the variety of local meanings – indeed, it renders them illegitimate since (by virtue of their provisional and partial nature) they are too diverse and ambiguous to conform to any single workable definition.

Analysis: power and metadata

The struggle for power takes various forms in this particular arena. Some, such as the expectation that academics will internalise specialists' language, have already been mentioned. Others will be discussed here.

The clearest exercise of power lies in the re-definition of roles. The idea in Dearing that materials will 'enshrine' lecturers' teaching' is a good illustration of this (Smith and Oliver 2002). Here, the development of materials is naturalised; it goes without question or comment. There is also a subtle but powerful re-drawing of lecturers' involvement with teaching; once enshrined, the core of their teaching will not need to be regularly 're-shrined'. This once-and-for-all abstraction of teaching stands in stark contrast to the curriculum practices of academics, which involve constant modification, both annually, through a cycle of renewal, and week-to-week, moment-to-moment, on the basis of the lecturer's reading of the student experience (Oliver 2002). The silences in this text are also notable; lecturers are not described (in relation to technology) as teachers. The emphasis is firmly on materials development, locating them in one aspect of an industrialised process with its own division of labour. However, this change in labour does not necessarily equate to a reduction in workload. Instead, academics could be made responsible for describing and cataloguing any materials they produce (Foster-Jones and Beazleigh 2002).

This emphasis is particularly interesting given the association of several authors of the Dearing Report (particularly Appendix 2) with the UK Open University – an institution whose history of industrialised course development stands in marked contrast to the *ad hoc*, 'craft' model of more traditional institutions (Plewes and Issroff 2002). When taken alongside the need for institutional collaboration to develop these materials, these recommendations seem only a small step from loosely-bound mega-universities becoming the future of UK higher education – a notion proposed by Daniel (1998), drawing on his experiences as Vice Chancellor of the Open University.

The Dearing example is the clearest, but not the most extreme. In Merrill's text (2001), lecturers no longer hold responsibility for curriculum design; instead, they become resources for Instructional Designers, who then build systems which hold no place for student–tutor interaction. Noble (1997) feared the sidelining of academics by administrators, but failed to foresee that a potent threat might come from traditionally marginal support staff.

In spite of this rhetoric, metadata developers have no direct influence over academics. How, then, can this agenda influence practice? One obvious example is provided by the Dearing Report. By virtue of being a governmental policy, it is easy to view its expectations as 'normal'. The same process holds for institutional policy. Thus the rhetoric discussed above influences practice whenever policy requires changes to roles in line with the agendas of metadata specialists.

First, however, those who set policy must be persuaded that these agendas are worth listening to. Higher education is viewed increasingly as a market (Smith and Oliver 2002) and, consequently, economic arguments hold particular sway. These can be seen in Dearing's recommendations, which are intended to influence institutions' patterns of curriculum development:

> This kind of development requires a staff:student time ratio of more than 100:1, rather than the 20:1 assumed above. Many staff would seek to spend some of their time on development of learning materials, because these will enshrine the core of their teaching. But for the high quality materials needed for the majority of university study, development will have to be of a high order, and therefore not in-house, in general. IT methods must achieve their promise of greater efficiency both by improving the quality of student learning, and by amortising the cost of development over large student numbers.
>
> (NCIHE 1997: Appendix 2)

This economic imperative is prevalent in many metadata texts, influencing how education is portrayed:

> From a certain perspective, an online course is nothing more than just another application, and software developers have long since learned that it is inefficient to design applications from scratch. [...] An online course, viewed as a piece of software, may be seen as a collection of reusable subroutines and applications. An online course, viewed as a collection of learning objectives, may be seen as a collection of reusable learning materials. The heart – and essence – of a learning object economy is the merging of these two concepts, of viewing reusable learning materials as reusable subroutines and applications. Educators in the corporate and software communities have known about this concept for some time. As Wayne Wieseler, an author working with Cisco Systems, writes, 'reusable content in the form of objects stored in a database has become the Holy Grail in the e-learning and knowledge management communities.'
>
> (Downes 2001: 6–7)

There is no recognition that higher education and corporate training have distinct cultures and aims. Higher education is positioned as lacking, with metadata the only sensible way forward. However, to make this argument convincing, it is necessary to presuppose the market discourse of higher education and position academics as lagging behind business.

This economic rationale paints an impoverished picture of re-use:

> We should not lose sight of the ultimate objectives of this exercise, which are to locate, share and reuse the learning resources that are the assets of our organization. Like information, a resource is only valuable if it can be found and utilized in time.
>
> (Foster-Jones and Beazleigh 2002: 59)

Gone is all possibility for serendipity; gone too is the role of resources as inspiration, sparking off ideas or prompting radical modification or re-purposing. In fact, all the elements identified by Wenger (1998) as being important for personal or organisational learning are missing.

This economic imperative is used to claim a moral high ground for metadata advocates. Many texts discuss the need to facilitate searches without specifying who might be searching (for example Foster-Jones and Beazleigh 2002). Others talk in general terms about benefits to 'the world' (Downes 2001: 1). How can academics be so churlish as to refuse to support an initiative with such generic benefits? However, the benefits are *not* generic. Downes, for example, draws all his examples from American or Canadian institutions. Few texts consider the potential impact of such initiatives outside of the Western, English-speaking world, ignoring the literature on globalisation and raising the spectre of cultural imperialism (Edwards 2002).

Finally, it is ironic that these texts paint a picture of unrestricted access when current research into web-based portals suggests that too many resources are available, emphasising the importance of experts' insights into which might prove valuable to specific audiences (Beckett 2002).

Implications for practice

There are two ways in which practice may change as metadata is introduced. If metadata, as currently understood, is embraced, academics' traditional teaching role will be eroded. In the extreme, they would be marginalised to the point where they were excluded from students' learning entirely. This tendency can be seen in the industrialised models of course development in place (or emerging) in a range of UK institutions (Plewes and Issroff 2002).

The alternative is that metadata practice will have to change to accommodate academics' values and patterns of work. Some work in this direction has already taken place. Friesen's (2002) proposed solution, drawing on

Wenger (1998), involves developing metadata within the context of specific communities. He proposes that the extent to which these can be shared across communities will vary depending on the degree to which their cultures differ. However, his argument that 'the focal communities constituted by schools, technical colleges and universities [...] would together form an extended educational community' (section 6) fails to capture the close engagement, mutual accountability and negotiation that characterise a community of practice. (A revision of this model involving smaller communities or a constellation of practice might address this, however.) This would allow metadata descriptions to act as boundary-crossing objects, a reification of practice that supports the process of negotiating meaning.

A second area of work complements and extends Friesen's idea of community-based metadata. Nilsson *et al.* (2002) start by identifying what they see as misconceptions about metadata, many of which relate directly to claims challenged in this chapter:

> We have encountered objections of varying kinds to the concept of meta-data and its use. It seems to us that many of those objections stem from what we regard as misconceptions about the very nature of meta-data [...]:
>
> * meta-data is objective data about data
> * meta-data for a resource is produced only once
> * meta-data must have a logically defined semantics
> * meta-data can be described by meta-data documents
> * meta-data is the digital version of library indexing systems
> * meta-data is machine-readable data about data.
>
> (Nilsson *et al.* 2002: section 2)

Rejecting outright the notion that metadata is anything but a personal interpretation of a resource, they propose that single resources be accompanied by numerous classifications, each reflecting the interpretation of a different user.

> When meta-data is viewed as authoritative information about a resource, adding descriptions of such features becomes not only counter-productive, since it excludes alternative interpretations, but also dishonest, forcing a subjective interpretation on the user. The ongoing debate is creating conflicts and is seriously hindering the adoption of meta-data technologies. When meta-data descriptions are instead properly annotated with their source, creating meta-data is no longer a question of finding *the* authoritative description of a resource. Multiple, even conflicting descriptions can co-exist. This amounts to a realization that meta-data descriptions are just as subjective as is any verbal description. In fact, we *want* people to be able to express

personal views on subjects of all kinds. It is a simple fact of life that consensus on these matters will never be reached, and the technology must support that kind of diversity in opinion, not hinder it.

(Nilsson *et al.* 2002: section 2.1)

However, whilst Nilsson *et al.* provide mechanisms for tackling such complexity, they fail to develop a conceptual grounding comparable to Friesen's. Combining these would give a powerful new way of conceptualising metadata that complements academic practice and addresses the issues discussed above.

To summarise, there are two possible directions in which practice could develop: the re-definition (marginalisation) of the role of the academic, or the complication and limitation of the role of metadata. These two directions stand opposed, with power being exercised by both camps to influence or protect the *status quo*.

Conclusions

Metadata may be described as having the potential to transform ('redeem') higher education, but such descriptions are problematic. They form part of a wider struggle to legitimate the role of educational metadata, a struggle that pits its potential against educational diversity and complexity.

By analysing this situation, the following conclusions can be drawn:

1   Metadata cannot solve the problem of educational re-use, because it cannot accommodate tacit knowledge or reflect cultural diversity. It can, however, facilitate the process of intentional, rational searching for resources within communities where meanings are shared.
2   Metadata cannot solve the complex problems attendant on learning, even when incorporated into adaptive systems incorporating user models. Its claims to facilitate education rest on an over-simplistic model in which access to information (or at best, to instruction) is equivalent to learning. However, since access to resources represents one element of learning it may facilitate part of the learning process.
3   Metadata does not resolve problems of semantics and searching. Instead, it ignores the complexity of semantics by seeking to impose a hegemonic terminology thus reducing the process to a simple matter of syntactic matching.
4   Metadata has located itself as part of a wider discourse in which higher education is re-conceived as a market economy. As part of this discourse, it contributes to a politicised process of re-defining the role of academics, marginalising them in the learning and teaching process.

Given these limitations, it must be asked whether pursuing the promise of metadata is worth the price.

Rather than dismiss metadata entirely, however, it is important to recognise developments that offer conciliation between these opposing positions. Developing culturally-sensitive, evolving metadata in which multiple accounts (rather than single 'authoritative' descriptions) can be attached to resources would help to address the concerns above. Conflicts over whose responsibility it would be to provide these accounts would still need to be resolved. Indeed, if handled appropriately by skilled information specialists (as advocated, for example, by Beckett 2002), such a process could make a valuable contribution to the processes of informal learning and curriculum development.

> The aim of all metadata is to make resource location possible. We value libraries for structuring and managing books for research, therefore we should no less value metadata creators for structuring and managing our learning resource assets.
>
> (Foster-Jones and Beazleigh 2002: 59)

References

Anido-Rifón, L., Santos-Gago, J., Ródríguez-Estévez, J., Caeiro-Rodríguez, M., Fernández-Iglesias, M. and Llamas-Nistal, M. (2002) 'A step ahead in e-learning standardization: building learning systems from reusable and interoperable software components', in *WWW2002 Alternate Paper Tracks Proceedings*, http://www2002.org/CDROM/alternate/136/index.html (date of access: 20 February 2004).

Barnett, R. (1994) *The Limits of Competence*, Buckingham: Open University/SRHE Press.

Beckett, D. (2002) 'Web crawling high-quality metadata using RDF and Dublin core', in *WWW2002 Alternate Paper Tracks Proceedings*, http://www2002.org/CDROM/alternate/747/index.html (date of access: 20 February 2004).

Beetham, H. (2002) 'Developing learning technology networks through shared representations of practice', in Rust, C. (ed.) *Improving Student Learning Using Technology: Proceedings of the 2001 9th International Symposium on Improving Student Learning*, Oxford: Oxford Centre for Staff and Learning Development, pp. 417–430.

Daniel, J. (1998) *Mega-Universities and Knowledge Media: Technology Strategies for Higher Education*, London: Kogan Page.

Downes, S. (2001) 'Learning objects: resources for distance education worldwide', *The International Review of Research in Open and Distance Learning*, 2 (1). http://www.irrodl.org/content/v2.1/downes.html (date of access: 20 February 2004).

Earle, A. (2002) 'Designing for pedagogical flexibility – experiences from the CANDLE Project, *Journal of Interactive Media in Education,* 2002 (4). www.jime.open.ac.uk/2002/4.

Edwards, R. (2002) 'Distribution and interconnectedness: the globalisation of education', in Lea, M. and Nicoll, K. (eds) *Distributed Learning: Social and Cultural Approaches to Practice*, London: RoutledgeFalmer, pp. 98–110.

Foster-Jones, J. and Beazleigh, H. (2002) 'Metadata in the changing learning environment: developing skills to achieve the blue skies', *ALT-J*, 10(1): 53–60.

Foucault, M. (1977) *Discipline and Punish: The Birth of the Prison* (trans. Alan Sheridan), New York: Vintage.

Freire, P. (1970) *Pedagogy of the Oppressed* (20th Anniversary Edition, 2000), New York: Continuum Publishing.

Friesen, N. (2002) 'Semantic interoperability, communities of practice and the CanCore learning object metadata profile', *Alternate Paper Tracks Proceedings of the 11th World Wide Web Conference*, Hawaii.

IEEE (Institute of Electrical and Electronic Engineers) (2001) *Current LTSA Specification; Draft 9*, http://ltsc.ieee.org/wg1/ (date of access: 20 February 2004).

Kuutti, K. (1996) 'Activity theory as a potential framework for human–computer interaction research', in Nardi, B. (ed.) *Context and Consciousness: Activity Theory and Human–Computer Interaction*, Massachusetts: MIT, pp. 17–44.

Lyotard, J.-F. (1979) *The Postmodern Condition: A Report on Knowledge*, Manchester University Press.

McMahon, A. (2000) 'The development of professional intuition', in Atkinson, T. and Claxton, G. (eds) *The Intuitive Practitioner: On the Value of Not Always Knowing What One is Doing*, Buckingham: Open University Press, pp. 137–148.

Merrill, M. (2001) 'Components of instruction: towards a theoretical tool for instructional design', *Instructional Science*, 29(4/5): 291–310.

NCIHE (National Committee of Inquiry into Higher Education) (1997) *Higher Education in the Learning Society*, London: HMSO.

Nilsson, M., Palmér, M. and Naeve, A. (2002) 'Semantic web metadata for e-learning – some architectural guidelines', *Alternate Paper Tracks Proceedings of the 11th World Wide Web Conference*, Hawaii.

Noble, D. (1997) 'Digital diploma mills – part 1: the automation of higher education', *FirstMonday*, 3 (1), http://www.firstmonday.dk/issues/issue3_1/noble/index.html (date of access: 20 February 2004).

Oliver, M. (2002) 'Creativity and the curriculum design process: a case study', *LTSN Generic Centre Resources Database*, http://www.ltsn.ac.uk/genericcentre/ (date of access: 20 February 2004).

Oliver, M. and Conole, G. (2002) 'Supporting structured change: toolkits for design and evaluation', in Macdonald, R. (ed.) *Academic and Educational Development: Research, Evaluation and Changing Practice in Higher Education*, SEDA Research Series, London: Kogan Page, pp. 62–75.

Plewes, L. and Issroff, K. (2002) 'Understanding the development of teaching and learning resources: a review', *ALT-J*, 10(2): 4–16.

Quinn, C. and Hobbs, S. (2000) 'Learning objects and instruction components', *Educational Technology and Society*, 3(2), 13–20, http/ifets.massey.ac.nz/periodical/vol_2_2000/discuss_summary_0200.html.

Rowland, S. (2000) *The Enquiring University Teacher*, Buckingham: Open University/SRHE Press.

Smith, H. and Oliver, M. (2002) 'University teachers' attitudes to the impact of innovations in ICT on their practice', in Rust, C. (ed.) *Improving Student Learning Using Technology: Proceedings of the 2001 9th International Symposium on*

Improving Student Learning, Oxford: Oxford Centre for Staff and Learning Development, pp. 237–246.

Thorpe, M. (2002) 'From independent learning to collaborative learning: new communities of practice in open, distance and distributed learning', in Lea, M. and Nicoll, K. (eds) *Distributed Learning: Social and Cultural Approaches to Practice*, London: RoutledgeFalmer, pp. 131–151.

Wenger, E. (1998) *Communities of Practice: Learning, Meaning and Identity*, Cambridge: University of Cambridge Press.

Whitson, J.A. (1997) 'Cognition as a semiotic process: from situated mediation to critical reflective transcendence', in Kirshner, D. and Whitson, J.A. (eds) *Situated Cognition: Social, Semiotic and Psychological Perspectives*, Mahwah, New Jersey: Lawrence Erlbaum Associates, pp. 97–149.

Wiley, D. (2000) 'Connecting learning objects to instructional design theory: a definition, a metaphor, and a taxonomy', in Wiley, D. (ed.) *The Instructional Use of Learning Objects* (online version), http://www.reusability.org/read/chapters/wiley.doc (date of access: 20 February 2004).

Part 3
Environments

6 Words, bridges and dialogue

Issues of audience and addressivity in online communication

Colleen McKenna

Introduction

Who is our audience for online discourse and how much control do we have in determining it? Perhaps more importantly, to what extent do our perceptions of audience in online environments influence how and what we write? Online text exists in formats that can be copied, forwarded, transmitted and archived with relative ease, and while such flexibility offers new textual opportunities for writers, it also alters more traditional notions of audience: as recent cases of misdirected email show, audience for online discourse can be a fluid and uncontrollable entity. (Examples abound of email messages written with particular correspondents in mind that are subsequently circulated either inadvertently or deliberately to readers unimagined by the original author.[1]) Given the role of audience in meaning-making, particularly in Bakhtinian constructs of the writer–reader relationship (to be described below), this chapter asks what an awareness of the changed nature of audience in online environments might mean for writing, particularly in educational contexts where digital communication is increasingly encouraged.

This chapter will draw on theories of dialogic discourse, specifically the notion of addressivity, to explore the complexity and impact of audience upon communication and identity construction in email, virtual learning environments (VLEs) and web-based, hypertext documents. Following a consideration of dialogism and reader–writer interaction in conventional academic writing, the discussion will turn to ways in which audience is conceptualized and constructed in email exchanges and will then move to briefer explorations of audience in VLE discourse and web-based documents. Throughout, I will attempt to raise questions about the ways in which audience is determined (both technologically and socially) and how online writers feel that a perception of audience influences their written expression. The chapter will also draw on interviews with university staff and students, some of whom occupy dual roles (such as postgraduate and administrator), to consider how ideas about audience (particularly the multiple or unknowable audience) affect their writing in online environments.[2]

Theories of addressivity and 'conventional' academic writing practices

Bakhtinian theory argues that an awareness of audience or addressee in a linguistic relationship is essential to the construction of meaning. The addressee, real or imagined, stimulates and partly determines what Bakhtin would call an utterance:

> Orientation of the word toward the addressee has an extremely high significance. In point of fact, word is a two-sided act. It is determined equally by whose word it is and for whom it is meant. As word, it is precisely the product of the reciprocal relationship between speaker and listener, addresser and addressee. Each and every word expresses the 'one' in relation to the 'other'. I give myself verbal shape from another's point of view of the community to which I belong. A word is a bridge thrown between myself and another. *If one end of the bridge depends on me, then the other depends on my addressee. A word is a territory shared by both addresser and addressee, by the speaker and his interlocutor.* (emphasis added)
>
> (Voloshinov 1929, cited in Pearce 1994: 43)

Bakhtin argues that the addressee determines both the content of what is said/written (the 'word' above) as well as the speaking subject (for Bakhtin subjectivity is always socially constructed through discourse). Furthermore, he argues that such relationships between addresser and addressee are inscribed with power dynamics, and that these too have an impact upon what is said or written. In this model, dialogue is frequently characterized as struggle which takes place within a multi-voiced or 'heteroglossic' environment.

There has, over recent years, been an increased interest in computer-mediated communication and online discourse, particularly from the perspectives of language and identity. For instance, much work has focused on the linguistic nature of online discourse, particularly in email correspondence and computer conferencing (Kress 1998; Lea 2001; Crystal 2001). More general issues of knowledge construction in online communities, including topics such as multimodality, electronic literacies and writer identity, have been widely theorized (Bolter 2001; Kress 2003; Warschauer 1999). However, if we accept the premise of addressivity and the notion that audience plays a significant role in the development of meaning, then it seems useful to explore the ways in which audience can be envisaged and constructed in online environments.

Addressivity in conventional HE writing

Much recent research into writing in higher education has focused on writing as a social act as opposed to a generic activity which happens without reference to wider institutional and disciplinary contexts (Lea and Stierer 2000; McKenna 2003). Of particular relevance to this chapter is the work on addressivity in student writing by Ivanic (1998), Clark and Ivanic (1997) and Lillis (2001). Starting from the Bakhtinian position that language is fundamentally dialogic, 'shot through with shared thoughts, point of view, alien value judgements and accents', Lillis considers the extent to which student writers are aware of and cope with the dialogic nature of writing practices in higher education. She argues that a dialogic model of writing development in which addressivity is a prominent feature, enables us to appreciate more fully the impact the reader (actual or imagined) has upon what a student-author writes and, perhaps equally importantly, what she does not:

> In this framework, the real or potential addressee contributes to what can be meant as much as does the addressor. To acknowledge the centrality of addressivity, in and for meaning making, is to challenge the dominant way in which the writer/reader relationship's impact on the construction of texts is often construed, in several ways. Firstly, addressivity challenges the conduit model of language in use ... Secondly ... it problematises the way in which the addressee is often conceptualised as an additional factor, giving instead the addressee a central role in and for meaning making.
>
> (Lillis 2001: 43)

Thus a sense of one's reader(s), both real and imagined, is critical to how and what is written.

Ivanic, in her influential work on writing and identity, also looks at these relationships between writers and readers. She argues that the power differential is of particular importance in terms of the extent to which a writer feels he or she must construct a particular account of 'self' in the writing: 'the discoursal self which writers construct will depend on how they weigh their readers up and their power relationship with them' (Ivanic 1998). She suggests that student writers partly accommodate their reader-assessors, but not entirely. Elsewhere she makes the point that the power relations between readers and writers are context-dependent. Whereas in the higher education construct of student-writer/teacher-reader, the writers tend to view themselves as less powerful than their readers, in other situations readers of published writing often view the writer as being more powerful than they are (Clark and Ivanic 1997). For both Lillis and Ivanic, the understanding of the complexity of audience and its involvement in the writing process is crucial to a discussion of academic writing practices. A number of the broad principles of addressivity and construction of meaning can also be applied to writing in online environments.

Audience in online environments

Given such emphasis on the importance of audience, we might usefully ask how audience is perceived and constructed in online writing. In his consideration of the relationship between writers and readers in digital environments, Gunther Kress (1998) argues that online discourse is socially rather than technologically determined. Looking at supposedly new discourses emerging in online communication, particularly the written–spoken hybrid discourse that frequently characterizes email exchanges, he suggests that rather than attributing such change to the speed with which technology transmits messages, shifts towards informality in online discourse are a function of a perceived 'social proximity':

> From such a position email produces new social relations – it effectively puts me in the temporal even if not geographical co-presence of my interlocutor, somewhat like a situation typical of the use of speech. And it is this remaking of the social situation which then reshapes language in the direction of speech-like form.
>
> (Kress 1998: 54)

While I would agree with this, I do think, nonetheless, that aspects of online communication – particularly instances of audience – are constructed to an extent by technology.

If we consider email, there are a number of ways in which technology plays a part in determining the addressee or audience. For example, recipients can appear in the 'To' line or the 'Cc' line (which already complicates Bakhtin's notion of the addressee by establishing a strict hierarchy of readers). Audiences can be single, multiple and even unknown. (In lists, there is the further complication that the addressee can be a named individual, but with the intention that the message is read by all list members.) Furthermore, the message can be 'blind copied' ('Bcc') which creates the condition of an invisible audience as far as other addressees are concerned. Beyond that, a writer/speaker must be aware that the words could easily have another, unintended audience through forwarding. If the messages are part of an archived list, there may be another, future audience, which is equally unknowable. Additionally, managers of institutional networks ultimately have access to users' correspondence (Moran and Hawisher 1998) and electronic messages are increasingly recovered from computer systems in investigations and legal cases. In fact, Moran and Hawisher go so far as to say 'the audience for email is, potentially, the world'. This would seem to be the position that many manuals on email practice take (Moran and Hawisher 1998; Whelan 2000). Given all this, it is perhaps paradoxical that a number of commentators suggest that email correspondence is often characterized by a certain intimacy (Moran and Hawisher 1998) and that people are more willing to 'self-disclose' in online communication than in telephone or face-to-face conversation (Wallace 1999; Bacon 2000, cited in Crystal 2001).

Who's in the audience?

Increasingly, the issue of audience is being explicitly addressed by organizations, including universities, through the placement of corporate footers within email messages. For example, the following statement, typical of its genre, appeared at the bottom of a message sent to a list recently from a contributor who works for a UK university:

> Privileged/confidential information may be contained in this message. If you are not the addressee indicated (in this message/or responsible for delivery of the message to such person), you may not disclose, copy or deliver this message to anyone and any action taken or omitted to be taken in reliance on it, is prohibited and may be unlawful. In such case, you should destroy this message and kindly notify the sender by reply email.
>
> (Personal communication)

This text raises a number of questions. On the one hand, most readers would probably take this statement to mean that should a message come your way inadvertently, as the unintended recipient the onus is on you to ignore or destroy it and certainly not to act upon it. (Whether this is actually legally binding or not – as implied – is another issue.) But upon further reflection, the section which says 'If you are not the addressee indicated in this message/or responsible for delivery of the message (to such person), you may not disclose, copy or deliver this message to anyone' is highly ambiguous. Does this apply if the message has been forwarded to you by the first addressee without the knowledge of the original sender? At what point do you stop being a legitimate addressee? And does it matter?

Clearly the thought that the entire world is a potential audience is seen as problematic. This attempt to restrict readership (although the very existence of the footer implies that this cannot be done) perhaps has a correlative in postal mail. As Moran and Hawisher point out, knowingly tampering with post can incur penalties, and we have long attempted to protect letters from others' eyes by sealing envelopes (Moran and Hawisher 1998).

Such an attempt to restrict and control readership of email seems an implicit admission that audience seriously influences meaning and has an impact upon what can be written. Significantly, one of the people with whom I spoke said that the thought of being held legally responsible (by an unknown reader) influenced both what she said and the language she used:

I am very conscious of the legal side ... If I was giving some kind of view of something ... I would tend to say 'would usually' or 'would normally', 'in my experience' or something like that just to mean this is the situation as far as I know but it may not apply in ... every case.

(Interview respondent)

This use of hedging in anticipation of a possible legal threat seems to constitute an act of self-regulation motivated by both an awareness of a potential audience and the status of an electronic message which may have some legal standing.

To, Cc or Bcc

Earlier in the chapter it was suggested that the way in which email software sets out fields for recipients may contribute to a sense of audience for both writer and reader. Most of the people with whom I spoke initially expressed fairly clear-cut rules governing the ways in which they determined whether to position someone in the 'To' or 'Cc' lines. A person (or persons) to whom a message was directly addressed and from whom they might expect a response or action was placed in the former ('To'). Those in the latter ('Cc') were generally included for information only. However, there were some issues of power that seemed to inform the perceived difference between the two lines. For example, one participant mentioned feeling uneasy about putting names of more senior colleagues in the 'Cc' line, in case they felt they were being 'fobbed off' with a 'Cc'. Additionally, another suggested that individuals were sometimes 'Cc'ed in order to send an implicit message to the main recipient – either to signal a broad level of support (on behalf of the writer) by including more senior colleagues or to draw others (again often more senior colleagues) as witnesses in a contentious or controversial exchange. I will return to this differentiation of audience in the conclusion and consider it in light of what Lynn Pearce has called 'a system of shifting address' (Pearce 1994).

If we accept, following Bakhtin's ideas of addressivity, that such constructions of audience are bound up with intent and development of meaning when *composing* messages then we might also think about audience in terms of where we, as readers, have been *positioned*, drawing on a sort of reader-response theory perspective which considers the positioning of the reader by the writer as significant to interpretation. Can audience foster a sense of exclusivity or inferiority for the reader? Does such a sense affect one's reading of the text? If we examine the placement of readers within email we might, for example, ask the following:

- Does an awareness of having been placed in the 'To' line rather than the 'Cc' line change the way a reader approaches the content and whether or not he or she responds? Perhaps there is meaning in the knowledge of others with whom one has been grouped. If I have been positioned within a list of senior academics as part of a visible audience I might engage more fully with a text than if I have been grouped with more junior colleagues.

- Does a full awareness of audience give the reader a certain amount of control (which has thus been relinquished by the writer)? If, for example, an email is circulated which is addressed to a group of decision-makers (referees, reviewers, etc.) who would otherwise remain unknown to one another, is there a certain prestige and empowerment that is gained?

I would suggest that in all such cases, an awareness of audience would have an impact on the reading and interpretation of a message, thus affecting its meaning.

At least, in the examples above, everyone is aware of who the audience is. What about the 'Bcc' (Blind carbon copy) function? Among the people with whom I spoke, there seemed to be two very different ways of using this function. One was to protect the privacy of other recipients, so that no one saw in a 'To' or 'Cc' line the email addresses of others. The other was to include within the audience members of whom the primary recipients would be unaware. In the latter use, one might ask what the relationship between the 'Bcc' recipient and the sender is, and to whom the message is actually addressed? Such use of the 'Bcc' function actively constructs an additional layer of audience, and it is hard to think of an analogue in other forms of communication (except perhaps a form of phone tapping in which a third party is listening at the request of the caller, however benignly). Furthermore, there again seem to be clear questions about control and power dynamics here. To what extent, if at all, is a recipient of a message which has been 'Bcc'ed to others disempowered by his or her partial knowledge of audience?

Blind carbon copy seemed to raise the strongest views about audience with interviewees:

> I use blind carbon copy very rarely and usually only when I feel I've got something important of maybe a strategic type nature – like a decision that might have been made about a project or something that we're doing ... it would be to someone like [line manager or head of department] or someone in the department that I would want to know what I've done or exactly what I've said to somebody without that person knowing that we're keeping that little tracking process going on [hesitation] so I would do it for that – for a record really – but I don't like using it because I wouldn't like it to be used on me very much, and I don't think it's very nice.
>
> ...One of my [friends] never knew that blind carbon copy existed and got a terrible shock when she realised it did and seemed to be

very fearful of email for a while. I think it was the idea that something was sent to her that she might have viewed as personal or for her own work or her own eyes could actually go to lots of different people depending on what the sender had decided and she never realised that before ... it's a bit of a shock to the system sometimes maybe when you realise that ... I think that's one reason I don't use it very much, because it seems a little bit underhand.

(Interview respondent)

Another interviewee said that while initially she felt that the 'Bcc' facility was 'sneaky', she now uses it as a means of keeping email addresses and names private when sending messages to a group of people. She disliked the idea that someone might use 'Bcc' (in its 'sneaky' mode) when sending email to her. What interests me here is not so much the act itself (after all, you could always keep copies of letters and show them secretly to a third party), rather it is the extent to which such activity is normalized and made so easily available by the software. Like Land and Bayne, in their analysis of surveillance tools routinely packaged in virtual learning environments (see Chapter 11 of this book), I think it is useful to 'render strange' this aspect of online discourse which, as far as I can tell, is rarely discussed.

Not surprisingly, acts of self-regulation are predicted in such an environment. Moran and Hawisher (1998) write that 'this lack of privacy, or security, can shape the message that has been written: it can force gaps and omissions, make a writer hold back, obfuscate, withdraw ... The writer needs to hold in mind a complex audience situation'. It seems a short step from this position to that of Foucault's notions of self-surveillance (via Turkle 1995) as applied to online discourse:

power in modern society is imposed not by the personal presence and brute force of an elite caste but by the way each individual learns the art of self-surveillance. Modern society must control the bodies and behaviors of large numbers of people. Force could never be sufficiently distributed. Discourse substitutes and does a more effective job.

(Turkle 1995: 247)

Among the people I spoke with, a sense of self-regulation was also practised when addressing email lists:

If it's a public list ... I'm very conscious of who might be there and I think it could be almost anyone and they could be from anywhere and I'm sometimes really surprised by the messages that get sent to [X] by people in institutions and I think 'Do they not know who could be reading this?'. Their own managers or whoever ... And they could be quite upfront about what's going on in their own institutions.... I would usually be very careful about writing ... to a list like that ... because you never know who's going to [be there].

(Interview respondent)

Furthermore, the potential durability of email motivates some self-regulating practices. Turkle quotes a student who, although writing for a non-academic list, changed his approach to email when he realized that the list was archived and that his messages might have new audiences in future:

> Then I found out that the list is archived in three places. Email makes you feel as though you are just talking. Like it will evaporate. And then what you say is archived. It won't evaporate. It's like somebody's always putting it on your permanent record. You learn to watch yourself.

(Turkle 1995: 248)

This final point returns us to the paradox of the intimate yet potentially public nature of the medium mentioned above. Significantly, the idea of forwarding a message to a new recipient other than the originally intended addressee did not raise the same sense of anxiety among participants as 'Bcc' and list archiving, although the awareness that something could be forwarded had an impact on what and how people wrote in email (most had at least one story of an unfortunate forward) and did seem to result in a certain degree of self-regulation.

Virtual learning environments and web-based writing

Similar lines of enquiry can be followed with virtual learning environments (VLEs) and the writing and publication of hypertext documents on the internet. According to dialogic theory all such instances of addressivity have an impact upon both the writer and the resultant utterance or text. It should be noted that aspects of dialogism, particularly Bakhtin's notion of heteroglossia and the related concept of discourse as struggle with another's words, have been part of the recent theorizing of online conferencing (Herring 1996; Galin and Latchaw 1998; Lea 2001). Nonetheless, it does seem that here, too, issues of audience – particularly the way in which audience is constructed in online environments – have perhaps been under-represented. For example, Howard (1998) describes the multi-voiced nature of an online conference in terms of the students' difficulty with the shift of authority away from the teacher:

> In one online forum, students complained that the lecturer's role was diminished ... students often resist our attempts to fade into the background. Students consider it their job to 'psyche out' the professor,

and when the teacher's voice gets lost in the polyphony of an electronic mail conference, the students feel confused and frustrated by the lack of guidance.

(Howard 1998: 220–221)

However, although Howard describes this as a misunderstanding about role, it may be a difficulty with conceptualizing audience and managing the shift from a singular to a multiple audience, one in which the students still desire to address ('psyche out') the teacher while also engaging with other students. For them, it would seem, the teacher is still the primary addressee. Furthermore, they haven't developed strategies for addressing different audiences simultaneously.

One person whom I interviewed suggested that the dialogic nature of a discussion board, and the different – in this case aggressive – nature of some of the postings had a direct impact upon the participant's wording of contributions:

I had to email and talk to the discussion boards in a way that was supportive of the other students. But ... they tended to challenge each other quite openly about different points and discuss in quite an open way and not always be very supportive. And you did have people, not shooting each other down in flames, but they could be quite strong about things they believed in and so there was a temptation to not always be very supportive and to be very assertive ... we had one person in there who was very, very assertive ... people like that made it quite difficult sometimes to know how to word things exactly.

(Interview respondent)

The more obvious and insistent presence of audience in such an environment clearly has an impact on writing here, and, as such, may have implications for the assessment of student writing produced in online spaces. Furthermore, there's a suggestion that the interface itself has an impact on the construction and understanding of audience:

I did feel in general using that system that the audience and the way they talked to each other was determined by the system because you had these discussion strands and but also by the content that was already in there because there were students there who had already done say [part of the course] ... So ... we were new people mixed with someone who had been there a year and a half already. And I felt that a lot of things had already been set by them like what was talked about to some extent and the tone and the attitudes towards the course in general and that maybe you shouldn't move very far away from those if you wanted to be part of the discussion. And I found that sometimes quite constraining in a way because I couldn't just say 'I'm

... a new person can anyone fill me in on what goes on here a bit more?' but I felt there was already a community there in a sense and it was quite hard to join it to begin with.

(Interview respondent)

One possible interpretation here is that virtual learning environments can overdetermine audience and create a hierarchical and historical account of discourse which inhibits future participants.

Finally, I want to consider briefly some observations about audience and web-based documents. Although with website publishing we might initially conclude that writers are knowingly publishing to an unlimited pool of readers, Daniel Chandler, in his work on homepages and identity, suggests, conversely, that many 'young' web page authors 'seem conscious only of an audience of their friends' (Chandler 1998). Related to this is the even more potentially counterintuitive observation that the audience for many online web page authors is the self: 'despite being a private person, I decided to publish what I wrote on my Home Page. I was the intended audience, as strange as it sounds. Somehow, publishing my feelings helped validate them for myself' (ibid.). That said, others have suggested that the notion of a limitless audience is almost silencing: 'What can I say about me that I would be equally happy to have read by all the categories of people I might want to relate to?' (ibid.).

This final account of audience being multiple and unknowable seemed to strike a chord with one participant in particular, and when asked whether audience has an impact on the production of web pages, she replied:

Yes definitely.... I'm doing a project web site at the moment ... and – I can't do it until I've figured out who this is for ... I probably do ... have an archetypal student in my head ... and I think probably if somebody were to analyse the way that I write for students ... that that affects all sorts of things: choice of words ... you have a tendency to generalise ... I think also you don't know who your audience is going to be on the web; whereas with email, at least you're emailing to someone ... if you've got materials on the web it's for the people you intend and anyone else who comes along and so I am sometimes conscious of the person who will not understand what you're trying to do and get very cross because anyone can find it.... I am conscious of an unknown audience in a way different to email.

(Interview respondent)

This person seems to be describing a variant of Bakhtin's superaddressee, a sort of imagined abstract, ideal reader, who exerts a shaping (and in this case potentially inhibiting) force upon the text that she puts online. Interestingly, she differentiates this concept of audience from that of email, where she feels more able to 'know' the reader.

Conclusions

How do we (and our students) think theoretically about multiple and unknowable audiences – both in terms of writing to them and being part of them? It has been suggested above that we practise acts of self-regulation, which are probably not dissimilar to analogous regulatory practices that have been observed in student writers, particularly those who position themselves 'outside' the academic culture (Turkle 1995; Lillis 2001). Additionally, I have suggested that we may have in mind a variation of Bakhtin's notion of the superaddressee. Finally, Lynn Pearce moves beyond the Bakhtinian approach of writing with a 'fairly particularized communicant' in mind, to argue that there is a system of 'shifting address' which to some extent enables the addressing of different, but related, audiences in the same text. She uses the example of writing an academic book as an instance in which multiple audiences – students, academics, interested others – must be kept in mind:

> As a consequence, you will find that many texts which are ostensibly meant for the student market ... are more obviously in 'dialogue' with fellow academics 'in the field' ... [T]he author has one ear anxiously directed to the authoritative scorn/approval of his or her peers.... Aside from the public and anonymous recipients of my discourse, there will also be the more intimate 'unofficial' readers: friends and colleagues ... whose dialogic contribution to this book ... will exist as a subtext only they recognize.
>
> (Pearce 1994: 21–22)

Such a shifting address approach would seem to characterize the following account given by an interviewee who regularly contributes to a special interest list which includes product developers, reviewers, users and detractors of the products. When writing to the list, the participant likes to communicate on one level with 'people in the know' on the list as well as with the more general audience:

> I may try and slip in some hidden references so that they know what I'm alluding to but not give so much away that [the detractors] will pick up on what's going on ... it's quite delicate ... some of the emails I redraft the heaviest are those that go to these informal lists.
>
> (Interview respondent)

This sort of sophisticated handling of audience is perhaps the very thing that the students discussed above in Howard (1998) seemed unable to do. Perhaps in the name of cybereducation then, we should aim more explicitly to teach students how to analyse and communicate to multiple audiences. The shift from writing an essay for a tutor to publishing a web-document to an unknowable audience surely has ramifications for writing and assessment in higher education which must be explicitly explored. Furthermore, although some writers acknowledge the impact of audience in contexts such as online conferencing, it is still to some degree treated in an undifferentiated way and not sufficiently investigated from the student perspective.

Finally, it is also necessary to remember that even the imagined, individual addressee or cyber-reader is not a stable, unchanging force, but one who is never entirely known. As one respondent put it:

> I do often think about whether if they've just come back from a horrendous meeting or their computer has just crashed or they have just spilled coffee all over the desk and then they get an email from me what's going to be the reaction?
>
> (Interview respondent)

Notes

1 Recent events such as the Hutton Inquiry in the UK, in which electronic messages written by government officials and journalists have been made public (both on a high-profile website and as part of the evidence submitted to the Inquiry), reveal correspondence that clearly had specific readers in mind and which was written with little or no sense of the very wide audience it now has. On the one hand it seems quite remarkable that journalists and government press officers would be so candid in a format which can be both copied and saved; on the other, it is perhaps indicative of the way that we've come to view the medium itself that this sort of informal and potentially damaging discourse can be written by professional communicators and/or image-makers, with seemingly little awareness of how it might appear to a broader readership. Significantly, Tom Kelly, the official spokesman for the UK prime minister who was quoted in email saying that the disagreement between the BBC and the government had become 'a game of chicken', later said that the message had been sent to 'a close colleague and, taken out of context, it was not the language he would normally use' (BBC Online 2003). Again, this would seem to be an example in which a certain conceptualization of audience results in a type of discourse which seems inappropriate and damaging when placed before a different audience. We might ask why writers who are highly media-literate might imagine only one type of audience for online discourse.
2 Quotations in this piece come from a small sample of in-depth interviews. The work is part of a larger enquiry into the role of audience in online spaces.

References

Bakhtin, M.M. (1988) *The Dialogic Imagination*, Holquist, M. (ed) (trans. C. Emerson and M. Holquist), Austin: University of Texas Press.

BBC online. The Hutton Inquiry http://news.bbc.co.uk/1/hi/uk_politics/3176267.stm (date of access: September 2003).

Bolter, J.D. (2001) *Writing Space: Computers, Hypertext and the Remediation of Print* (2nd edn), New Jersey: Lawrence Erlbaum Associates.

Chandler, D. (1998) 'Personal home pages and the construction of identities on the web', http://www.aber.ac.uk/media/Documents/short/webident.html (date of access: 20 October 2002).

Clark, R. and Ivanic, R. (1997) *The Politics of Writing*, London: Routledge.

Crystal, D. (2001) *Language and the Internet*, Cambridge: Cambridge University Press.

Galin, J. and Latchaw, J. (eds) (1998) *The Dialogic Classroom: Teachers Integrating Computer Technology, Pedagogy, and Research*, National Council of Teachers of English.

Herring, S.C. (ed.) (1996) *Computer-Mediated Communication: Linguistic, Social and Cross-Cultural Perspectives*, Amsterdam: John Benjamins.

Howard, T.W. (1998) 'Four designs for electronic writing projects', in Galin, J.R. and Latchaw, J. (eds) *The Dialogic Classroom: Teachers Integrating Computer Technology, Pedagogy and Research*, National Council of Teachers in English, pp. 210–239.

Ivanic, R. (1998) *Writing and Identity: The Discoursal Construction of Identity in Academic Writing*, Amsterdam: John Benjamins.

Kress, G. (2003) *Literacy in the New Media Age*, London: Routledge.

Kress, G. (1998) 'Visual and verbal modes of representation in electronically mediated communication: the potentials of new forms of text', in Snyder, I. (ed.) *Page to Screen: Taking Literacy into the Electronic Era*, London: Routledge, pp. 53–79.

Lea, M. (2001) 'Computer conferencing and assessment', *Studies in Higher Education*, 26(2): 163–179.

Lea, M. and Stierer, B. (eds) (2000) *Student Writing in Higher Education: New Contexts*, SRHE/Open University Press.

Lillis, T. (2001) *Student Writing: Access, Regulation, Desire*, London: Routledge.

McKenna, C. (2003) 'From skills to subjects: the reconceptualisation of writing development in higher education', in Rust, C. (ed.) *Improving Student Learning: Ten Years On*, Oxford: OCSLD, pp. 67–74.

Moran, C. and Hawisher, G. (1998) 'The rhetorics and languages of electronic mail', in Snyder, I. (ed.) *Page to Screen: Taking Literacy into the Electronic Era*, London: Routledge, pp. 80–101.

Pearce, L. (1994) *Reading Dialogics*, London: Edward Arnold.

Turkle, S. (1995) *Life on the Screen: Identity in the Age of the Internet*, New York: Touchstone.

Voloshinov, V.N. (1929) *Marxism and the Philosophy of Language* (trans. L. Matejka and I.R. Titunik), Cambridge: Harvard University Press, 1986, p. 86, cited in L. Pearce, *Reading Dialogics*, London: Edward Arnold, 1994, p. 43.

Wallace, P. (1999) *The Psychology of the Internet*, Cambridge: Cambridge University Press.

Warschauer, M. (1999) *Electronic Literacies: Language, Culture, and Power in Online Education*, New Jersey: Lawrence Erlbaum Associates.

Whelan, J. (2000) *Email at Work*, London: Pearson Education Ltd.

7 Nobody knows you're a dog

What amounts to context in networked learning?

Christopher R. Jones

Introduction

In a famous cartoon in the *New Yorker* a dog is pictured sitting in front of a computer screen. The text reads, 'On the internet nobody knows you're a dog' (Steiner 1993). This cartoon symbolises readings of the internet that stress the anonymity of the user who is able to send and receive messages over the internet in relative obscurity. Cyberspace has been described as an altered reality, a virtual space, in which the normal rules of the real are changed, where in some senses anything goes. One criticism of this view identifies just how little anonymity the internet *actually* provides to its users (see Chapter 12 of this volume). Another reading, explored in this chapter, would stress the designers of internet activities rather than the user. It would point out how little control designers may have over the eventual users of their products and services. It is in this sense that I draw the reader's attention to this cartoon. I want to ask whether those who wish to exercise control over users in networked learning have their perceived capacity to control students disrupted or reduced by the application of computer networks.

The internet has the potential to disrupt the capacity that designers usually believe that they have to control the context of the user. This disruption may have a particular relevance in higher education. Teachers and designers of learning materials and services have traditionally held some control over the contexts in which their students learn. In so far as students in networked environments have been portrayed as being able to study flexibly, at 'any time, any place, any where', the context of learning may be increasingly diverse and uncontrollable. This chapter examines the issue of context in terms of the internet and in relation to the specific environment of higher education.

Higher education is a setting that is increasingly affected by new technologies and it is also the site for the development of a new professionalism. The work of academic staff is increasingly defined in terms of teaching alongside the traditional focus of research and disciplinary expertise. Higher education is under pressure to deliver a larger number of student outputs, to make them more employable and to widen access to increase the participation rates of selected social groups. Teaching in this setting is increasingly planned and designed rather than reliant upon a vague and under-specified professionalism. For planning to make sense and design to be successful there has to be some guarantee of correspondence between the plan or design and the anticipated conditions under which it could be realised.

This chapter will examine the potential tensions, conflicts and contradictions between a desire to plan and control learning environments and the development and deployment of technologies that potentially disrupt the usual ability to control. This chapter explores the ways in which internet technologies might be theorised in relation to context. This exploration is related to the persistence of technological determinist approaches, in the statements of policy makers, researchers and practitioners of networked learning in higher education. Context is also examined in relation to the use of internet-based resources and services in higher education by exploring the ways in which context is relevant to common theories of teaching and learning. It examines in particular the relational approach to teaching and learning and the ways in which this approach relies upon relatively stable interpretations of context. The chapter will also draw on a number of empirical studies to illustrate aspects of context as they are constituted in and through interactions on- and off-line.

Learning in context

Recently I had the pleasure of interviewing Yrjo Engeström who was a visiting professor at Lancaster University. I conducted the interview for use on an MSc programme in Advanced Learning Technology. The final question I asked him was 'What would your message be if you had one thing for students of networked learning to think closely about?' His response was as follows:

> I would say personally, but it is a very theoretically-driven concern of mine, be aware that networks, networked learning, virtual worlds, digital worlds, etc., should not be conceived of as closed worlds. In other words there is a tremendous temptation to think of those networks as complete worlds unto themselves in which anybody can assume any identity, everybody can play any role, any information is available, you can do anything. However the connection, the interface to the other world, our physical existence, the fact that we have to eat and walk and live with real people oftentimes tends to be suspended or nearly excluded. The closed world phenomenon is a real challenge, and I think we need mixed worlds. We need worlds which cross those boundaries and become hybrids.... If you think of fantasy, good fantasy books, the Narnia books of C.S. Lewis. They were pretty much

a closed world, I think you had to enter through a closet and then you were there. But Harry Potter's world was different; it is in the everyday society, the magicians' school is a place where they actually have to cross the boundary. So that is a good lesson we should learn from Harry Potter. We should not construct our Narnias; we should construct our magicians' schools where you have the trouble of facing your parents and dealing with your livelihood along with those magical possibilities that are offered by the web.

Boundary crossing is the issue I want to deal with here. For me it concerns the ways in which networked environments challenge our perceived conceptions of the nature of reality. In particular I want to examine the ways in which the boundary between learning and its contexts might be revised in terms of networked learning and policy towards networked learning.

A particular concern in the writing of this chapter has been an examination of student experiences of networked learning in higher education. This research has involved me in observations and interviews with students studying on a variety of courses taught both on and off campus. I was impressed during this research by the variety of physical and social spaces in which study took place. For example in one instance a student studying at home had his computer under the staircase in an open plan ground floor with two small children in the family unit. Not a standard image of a study environment. Overall I was impressed by the ways in which student activity was highly contingent in a networked learning environment (Jones and Bloxham 2001; Jones and Asensio 2001). However, such contingencies tend to be overlooked, or absent, within the accounts of student learning and the student's 'situation' to be found in currently prevailing 'relational' theories of student learning. These theories will be examined in a more detailed fashion later in the chapter.

Approaches to the theory of learning

The late 1980s and 1990s saw the development of a set of related theoretical approaches in social sciences that grappled with both new technology and learning. For convenience I will reduce them here to three: a situated view of learning and action (Brown *et al.* 1989; Lave and Wenger 1991; Suchman 1989), (historical cultural) activity theory (Engeström 2001; Nardi 1996; Nardi and O'Day 1999) and distributed cognition (Hutchins 1995; Salomon 1997). Though there are significant differences within and between these different schools they all focused on the social aspect of learning. They displaced learning from the head of the individual out into the social and physical world. Learning ceased to be a 'one-person act' (Lave and Wenger 1991: 15). By placing learning in the community and at times within a complex of tools and artefacts these social and situated views of learning placed the context of learning at centre stage.

Lave and Wenger defined the concept of legitimate peripheral participation as 'engagement in social practice that entails learning as an integral constituent' (1991: 35). In advancing this view Lave and Wenger were also explicit in rejecting abstractions and generalisations. For Brown *et al.* abstractions were also a problem:

> Many methods of didactic education assume a separation between knowing and doing, treating knowledge as an integral, self-sufficient substance, theoretically independent of the situations in which it is learned and used.
>
> (Brown *et al.* 1989: 32)

They argued that the primary reason for learning failure was to do with the abstract approach to cognition taken in schooling and they advocated, like Lave and Wenger, a variety of apprenticeships, whereby learning takes place in a 'real world' context as more appropriate and effective.

> Abstractions *detached from practice* distort or obscure intricacies of that practice.
>
> (Brown and Duguid 1996: 59)

To emphasise the real world nature of learning, Brown and Duguid (1996) likened learning to theft. Knowledge was 'stolen' and a particular example was identified in the driving of a car.

> Cars are socially so well integrated that the learning becomes almost invisible. The success of learner drivers – with or without instruction – should undoubtedly be the envy and object of many who design far less complex consumer or workplace appliances.
>
> (Brown and Duguid 1996: 51)

I have pointed out before that much of the work conducted in an educational setting contrasts with real world informal learning *because* it is oriented towards the documenting and validating of the practices of the participants (Jones 1999). Indeed Brown and Duguid have themselves identified the central function of the university as being warranting and credentialing students. They go so far as to suggest that a core activity of the university is to act as a degree-granting body (Brown and Duguid 2000). More generally, most of us would recognise that though learning to drive a car may rely on informal processes we would prefer drivers to be qualified rather than self-taught. The processes of educational practice exhibit an orientation towards achieving not simply knowledge but *accredited* knowledge. Stolen knowledge is uncertain knowledge.

The place of abstractions and generalisations in the process of education using networks presents an interesting problem for social research.

Steve Fox has suggested adopting the approach of Actor Network Theory because of the integration into that theory of objects and artefacts as actants (Fox 2002). Fox argues that abstraction is a practical accomplishment that is reliant on new technology. In particular he emphasises the role of standardisation, immutability and mobility in the process. Networked learning, understood as a situated process, has emphasised process issues and the negotiation of meaning. At the same time the development of networked and e-learning has led to the construction of a range of learning objects tagged by metadata and intended for re-use (see Oliver's account in Chapter 6 of this volume). More particularly for the purposes of this chapter the emphasis on the socially situated nature of learning has downplayed the importance of policy and politics as these arenas, like abstractions and generalisations, appear detached from local practice.

To explore these issues further I want briefly to examine two different contexts for networked learning. For the purposes of this chapter, when I am talking about context I am referring to the idea that actions, designs and artefacts cannot be interpreted in isolation. Context in this sense refers to those features in a setting that are understood to have an impact on the central feature under examination. The first is an aspect of the national policy framework for higher education in the UK. The point of interest for this chapter is to what degree policy from government can configure the user in a networked learning environment. The second examines another locus of control at a more local level. How can designers of networked learning environments constitute settings in which student and learner activity can be reasonably predictable?

Contexts of higher education: policy

It is widely suggested that educational institutions have to restructure as a consequence of the introduction of new technologies. This technological determinism gains some strength from the contrast between the outmoded structures and buildings of real educational organisations that have had their day and the new virtual or e-learning that will emerge, designed to conform to the new technological environment. To give a flavour of how these views impact on policy I include a quotation from a UK government minister (now resigned) responsible for education:

> When you look back at the development of our schools it has been very strangely evolutionary. One of the reasons for that is there has not been a development, there has not been an invention which has brought about a transformation which has signalled the revolution and if you look at health it was maybe antibiotics or it was maybe the discovery of DNA. If you look at transport it was maybe the internal combustion engine and once those discoveries were made, once those changes happened nothing was ever the same again. I think ICT is our

DNA, it's our internal combustion engine; it is the trigger that can introduce a revolution in how we teach and in how we learn.

(Morris 2002)

There is at the heart of government policy a version of technological determinism. The policy idea is that changes in education are both necessary and inevitable as a response to new technologies. Of course government is alive to the effects of other pressures, globalisation in particular, but the technology of computer networks is seen as a key driver of change in the way that education is conducted. There is good evidence from the USA that for all the policy pressure (motivated by similar concerns) towards the use of computers and computer networks, classroom and university practices are highly resistant to radical change (Cuban 1986, 2001). Cuban notes that:

the primary reason given by university boards of trustees and presidents for investing money and time in an expensive technological infrastructure over the decades is to 'revolutionise' teaching and learning.

(Cuban 2001: 130)

Despite this investment Cuban comments that there has been only modest to little impact on the teaching strategies used. Hardly the revolution expected by Morris or the university boards.

There are a number of possible reasons for this failure of policy to impact on classroom and university practice. One has been recently reported in relation to a UK policy initiative, the Distributed National Electronic Resource (JISC-DNER) (Goodyear and Jones 2003). The DNER is:

a managed environment for accessing quality assured information resources on the internet which are available from many sources. These resources include scholarly journals, monographs, textbooks, abstracts, manuscripts, maps, music scores, still images, geospatial images and other kinds of vector and numeric data, as well as moving picture and sound collections.

(DNER 2001)

It is funded by the JISC – the Joint Information Systems Committee of the four UK funding councils for higher education – with an investment to date of over 30 million pounds. The DNER is aimed at users in tertiary education in the UK for learning and teaching and for research and scholarship. The DNER is an example of how policy at national government level is filtered through agencies with a flow of resources and a flow of ideas that form part of a policy framework.

One of the findings from the formative evaluation in relation to a set of projects (5/99) concerned specifically with teaching and learning was that:

> In the case of DNER, many of the projects are driven by beliefs about the value of improved access to electronic content. Access is primarily conceived in technical terms; it is addressed in terms of 'cross-searching', 'fusion services' and 'interoperability', for example. Access is not linked, conceptually, with pedagogically-informed beliefs about students' learning activities. There is no clear view of how learning activity and information resource (content) are meant to relate.
>
> (Goodyear and Jones 2003: 40)

A possible point of failure for government policies in relation to networked learning is that a form of technological determinism goes all the way down, even to individual projects preparing resources and materials for use in teaching and learning. This points to a reading of context in relation to networked learning that suggests that beliefs about technologies are as important as the technologies themselves in framing the objects and artefacts designed for educational use. It is government belief in computer technology that induces them to fund programmes that focus on beliefs about access to the technology rather than pedagogy.

There is, however, a second way in which such policies can fail. Cuban points out that:

> As constrained as teachers are by the history and contexts in which they work, they still exert substantial discretionary authority in classrooms.
>
> (Cuban 2001: 167)

Research I have conducted observing and interviewing teaching staff about their use of digital resources reinforces this observation. The take-up of digital resources relies on more than simple access. In particular it relies on how the individual academic integrates these resources into practices that can be highly resistant to change. This potential autonomy for the teacher in the classroom should remind us of the cartoon that gave this chapter its title. In government policy circles nobody knows that the teacher holds a critical gatekeeper role. In so far as the technology is identified as the driver for change the capacity for academic and teaching staff to resist is largely ignored.

Contexts of higher education: design

Recent government policy in UK higher education has promoted teaching and learning as an increasingly significant part of the practice of academic staff. This is an area of policy in which governments wish to exert increasing control through the promotion of the professionalisation and accreditation of university teachers. The process of accreditation has led to the development of an emerging canon of theory and research related to teaching practice in universities that places stress on teaching being both student-centred and more explicit and accountable. These changes alongside the introduction of networked technologies have placed a greater emphasis on the design of educational environments. Academics involved in the development of networked learning courses have been found to accept the idea of design in ways that might be uncommon elsewhere among academic staff (Jones and Asensio 2002).

The accreditation of teachers in universities and the development of a canon for research-based practice has drawn attention to particular schools of educational research. The relational approach, based on the phenomenographic strand of research, has provided a significant element of this emergent canon for teaching and learning in UK higher education. The relational approach to teaching and learning aims to optimise the conditions in which students can adopt the qualitatively better deep approach to learning. It is also an approach that offers a strong basis for design.

In the relational approach the learning and teaching context is conceived of as outside what is described as the student's situation. The student's situation is said to comprise:

- their evoked prior experience;
- their approaches to learning;
- their perception of their situation;
- their learning outcomes.

The learning and teaching context set beyond these elements would encompass all those factors beyond the student's own experience. It is recognised that there is a potential divergence between the context as designed and the situation as it is perceived and acted upon by the student. This view posits a separation of 'situation' as perceived by the student, from the broader socio-cultural 'context'. Within this body of work the approach a student adopts to learning is dependent on the student's awareness of their learning environment and the teacher's approach to teaching (Prosser and Trigwell 1999). In their account they distinguish between the context in which students are situated and the unique learning situation perceived by each student for himself or herself. Recently Keith Trigwell and Paul Ashwin have introduced the concept of 'evoked conceptions of learning' to bridge a perceived gap between overall environmental factors and a 'perceived learning task in a particular context' (Trigwell and Ashwin 2002: 183).

Several aspects of this popular theory concern us here. The relational approach relies upon the capacity of academic staff to design and control context. The introduction of the idea of evoked conceptions of learning attempts to sharpen the design focus from a general or generic conception of learning to the particulars evoked within a precise context (in the case offered by Trigwell and Ashwin, for example, the distinctive tutorial system of Oxford University). The relational approach relies on the separation of situation from context. This chapter explores this distinction from the perspective of the recipient of the designed elements and questions whether such a distinction is theoretically warranted.

My own research has indicated that the broader 'context' of learning is likely to contain a series of contingent factors which impact on the spaces used by students to conduct their work. Students asked to collaborate on a first-year law course found that the provision of computing on-campus made finding a public work area difficult (Jones and Bloxham 2001). In this particular case the computer labs, library provision and the law library did not provide an adequate environment for group work using networked computers. As a result many students found alternative locations, including the study-bedroom, but some students were inclined to meet entirely face-to-face despite the networked nature of the course.

In another study examining the limits of course design Charles Crook (2002) has used the term 'learning nests' to refer to student study-bedrooms. His particular interest was in these spaces when they formed part of the campus computer network. Like Cuban's study from the point of view of the teacher and the classroom, Crook found that the impact of networked resources and opportunities was 'hardly dramatic'. Little of the students' activity seemed particularly focused on study and he wondered if the convergence of study and recreational resources on one site through the networked computer might be disruptive to the learning of some students. Learning nests are one of the emerging spaces in which learning might take place. The significant points here are that within the learning nest networked computing forms one part of a complex study and recreational space and beyond the study-bedroom computing provision is often beyond the control of the course designer or the course tutor.

Not only was the physical location of the computers on campus a significant influence, so was the provision of a free on-campus telephone network. The flows of information among students were highly sensitive to contingent factors. Those students who lived on-campus would communicate freely using the free phones, those off-campus were less available to the group, especially those who used expensive mobile phones. This cost restraint affected both the calls to and from these students. In some cases students who worked off-campus compensated by greater use of email and the Lotus Notes database for their lack of access to the free phone system.

The interpretation of tasks was another feature identified from my research into student experiences. Distance students that were working on their final project in a single group were shown to have different understandings of the task they had been set (Jones and Asensio 2001). This was not the result of a poorly specified task; indeed the course documentation was in some ways exemplary and when students were shown the course documentation they would correct their mistaken reading of the task that had been set. Rather it appeared that students were reacting to local and contingent factors. For one student it was the group nature of the course that led him to interpret the task as group work rather than an individual assessment. For another it was the isolation of distance learning that he had experienced previously on other courses that led him to over-emphasise the group aspect of the task. In both cases the task that was specified was translated into student activity in relatively unpredictable ways.

If we take these two limited examples and contrast them to the model proposed by the relational approach proposed by Trigwell and others we can see a potential problem. In the relational approach as it has been developed by Trigwell and Ashwin (2002), context is interpreted as locally specific. Their study examined the conceptions of learning evoked in the Oxford tutorial system and related them to self-reports of expected degree classification. These results suggest a stable context that applies across a large number of students in a particular setting. The research reported here would suggest that we could expect contingent factors to disrupt such stable blocks of variation among students.

Conclusions

The notion of context that is applied in many studies of networked or e-learning is one that could be described as requiring infinite extension. Context in this reading becomes anything beyond the local, beyond the focus of immediate concern that could have a bearing on what is being designed, researched or evaluated. In this chapter I have concentrated on more sophisticated readings of context that are compatible with situational and social approaches to learning. For socially situated learning theories context is a critical arena for learning, as learning itself is re-focused away from the internal and individual and onto the external and social.

The policy environment is one area of the context of networked learning that can appear remote from practice, relatively fixed and determined simply by technical and political forces. It is by now a well-rehearsed argument that technical features are themselves constituted by social activity in laboratories, projects and production teams. The brief example taken from the DNER 5/99 projects indicates that policy in the area of networked learning gives rise to activities that are intended to focus on teaching and learning but that emphasise access to technology over and above a pedagogical approach. This hints at the notion that context is constituted by action within policy frameworks in which local actions mobilise elements of the policy framework for use and re-use in a reflexive relationship between beliefs about the world and the world as it is constituted in and through activity.

The cartoon 'Nobody knows you're a dog' suggests that the internet and web allow users to constitute online identities that are separate from the physical identity carried in the real world. I have suggested that this freedom can be reconceived as freedom to resist those attempts to control that come from or through the virtual world. The discretion of the teacher is complemented by the capacity of the student to interpret tasks, instructions, places and organisations in ways that are fundamentally unpredictable. This degree of freedom increases in so far as networks remove students and teachers from direct personal surveillance and replace this with remote systems of control. We can expect this feature of networks to increase with the additional mobility of wireless networks and ubiquitous computing.

This chapter has suggested that educational research needs to take seriously the question of how the routine practical activities of members of educational settings constitute the context of their activities. It is suggested that design practices and theories that rely on the separation of design elements (described as 'context') from activity that is allowed to remain situationally specific are an area that needs careful research. The idea that there is a definite relationship between teachers' approaches to teaching, the evoked conception of learning in students, and results, is highly attractive to planners and policy makers. This relationship is not disproved by what is reported here but the suggestion is made that it requires careful research. We might expect networked learning environments to be more unpredictable and local contexts to be less stable than the relational approach might imply.

One way that context within socially situated theories can be thought of is as a resource for action, mobilised by members of a setting as part of their situationally specific practical reasoning. Practical reasoning is taken to include the ways in which regularities such as policies towards learning and approaches to study are taken to be the practical accomplishments of people in particular settings rather than, in principle, features of the world.

References

Brown, J.S. and Duguid, P. (1996) 'Stolen knowledge', in McLellan, H. (ed.) *Situated Learning Perspectives*, Englewood Cliffs, NJ: Educational Technology Publications.

Brown, J.S. and Duguid, P. (2000) *The Social Life of Information*, Boston, MA: The Harvard Business School Press.

Brown, J.S., Collins, A. and Duguid, P. (1989) 'Situated cognition and the culture of learning', *Educational Researcher*, 18(1): 32–42.

Crook, C. (2002) 'The campus experience of networked learning', in Steeples, C. and Jones, C. (eds) *Networked Learning: Perspectives and Issues*, London: Springer, pp. 293–308.

Cuban, L. (1986) *Teachers and Machines: The Classroom Use of Technology Since 1920*, New York: Teachers College Press.

Cuban, L. (2001) *Oversold and Underused: Computers in the Classroom*, Cambridge, MA: Harvard University Press.

116   *Christopher R. Jones*

DNER (2001) *JISC Distributed National Electronic Resource*, available at: http://www.jisc.ac.uk (date of access: 18 August 2003).

Engeström, Y. (2001) 'Expansive learning at work: toward an activity theoretical reconception', *Journal of Education and Work*, 14(1): 133–156.

Fox, S. (2002) 'Studying networked learning: some implications from socially situated learning theory and actor network theory', in Steeples, C. and Jones, C. (eds) *Networked Learning: Perspectives and Issues*, London: Springer-Verlag, pp. 77–92.

Goodyear, P. and Jones, C. (2003) 'Implicit theories of learning and change: their role in the development of e-learning environments for higher education', in Naidu, S. (ed.) *E-Learning: Technology and the Development of Learning and Teaching*, London: Kogan Page, pp. 29–48.

Hutchins, E. (1995) *Cognition in the Wild*, Cambridge, MA: MIT Press.

Jones, C. (1999) 'Taking without consent: stolen knowledge and the place of abstractions and assessment in situated learning', in Hoadley, C. and Roschelle, J. (eds) *Proceedings of the Computer Support for Collaborative Learning (CSCL) 1999 Conference*, Dec. 12–15, Stanford University, Palo Alto, CA and Mahwah, NJ: Lawrence Erlbaum Associates. http://kn.cilt.org/cscl99/A35/A35.HTM (date of access: 18 August 2003).

Jones, C. and Asensio, M. (2001) 'Experiences of assessment: using phenomenography for evaluation', *JCAL, Journal of Computer Assisted Learning*, 17(3): 314–321.

Jones, C. and Asensio, M. (2002) 'Designs for networked learning: a phenomenographic investigation of practitioners' accounts of design', in Steeples, C. and Jones, C. (eds) *Networked Learning: Perspectives and Issues*, London: Springer-Verlag, pp. 253–278.

Jones, C. and Bloxham, S. (2001) 'Networked legal learning: an evaluation of the student experience', *International Review of Law, Computers and Technology*, 15(3): 317–329.

Lave, J. and Wenger, E. (1991) *Situated Learning: Legitimate Peripheral Participation*, Cambridge: Cambridge University Press.

Morris, E. (2001) Speech at London Guildhall University, http://www.dfes.gov.uk/speeches/index.shtml (date of access: 18 August 2003).

Nardi, B.A. (ed.) (1996) *Context and Consciousness: Activity Theory and Human–Computer Interaction*, Cambridge, MA: MIT Press.

Nardi, B.A. and O'Day, V. (1999) *Information Ecologies: Using Technologies with Heart*, Cambridge, MA: MIT Press.

Prosser, M. and Trigwell, K. (1999) *Understanding Learning and Teaching: The Experience in Higher Education*, Buckingham: SRHE and Open University Press.

Salomon, G. (ed.) (1993) *Distributed Cognitions: Psychological and Educational Considerations*, Cambridge: Cambridge University Press.

Steiner, P (1993) 'On the internet nobody knows you're a dog', *New Yorker*, 69(20): 61.

Suchman, L. (1987) *Plans and Situated Actions: The Problem of Human–Machine Communication*, Cambridge: Cambridge University Press.

Trigwell, K. and Ashwin, P. (2002) 'Evoked conceptions of learning and learning environments', *Improving Student Learning Symposium: Theory and Practice Ten Years On*, Oxford: OCSLD, pp. 183–193.

8 Learning from cyberspace

Glynis Cousin

Introduction

Many higher education curriculum design initiatives involving Information and Communication Technology are conducted within the spirit of a much declared principle that the pedagogy must lead the technology. This principle has become something of a mantra to be recited gravely at any event that invites dissociation of traditional academic practices from geekly interference. It is also embodied in a number of e-learning strategy documents which insist that e-learning should be driven by pedagogical considerations rather than the demands of the technologies themselves. Take, for instance, the following statement from the Higher Education Funding Council for England's consultation document on a UK e-learning strategy:

> We believe that the technology should follow the learning and teaching objectives and not the other way round.
>
> (HEFCE 2003: 11)

The purpose of this chapter is to critique statements like these because, first, they neglect the fact that the medium *is* the pedagogy; second, they posit a division between humans and technology in which the latter is neutral and in the service of the former; third, they contain a luddite drift which I will exemplify in the case of virtual learning environments (VLEs); and fourth, they block our view of the full potential of computer technology for educational purposes.

The dialectics of pedagogy and technology

As Murphy *et al.* point out (2001), all pedagogies necessarily involve technologies of communication and thus the history of pedagogy is inextricably linked to the history of media. Both the scope and the limits of pedagogic methods are influenced by the media involved. For example, before the ascendancy of print, advanced learning relied on memorising and recitation supported by the ancient techniques of *Ars Memoria*, where the imagination was turned into a structured, virtual database in which poems, ideas, facts and so on would be tagged to images. In the words of Augustine, students were advised to deposit information and stories in 'well-lighted, clearly set out' places in their heads 'which have the power of speedily encountering and penetrating the psyche' (in Davis 1998: 200).

With the advent of print culture scholars of *Ars Memoria* lamented this fading complex technology of the mind and the careful face to face coaching it required. Doubtless many of these scholars argued that the adoption of print needed to be driven by the pedagogic imperative to train the mind to remember and retrieve. But pedagogies never live independently of prevailing media and defensive arguments of this sort are destined to be lost. My point is that technologies work dynamically with pedagogies, not for them, and in the process they become mutually determining. A modern illustration would be the pedagogic method of brainstorming which is strongly associated with flipchart technology. It is fruitless to assess from this association whether the pedagogy is driving flipcharts or the flipchart the pedagogy because, whatever their origins, they have now become intertwined. Similarly, the pedagogic strategy of breaking down information and concepts into bite size, slow-release chunks is so interwoven with the striptease function of Microsoft PowerPoint that we can confidently judge them to be jointly culpable for the current reign of the bullet point.

The view that technology is just lying there, waiting for pedagogues to put it to good use, is at the root of the second issue I have raised because this posits technology as inert and separate from human beings. The frequent use of the terms 'tools', 'toolkit' or 'toolbox' with reference to learning technology reinforces this view of technology.

Technology and ontology

The following perspective on computer technology from the UK's Learning and Teaching Support Network (LTSN) provides a good illustration of a conception of technology as subordinate to and separate from humans:

> The WWW and its applications are mere instruments without any intrinsic educational value. Their effectiveness as educational tools relies on the use that is made of them, both by educators and by students.
>
> (Rius-Riu 2002)

The notion that the medium, be it pencil, Morse code or laptop computer, is simply awaiting human use as a 'mere instrument' was much undermined by McLuhan's (1964) demonstration that all media change our self-relation and our social relations. McLuhan pointed out that different media demand different levels and forms of engagement of our senses and social relations, changing the ways we live and perceive. As Davis, following McLuhan put it:

> The moment we invent a significant new device for communication – talking drums, papyrus ... – we partially reconstruct the self and its world, creating new opportunities (and new traps) for thought, perception and social experience.
>
> (1998: 4)

And thus:

> Technology is neither a devil nor an angel. But neither is it simply a tool, a neutral extension of some rock-solid human nature.
>
> (9)

For the LTSN, technology is asocial. For McLuhan, every kind of technology is an extension of our nervous system, which imprints our imagination with the realm of the possible. Understanding technology involves an appreciation of the ontological because how we are with television, radio, the telephone importantly shapes who and what we are. Being a teenager in contemporary Western society involves different ways of being because it involves different ways of being-with technology than it did for former generations. The social life of the juke box generation of the 1950s considerably varied from that of the 'net generation' (Tapscott 1998) of today. In short, far from being 'mere instruments', technologies are constitutive of our identities.

At some UK universities there is talk of hiring students to supervise other students to ensure the 'proper use' of computers and to block them from getting into Hotmail. This talk wants pedagogy to be the exclusive driver of computer use and includes no consideration of the new cultural norms of communication of much of the present student generation. Whereas in my day I might have broken up my library study time with regular trips to a campus café, today's students are more likely to intersperse work and play online. Computers in libraries provide space for chatting in ways that were not possible for earlier generations of students.

Discussion about how to address questions of student engagement with a new medium cannot be based on norms set for an older medium. The original monastic conditions of a library, which were geared towards quiet and close attention to the printed word, may no longer be appropriate. At any rate, educationalists need to ask how computer technology has changed social practices in order to formulate responses to student usage. For instance, Tapscott's (1998) research into 'the rise of the net generation' provides compelling evidence that electronic media have transformed the way children learn:

> When we observed our N-Gen (Net Generation) sample surfing the
> Net, they typically participated in several activities at once. When
> surfing some new material, they hyperlinked to servers and informa-
> tion sources all over the place.... Seven year old Robert looked up
> the movie Independence Day, followed links to fans' pages and
> returned to the search engine. Interestingly, Robert entered three dif-
> ferent searches, but he never went more than two pages away from the
> Independence Day site. If a download took too long or a page disap-
> pointed him, he hit the back key to return to the site.
>
> (Tapscott 1998: 142)

In making sense of observations of this kind, Tapscott is able to show
how children's learning is more 'interactive and nonsequential' than that
which is supported by traditional, book-based pedagogies. An exploration
of this kind into how people learn can be harnessed to an inquiry into what
new technologies expand in the way of opportunities and capacity.
Without such an exploration, the default position will be inherently
conservative. As I discuss next, I think that this is a risk in the case of
virtual learning environments in higher education.

Looking backwards with virtual learning environments

With the ascent of one media form, another begins to take a back seat,
perhaps eventually sliding into obsolescence. A further indication of the
ontological dimension to our being-with technology is that the declining use
of any media which have played a part in our identity formation is under-
standably experienced as loss. For some this loss prompts a luddite yearning
for the apparent safety of the past. Consciously or not, are higher education
e-learning strategies plugging into this yearning? Does the insistence that
pedagogy is running the show calm fears that headstrong learning technologists might dethrone the thoughtful, bibliophilic academic? Another possible way of reassuring academic colleagues that the past is intact lies in the
reference to technology as an 'enhancement tool'. Here the attempt is to
avert any possible protest about technology usage with the compliment that
it will only make better what is already good. It will not alter the status quo;
it will simply dress it in finer clothes, as suggested, for instance, in an
e-learning guide at Oxford University which describes the use of IT in
teaching on campus as assisting 'the "traditional" teaching methods of
Oxford – tutorials, seminars, lectures, lab-work, etc.' (Oxford 2003b: 1).
    Or this from the UK Minister of Education:

> I don't think ICT can replace teachers and lecturers but, alongside
> existing methods, it can certainly enhance the quality and reach of
> their teaching.
>
> (JISC 2003)

Reassurances about the primacy of pedagogy and the purely enhancement value of technology offer false protection to academics because they promise a stable transition in an inherently unstable process of change from one media age to another (Poster 1996), and they promise no loss where there is always loss. This creates an unexamined friction between past and future and, in consequence, inhibits a debate about the losses and the hopes held out by learning technology. One way in which I think this debate remains subdued is in the adoption of virtual learning environments in academe.

I should acknowledge that I am bending the stick in my characterisation of VLEs to allow my argument to work at an ideal typical level. From my experiences, I know that the campus-wide provision of a VLE, together with robust educational development support, has enabled the experimentation of online learning in a variety of innovative ways (for example, Orsini-Jones and Davidson 1999). But unless this kind of experimentation is encouraged, VLE environments tend to be skewed towards the simulation of the classroom, lecture hall, tutor's office and the student common room. The following description of the principal components of a VLE comes from the British Joint Information and Science Council (undated briefing paper). The VLE enables:

- controlled access to curriculum that has been mapped to elements (or 'chunks') that can be separately assessed and recorded;
- tracking student activity and achievement against these elements using simple processes for course administration and student tracking that make it possible for tutors to define and set up a course with accompanying materials and activities to direct, guide and monitor learner progress;
- support of online learning, including access to learning resources, assessment and guidance – the learning resources may be self-developed, or professionally authored and purchased materials that can be imported and made available for use by learners;
- communication between the learner, the tutor and other learning support specialists to provide direct support and feedback for learners, as well as peer-group communications that build a sense of group identity and community of interest;
- links to other administrative systems, both in-house and externally.

It is clear from this description that the technology is connecting users to the conventional academic centralising practices of teaching, assessment and supervision. Another clue to the resonance VLEs establish with the old world can be found in their brand names or symbols: Blackboard and FirstClass are two obvious ones and in the case of the WebCT logo we have the image of a little white, male professor complete with mortar board and gown, clutching the sturdy medium of paper. A set of images and vocabularies concerning VLEs trigger associations with a safe and known academic world. Commenting on this kind of association in relation to the evolution from print to electronic scholarship, Burnett writes:

> Historical metaphors, such as pioneers exploring the wilderness, settlers and homesteaders of the Old West, and Forty-niners scrambling to make their fortune in the gold mines – have been employed in both print and electronic forums to describe the contemporary role of the scholar/networker. These unexamined attempts to find analogies in the past which will help us to stride more confidently into the future – while comforting – are potentially misleading.
>
> (1993: 1)

Though the online medium can allow forays into unchartered territory, there is a level at which the VLE pulls up the drawbridge, enclosing the student and tutor within a familiar university building. The following quotation from a guide to the use of VLEs, for instance, carries the reader into the safe realm of tradition:

> A virtual learning environment can be compared to the empty shell of a building. It is a virtual structure created on the web *into which all aspects of a traditional learning environment can be placed.*
>
> (my emphasis) (Haynes and Anagnostopoulou 2002)

Or this from Oxford University:

> WebLearn is built around the metaphor of a campus containing multi-storied buildings. This flexible structure allows the virtual partitioning of the Oxford electronic campus into a number of divisional and collegiate 'buildings', in which departmental 'floors', and further 'suites' and rooms', can be created practically ad infinitum.
>
> (Oxford 2003b)

This invitation to use VLEs does not require teachers to leave 'traditional learning' or indeed the building. All the prospective adopter of VLEs need do is to locate these environments in the academic womb:

> So the easiest way in which to visualise a virtual learning environment is to think of the plan of the campus of any educational establishment with which you are familiar.
>
> (Oxford 2003b)

Besides the simulation of the architecture of the old world, VLEs were originally designed within the spirit of the broadcast phase of technology in that, like television and radio, they tend to be unidirectional (a small number of producers, too many consumers). Typically, the tutor constructs the curriculum for the student audience to consume. In many VLEs, for instance, three identities are available for reinforcement/construction: designer (she has control over the material to be uploaded, changed, etc.), the teaching assistant (he can get access to the student database for marking purposes) and the students (they can have a private room for groupwork but have access-only to resources). In this way, the identities encouraged by VLEs derive from a protectionist view of the university as the centre and controller of knowledge production. They have also been charged with accommodating a narrow instructional design framework. For instance, in a recent review of learning technology development projects (Conole 2002), VLEs are said to have an inbuilt pedagogic bias towards traditional didactic methods. The review reports on the decision by some universities to develop their own VLE, to correct this bias:

> Many of the commercially available VLEs put learning materials at the centre of the system, whereas some of the home grown VLEs ... were adopting a more learner-centred approach of supporting collaborative learning.
>
> (Conole 2002: 24)

In truth, even the VLE, the report labels as 'traditional' (WebCT), yearly extends its capacity to enable a student-centred approach, and the differences between the various VLEs are insubstantial, not least because few academic learning technologists would defend a content-centred approach. Most technologists now argue for student-centredness, often from a constructivist learning theory approach. Noteworthy for my discussion is that they remain exercised by assumptions about the primacy of pedagogy in the development of online learning. The key debate in online learning in higher education concerns arguments about the nature of its educational underpinning from the viewpoint of pedagogic paradigms developed in conditions of modernity. While this debate permits the kind of critique of VLEs expressed in the review above, it tends to proceed from the negative reference point of instructional design rather than the positive reference point of the media itself.

I think that we need a more fluid interrogation of the pedagogy and the technology, one that does not ask each to fit or serve the other but explores their movements as overlapping, complementary, conflictual, dynamic. We should expect each to be changed by the other:

> E-learning is distinguished, in a paradigmatic sense, from what went before. It represents a new 'learning ecology.' This is not just another add-on, but a technology that is transforming our educational institutions and how we conceptualise and experience teaching and learning.
>
> (Garrison and Anderson 2003: 122–123)

In terms of this 'new learning ecology', I share the position hinted at by Bayne, in Chapter 2 of this volume, that the prevailing conception of online learning technology tends to be modernist, and that this is in tension with a medium which Jencks has described as 'the definitive technological expression' of the postmodern condition (in Woolley 1992: 169). This question brings me to my final argument which is about the extent to which educationalists can explore the potential of communication and information technology for a paradigm shift in teaching and learning which might, somewhat more boldly, let go of the past.

Learning from cyberspace

Cyberspace is often characterised as postmodern because it allows playful and deceitful identity performances (see Chapter 2 of this volume) and is labyrinthine rather than linear. One metaphor that might be invoked to convey these characteristics of the internet is that of the rhizome.

In the postmodern view of Deleuze and Guattari (1987), most texts (exceptions would be from writers like James Joyce and William Burroughs) occupy positions within a hierarchical tree structure, with the canonical text providing the 'root-book' that 'endlessly develops the law of the one that becomes two, then of the two that becomes four ... Binary logic is the spiritual reality of the root-tree' (5). Certainly, this is often the way subjects are approached in higher education where conceptions of foundational knowledge are strong in most disciplines. For Deleuze and Guattari, arborescent imagery has structured and inhibited our imagination; it frames binary thinking and drives us towards a need for genealogies, a need to ask questions like 'Where are you going?', 'Where are you coming from?', 'What are you heading for?' (25). Certainly, this claim accounts for the 'learning outcomes' culture of higher education curriculum design in the UK where a hierarchy of knowledge is respected, the future colonised (in theory) and room for the unexpected and the surprising to manoeuvre is rather limited, at least at the formal level. The search for beginnings and endings, insist Deleuze and Guattari, never 'reaches an understanding of multiplicity' (5), its 'too busy looking for signs and signifiers, for conceptual capture, for origins, to allow understandings to accommodate additions, the "and ... and ... and" of things' (25).

Before briefly expanding on Deleuze and Guattari's image of the rhizome, it is important to acknowledge the danger of exaggerating the scope of the internet, of representing its nomadic capacities as intrinsic threats to the restrictive perspectives of modernity. Before we get too postmodern fanciful, we need to note, for instance, Jacoby's (1997) protest that the critique of binarism is often 'cranked out on computers constructed out of binary switches, routines and numbers' (61). And while the image of the rhizome may reduce our concern for unity and linearity, it may also encourage us to get lost in a polymorphously perverse underworld in which decisions about meanings are never consummated because all is so negotiable and distributed, that we cannot land somewhere to get started. The sheer abundance of idiosyncratic information on the internet can produce nomadic learners who succumb to an endless search for a knowledge oasis rather than enter into the process of digging for one. Indeed, students are frequently issued warnings about the promiscuous nature of the internet search because it strays from sensible associations, often throwing up wild, silly, interesting and sometimes offensive and whacky, linkages that are felt to inhibit getting down to learning. To surf is also, after all, to skim the surface. With this qualification in mind, the metaphor of the rhizome invites us to think of the potential of the internet. A rhizome, write Deleuze and Guattari, 'assumes very different forms, from ramified surface extension in all directions to concretion into bulbs and tubers' (Deleuze and Guattari 1987: 7). For Deleuze and Guattari there are six principles of the rhizome, as follows.

The first two principles concerning 'connection and heterogeneity' state that any point of a rhizome can be connected to any other, and must be. This is very different to a tree or root, which plots a point, fixes an order (7). A rhizome is less likely to be locked in a 'regime of signs' and 'ceaselessly establishes connections between semiotic chains' (7). A semiotic chain 'is like a tuber agglomerating very diverse acts, not only linguistic, but also perceptive, mimetic, gestural and cognitive: there is no language in itself ... only a throng of dialects, patois, slangs and specialized languages' (7). The pace, spread and nature of connectivity allowed by the internet permits all kinds of associations with people, ideas, texts and conversations that resonate with this image of a 'throng of dialects', particularly, perhaps in its chat rooms. Heterogeneity and connectivity, translated into online teaching and learning, potentially concerns the softening of author/reader oppositions, valuing what Deleuze and Guattari describe as change through 'additions'. This refers to ways in which humans add to given scripts, bringing in unexpected amendments by borrowing strategies from elsewhere as in the case of the soldier who indicates alternative possibilities for a different development of the plot because he brandishes a pack of cards to the 'enemy' instead of a gun (Goodchild 1996: 2). In the more prosaic context of the virtual classroom, the medium facilitates the development of multiple 'additions' to a text, as learners post their comments from their own position so that the connectivity principle is more horizontal than vertical.

The third principle is that of multiplicity and is closely tied with that of heterogeneity, as the following illustration suggests:

> Multiplicities are rhizomatic. . . . Puppet strings, as a rhizome or multiplicity, are tied not to the supposed will of an artist or puppeteer but to a multiplicity of nerve fibres, which form another puppet in other dimensions connected to the first.

(8)

In online learning perhaps this would be about diminishing the quest for the 'right' answer or the ritualistic bows to the rival arguments of members of a discourse community, allowing learners to offer tentative responses, the annotation of texts and conversations with fresh questions and/or other texts. As Deleuze and Guattari put it 'the point is that a rhizome or multiplicity never allows itself to be overcoded' (9). This principle of multiplicity, like the next discussed, challenges 'the tyranny of biblical authority' (Woolley 1992: 153) be it in the form of the text, the teacher or disciplinary authority.

The fourth principle is that of a 'signifying rupture' – 'a rhizome may be broken, shattered at a given spot, but it will start up again on one of its old lines, or on new lines' (9). This movement from the broken to the newborn is described as one of 'deterritorialisation' to 'reterritorialisation'. Deleuze and Guattari offer the example of an orchid which 'deterritorialises by forming an image, a tracing of a wasp; but the wasp reterritorialises on that image (10). Burnett (1993) suggests the case of feminist literary criticism which disrupted the established canon by introducing into it non-canonical texts and authors. But in a process of reterritorialisation, these non-canonical texts have become canonical (for example, leading feminist books have become set texts for UK examination boards) though they land in different places to spawn further deterritorialisations. This process of rupture and rebirth partially describes the way in which the surfer encounters broken links that serendipitously lead her to locate fresher or older links. But are these links necessarily fertile in the way Deleuze and Guattari suggest? The next principles give a partial answer perhaps.

The fifth and sixth principles are that of cartography and 'decalcomania'. A rhizome, write Delueze and Guattari, 'is not amenable to any structural or generative model. It is a stranger to any idea of genetic axis or deep structure' (12). In distancing the rhizome from the attribution of a 'genetic axis' (in contrast to the tree), they insist that it is a 'map not a tracing'. 'The orchid' they continue,

> does not reproduce the tracing of the wasp; it forms a map with the wasp, in a rhizome ... what distinguishes the map from the tracing is that it is entirely oriented towards an experimentation in contact with the real ... it is open and connectable in all of its dimensions; it is detachable, reversible, susceptible to constant modification.
>
> (12)

This contrasts vividly with the 'infinite, monotonous tracings of the stages' (13) to which the psychoanalytic procedure is wedded in its attribution of human behaviour to infant traumas. Deleuze and Guattari scorn the psychoanalytic search for deep structures in their insistence that desire can depart from many 'lines of flight' but once the rhizome has been obstructed 'arborified, it's all over, no desire stirs; for it is always by rhizome that desire moves and produces' (14). By this definition, the well-argued text book can over-structure the learner journey, reducing curiosity and pleasure en route. Perhaps the hypertext function can overcome this difficulty by offering multiple exit and entrance points to a 'didactic object' (Shulman 1999). More generally, cyberspace travellers, suggests Burnett (1993), find their own journeys, drawing and redrawing their maps, replacing static networks with mobile ones, surfing and landing wherever the mood or interest takes them.

This idea of the cyberspace traveller carries the risks of an individualism at the expense of a more political and social perception of the internet. We need also to consider how cyberspace could help to produce new forms of cosmopolitanism among students for whom contact across seas, cultures and continents is possible. It could mean new partnerships across universities with, for instance, resource-rich institutions sharing their booty with more impoverished ones, privileged learners conversing with less privileged ones (see Tapscott 1998, for a vivid example of how this works at the schooling level). If the rhizome can 'connect any point to any other point' (21), it can nurture horizontal links across cultures, establishing a 'logic of the AND' (25) over the dichotomous good and bad or the right and wrong. As I have argued in the case of VLEs, it is ironic that most universities are using a medium that enables endless travel to construct learning within the confines of a module or course.

In touching on Deleuze and Guattari's perspective, I have sought to follow their counter-positioning of the arboreal with the rhizomorphic, and to relate this to our thinking about learning in cyberspace. 'We are tired of trees' conclude Deleuze and Guattari:

> They've made us suffer too much. All of aborescent culture is founded on them, from biology to linguistics. Nothing is beautiful or loving or political aside from underground stems and aerial roots, adventitious growths and rhizomes.
>
> (15)

While this declaration appears to request the exchange of one fundamentalism for another, its rhetorical structure allows us to think big about the scope of the internet. If the web is worldwide, the university is the nation state. The latter finds safety in small numbers, proximity, intimacy, familiarity, definable boundaries, disciplinary and tutor authority, linearity, role separation, fixity and hierarchies. The former posits the limit beyond the skies, all is possible, the map is the territory, the medium is definitely the message, the message being that all contact, fleeting or sustained, is possible. All identities are fictional to any degree, and all points of departure are available. It is also more playful, more daring and perhaps more dangerous. In returning to my discussion of VLEs, it may be best to regard

VLEs as transitional objects, enabling academics to work with the new and the old simultaneously.

Chapter 2 of this volume, which includes research into tutors' experiences of online teaching, reveals their fears about losing control of their teacher authority in the online medium. In this context, VLEs allow a creative means by which paths between the new and the familiar can be negotiated. The issue is not to denounce or abandon them, but to see their limits as well as their potential. This would include an appreciation that the cry for the pedagogic determination of the technology may be rooted more in nostalgia for old media than in educational theory for/with the new.

In conclusion, shifts from one paradigm to another always require a transitional period in which the present is characterised by a tussle between the past and the future. In drawing attention to a policy drift that wants learning technology to do pedagogy's bidding, as if the latter were distinct and separate from the former, my aim has been to show how this subdues our understanding of the ontological, intellectual and professional shifts which are inevitable with every significant media revolution.

Acknowledgement

I would like to thank my colleagues Christine Smith, Mark Childs and Jay Dempster for their very helpful comments.

References

British Joint Information and Systems Council (undated briefing paper) *VLEs and MLEs Explained*, http://www.jisc.ac.uk/index.cfm?name=mle_briefings_1 (date of access: 21 February 2004).

British Joint Information and Systems Council: Conference (2003) *Exploiting the potential of ICT* (interview with Charles Clarke), http://www.jisc.ac.uk/index.cfm?name=pub_inform4#02futureElearning (date of access: 21 February 2004).

Burnett, K. (1993) 'The scholar's rhizome: network communication issues', *Electronic Journal on Virtual Culture*, 1(2): April.

Conole, G. (2002) *Review of JTAP Projects*, University of Southampton, Research and Graduate School of Education.

Davis, E. (1998) *TechGnosis*, Harmondsworth: Penguin.

Deleuze, G. and Guattari, F. (1987) *A Thousand Plateaus*, Minneapolis: Minnesota University Press.

Garrison, D.R. and Anderson, T. (2003) *E-Learning in the 21st Century*, London: RoutledgeFalmer.

Goodchild, P. (1996) *Deleuze and Guattari: An Introduction to the Politics of Desire*, London: Sage.

Haynes, M. and Anagnostopoulou, K. (2002) 'Virtual learning environments as tools in learning and teaching', in Fallows, S. and Bhanot, R. (eds) *Educational*

Development Through Information and Communication Technologies, London: Kogan Page.

Higher Education Funding Council for England (2003) 'Annex A', *Consultation on HEFCE E-Learning Strategy*, http://www.hefce.ac.uk/pubs/circlets/2003/cl21_03/ cl21_03a.pdf (date of access: 21 February 2004).

Jacoby, R. (1997) 'Intellectuals: inside and outside the academy', in Smith, A. and Webster, F. (eds) *The Postmodern University? Contested Visions of Higher Education in Society*, Buckingham: SRHE/OU Press.

McLuhan, M. (1964) *Understanding Media: The Extensions of Man*, London: Routledge, Kegan and Paul.

Murphy, D., Walker, R. and Webb, G. (eds) (2001) *Online Learning and Teaching with Technology: Case Studies, Experience and Practice*, London: Kogan Page.

Orsini-Jones, M. and Davidson, A. (1999) 'From reflective learners to reflective lecturers via WebCT', *Active Learning*, Issue 10, July.

Oxford University (2003a) *E Learning at Oxford: An Introduction*, http://www.oucs. ox.ac.uk/ltg/reports/elearn_index.htm (date of access: 21 February 2004).

Oxford University (2003b) *Virtual Learning Environments (VLEs) and Oxford*, http://www.oucs.ox.ac.uk/ltg/vle/ (date of access: 21 February 2004).

Poster, M. (1996) 'Postmodern virtualities', in Featherstone, M. and Burrows, R. (eds) *Cyberspace/Cyberbodies/Cyberpunk: Cultures of Technological Embodiment*, London: Sage.

Rius-Riu, M. (2002) *Using the WWW in Learning and Teaching*, Learning and Teaching Support Network, Generic Centre, Resources Database, UK.

Shulman Lee, S. (1999) 'Knowledge and teaching: foundations of the new reform', in Leach, J. and Moon, B. (eds) *Learners and Pedagogy*, London: Paul Chapman Publishing.

Tapscott, D. (1998) *Growing Up Digital: The Rise of the Net Generation*, New York: McGraw Hill.

Woolley, B. (1992) *Virtual Worlds: A Journey in Hype and Hyperactivity*, Oxford: Blackwell.

9 Towards highly communicative e-learning communities

Developing a socio-cultural framework for cognitive change

Andrew Ravenscroft

Introduction

The development of highly communicative online communities that engage in effective educational discourse leading to conceptual – or belief – change and development, or 'deep learning', presents a significant challenge to researchers and practitioners in e-learning. Thus far much research into collaborative online dialogue in the context of virtual learning communities has focused on particular cases. The emphasis has been given to describing these operations and contexts, rather than penetrating deeper issues, through considering more fundamental approaches to learning and communication or systematically comparing different discursive contexts. In contrast I argue that progress can be made by conceptualising online dialogue in terms of relevant theories, considering findings from empirical work in discourse analysis and evaluating the development of dialogical cognitive tools. So this chapter has four main aims. First, it will critically review socio-cognitive and socio-cultural approaches to learning (for example, Vygotsky 1978; Engeström 1987) and more analytic community and situated perspectives (for example, Wenger 1998; Lave and Wenger 1991). It will also consider behavioural[1] – or 'environmental' – perspectives (for example, Bandura 1977; Gibson 1977). This will assist our conceptualisation of effective educational dialogue and how it can be brought about. Second, I will consider the findings from empirical work in educational discourse analysis and dialogue modelling (for example, Pilkington 1999; Ravenscroft and Pilkington 2000) to examine our current understanding of educational dialogue processes and interactions. Third, I will evaluate work in dialogue design and cognitive tool development (for example, Ravenscroft 2000; Ravenscroft and Matheson 2002; Pilkington *et al.* 1992) to establish the progress made in fostering and promoting favoured dialogue processes using specially designed software systems. Finally, through reflecting on, applying and synthesising this previous and ongoing work, I will build upon my previous work (Ravenscroft 2004, 2002) to outline the state of development of a socio-cultural framework for cognitive change that is suitable for e-learning communities, which holds that learning should be redefined as the *transformation and development of cognition, identities and communities.*

Vygotsky: linking dialogue processes to cognitive change

Vygotsky's (1978) theory of the development of higher mental processes can provide a foundation and inspiration for approaches to e-learning that emphasise the necessity for collaborative, argumentative and reflective discourses. Although he conceived learning as an instructional process aimed at 'transforming the mind of the child into that of an adult', it is accepted nowadays that his ideas can equally apply to any relevant situation involving a learner and a more learned other.[2] This more learned other may be a teacher or a more capable student – which is often the case in higher education settings. Similarly, his theory is not bound to the 'traditional' concept of a school but can be applied more generally to online and other learning communities.

Vygotsky draws a clear distinction between lower level mental processes, such as elementary perception and attention, and higher level mental processes that include verbal thought, logical memory, selective attention and reasoning. He argues for a qualitative distinction between these two levels of mental performance, because unlike lower level activity, the higher level is mediated through cultural symbols and tools, self-regulated rather than bound to a stimulus context, social in origin, and the result of conscious awareness rather than an automatic response.

Critical in distinguishing higher and lower level activity is the qualitative developmental transition that occurs when language, or any other signification system, is internalised to operate as a mediating factor between environmental stimuli and an individual's response. This mediation *transforms* the lower level activity by *lifting it onto a higher plane* and can be achieved through the application of material or psychological tools. Further, in using such tools we become conscious and in control of our mental activities. However, Vygotsky considered language to be the most interesting and powerful of these semiotic mediators and the primary tool for thinking. He claims that these higher mental functions originate in the social. Development proceeds 'from action to thought' and therefore communication and social contact are essential. It is through the communicative process that external signification systems conveying interpersonal communication become internalised to operate as intrapersonal psychological tools that *transform* mental functioning. In other words, internal language and thought are transformed from the 'outside'. This idea is critical to Vygotsky's notions about conceptual development and the evolution of linguistic meaning as we develop our higher level mental processes.

The primary theoretical construct introduced by Vygotsky for 'engineering' this conceptual change is the zone of proximal development (ZPD). According to Vygotsky (1978), the ZPD represents the place where the student's empirically rich but disorganised, spontaneous or contextual concepts meet with the *systematicity* and logic of the tutor's reasoning. It is:

> the distance between a child's actual developmental level as determined by independent problem-solving and the higher level of potential development as determined through problem-solving under adult guidance or in collaboration with more capable peers.
>
> (Vygotsky 1978: 86)

Through tasks, exercises, discussions and dialogue within the ZPD, the weaknesses of the student's spontaneous concepts and reasoning are made explicit and compensated for by the strengths of the tutor's scientific conceptions and reasoning. Thus, in performing the task, the student 'appropriates' the more mature, scientific conceptualisations and becomes socialised into the expert practitioner's knowledge and approach to particular problems, subsequently operating as a more expert practitioner him/herself.

The notion of the ZPD is also a positive and powerful paradigm for evaluating and improving the teaching–learning process in co-operative contexts. Failure to complete a task successfully can be evaluated in terms of what 'extra' should be introduced to improve the ZPD, instead of simply assessing a 'failure' in performance.

This necessity for an instructional dialogue of a 'scaffolding' nature between the learner and a tutor, or more capable other, is clearly something we should attempt to replicate and operationalise within online learning communities.

Activity theory: a socio-cultural approach emphasising the role of context

Although Vygotsky's work is sometimes considered as socio-cultural, activity theory arguably provides a more rigorous account of relations between learners and their social and cultural context. Here, Vygotsky's (1978) work has been developed to provide a framework for learning and development which accepts that meaning arises and evolves during interactions that are influenced by the social relations within a community of practice. Or, 'you are what you do' (Nardi 1996: 7) in a natural context that is influenced by history and culture. Hence, human practices are conceived as developmental processes 'with both individual and social levels interlinked at the same time' (Knutti 1996: 25). It emphasises relationships between interactions, processes and outcomes and the relevance of social conditions, such as a shared enterprise and the need for mutual engagement of conceptualisations. Therefore, the relevance of conceptual similarities and differences, and changes and developments over time, are taken into account in the design of mediated activities (see, for example, Engeström 1987).

Issroff and Scanlon (2001) have recently assessed activity theory in the context of computer-supported collaborative learning (hereafter CSCL), and reconsidered some of their previous studies using this framework. They concluded that, as it stands, activity theory is more useful as a framework for describing and communicating findings, and less effective as a framework for uncovering 'further insights' into designing and interpreting collaborative learning activities. So, although Baker *et al.* (1999) have used it to analyse and examine different forms of grounding in collaborative learning, and Lewis (1997) has employed it in researching interdependent parameters in distributed communities, its value as a prescriptive design paradigm for e-learning remains open to question. Nevertheless, this and other research (Tolmie and Boyle 2000) has demonstrated that an activity theory framework does hold some significant value in shifting our attention to the relevance of social, cultural and historical influences and relationships that are implicated when we introduce and use innovative educational technologies such as CMC systems or dialogical cognitive tools. It also highlights the complexities associated with the way a design is operationalised within a context as its use develops over time, and has pointed out some of the limitations in theory that need to be addressed. Specifically, this approach forces us to focus on the necessity to conceptualise the relationship between dialogical activity and the learning communities in which it occurs. We need to address the requirements to form appropriate social relations between interlocutors, create and foster a suitable 'cultural' context online and also account for the constraints and potentialities governed by contextual factors surrounding the e-learning community.

Learning communities and collaborative discourse

According to Preece (2000: xii), 'The internet has given rise to a new community model of communication.' Currently, however, there is little agreement about what this model actually is, how we can conceptualise it, or how it can be operationalised and exploited for educational purposes. Preece (2000) herself argues for Community-Centred Development (CCD) that accepts the sociology and social psychology of community development and maintenance, putting the 'community' firmly at the centre of the design process in the same way that Norman (1986) conceived the 'user' as central. Within this scheme she points out that we need to support the evolution of communities, design for usability and plan for sociability. This approach seems to hold that learning should be conceived as a social process, but raises a crucial question about whether we can actually build online communities that truly satisfy the necessary social conditions for effective, and often dialectical, discourse interactions. Or, putting this another way, can we be sufficiently social online to have meaningful conversations, discussions and arguments that lead to conceptual change and development?

The recent work of Wenger (1998) on 'Communities of Practice' considers meaning, along with learning and identity, as important features in the educative process and holds that:

> engagement in social practice is the fundamental process by which we learn and so become who we are. The primary unit of analysis is neither the individual nor social institutions but rather the informal 'communities of practice' that people form as they pursue shared enterprises over time.
>
> (Wenger 1998: introductory notes)

Central to this notion, inspired by Lave and Wenger's (1991) work on 'situated cognition' (discussed later), is that these communities have knowledge about practice embedded within them, and therefore learning occurs through legitimate entry and participation within the community. 'Learning is a process that takes place within a participation framework, not an individual mind' (Lave and Wenger 1991: 15). Wenger (1998) argues that effective communities of practice are characterised by mutual engagement, joint enterprise, shared repertoire and the negotiation of meaning in practice.

Whilst this approach provides a useful analytic framework, this descriptive emphasis means that it cannot be readily articulated for e-learning dialogue design, a point that is emphasised by Wenger (1998) himself. However, as e-learning designers we have to be more prescriptive and promote learning as well as describe it. So the challenge is to stimulate and promote the engagement in social practice that in turn leads to the formation of an efficient community of practice. There is also a problem mapping some of Wenger's features to desired discourse practices in educational contexts. Whilst we obviously want to promote and identify features such as mutual engagement, shared repertoire and negotiation of meaning, other aspects such as joint accountability, diversity and partiality are not necessarily appropriate in many educational contexts – except perhaps for informal learning. One reason why it is not yet clear how to design, develop and maintain a community of practice supporting and engaging e-learning discourse is that in educational settings it is often unclear what the 'practice' actually is. In such contexts a greater emphasis is given to knowledge-based and conceptual activity rather than co-operative task-oriented activity. Finally, although Wenger's work has provided a valuable conceptual resource of socio-cultural features that should be considered when designing, cultivating and developing communication in online communities, I would argue that the central tenet of this approach is too simplistic. In an earlier review of learning theories and pedagogical approaches (Ravenscroft 2004) I have argued that when we consider the pedigree of, and support for, more cognitive and socio-cognitive approaches such as those described earlier, we cannot accept the claim that 'Learning is a process that takes place within a participation framework, not an individual mind' without significant qualification. Surely *learning is a process that takes place within a participation framework **and** an individual mind*?

McConnell's (2000) work focusing on 'Implementing Computer Supported Co-operative Learning' (CSCL) is one of the few practical approaches that considers Wenger's work. He proposes six design features for promoting and supporting co-operative learning: openness in the educational process (the learning community); self-determination in learning; having a real purpose in the co-operative process; a supportive learning environment; collaborative assessment of learning and assessment and evaluation of the ongoing learning process. He presents a specific design for a CSCL system that is successfully implemented in a UK higher education setting. The emphasis here is high level, placed on the learning management and organisation supporting CSCL, or the conditions and issues for co-operative learning in general. Lower level questions, such as whether the discourse processes that are fostered lead to genuine improvements in knowledge and understanding, remain largely unanswered in any systematic way. Nevertheless, this work makes useful progress in considering social processes in the design and management of computer-mediated activities, although McConnell points out that:

> CSCL is an idea that helps surface questions about the role of technology in learning, and about the nature and purpose of learning itself.
>
> (McConnell 2000: 2)

Similarly, Kirschner (2002), in reviewing the current state of CSCL research, points out that findings about the effectiveness of CSCL environments remain inconclusive.

Situated learning: participation in authentic social practice

The 'situated' nature of learning, and the requirement to participate in authentic activity and practice, have been emphasised by a number of researchers (Seely-Brown *et al.* 1989; Lave and Wenger 1991) and are often considered important tenets of approaches to learning based on notions of 'community' or 'communities of practice' (Wenger 1998; Wenger *et al.* 2002). This stance is often considered antithetical to more cognitive approaches to learning, a position concisely proposed, in relation to new media technology, by Pea and Seely Brown:

The *situated* nature of learning, remembering, and understanding is a central fact. It may appear obvious that human minds develop in social situations, and that they use tools and representational media that culture provides to support, extend, and reorganise mental functioning. But cognitive theories of knowledge representation and educational practice, in school and in the workplace, have not been sufficiently responsive to questions about these relationship.... In changing situations of knowledge acquisition and use, the new interactive technologies redefine – in ways yet to be determined – what it means to know and understand, and what it means to become 'literate' or an 'educated citizen'.

(1996: vii)

Whilst providing an incisive argument for turning our attention to the local, social and socio-cultural dimensions of learning, the approach also surfaces some difficulties for e-learning dialogue design, because, like Wenger's work on communities of practice, it is essentially analytic rather than predictive. A corollary of this, articulated in objections proposed by Anderson *et al.* (1996) is that situated approaches are *too* specific and authenticity-focused. They do not allow us to consider issues of transfer or the common necessity for independent training in sub-components of complex social activity. Nevertheless, the approach forces us to consider whether online educational dialogue should be as authentic, social, relevant and meaningful as possible to the interlocutors in their contexts. Given the noted difficulties with promoting participation in online communities (Ravenscroft 2004), more relevant and meaningful dialogue is likely to be more motivating, and easier to maintain and manage, than more abstract, knowledge-based discourse. We will have to introduce more about 'ourselves', 'our interests' and 'our lives' if we wish online dialogue to engage meaningfully with more generic and academic topics.

Social learning theory, affordances and emotion

Surprisingly, little work thus far has looked at the more behavioural, environmental and motivational approaches to learning in the context of online dialogue. Here, the term 'behavioural' refers to situations where activities result from a relatively close perception-action coupling, rather than being the result of more 'reasoned' processes. The neglect of these perspectives possibly relates to the current emphasis on constructivist approaches such as those of Fosnot (1996), Jonassen *et al.* (1993) and Duffy *et al.* (1993). Yet questions such as how our discursive behaviour relates to our perceptions of (and the influence of) the activities of those around us, and what really motivates us to engage intellectually with others or express ourselves online, deserve attention. What features of the online environment invite participation? A possible reason for not engaging with such questions is that many online learning communities are heavily structured and managed with clear extrinsic motivation. An online course, for example, has restricted and public membership, well-established practices, a set time-scale for activities, clearly assigned roles and implicit shared goals, such as to pass a course and achieve the best possible grade. However, as soon as e-learning dialogue becomes more informal and less 'enforced', participation and interaction tend to drop, often regardless of the potential conceptual gain from any active participation.

Thus it is crucial to consider motivational approaches to learning that stimulate interaction. Bandura's 'Social Learning Theory' (1977), which holds that we learn by modelling the behaviour of others, may be particularly valuable in this respect. Observing the online behaviour of exemplary interlocutors can lead us to model this activity and subsequently become effective interlocutors ourselves. Similarly, the notion of affordances (Gibson 1977), draws our attention to the 'invitational' qualities of the online environment, that may be a key factor in stimulating participation. Originally the term 'affordances' referred to relationships between the physical properties of objects and the characteristics of a potential user, which resulted in an interaction between the user and the object (Gibson 1977). Recently Kirschner (2002) has elaborated the concept significantly, pointing out that affordances can be educational and social as well as technological or physical. So affordances may be provided by the technology that is involved or the behaviour and social features of the online community or surrounding context.

Along related lines, the work of Cooper (2003), building on the emotional theories of de Masio (1999) takes an extreme stance on the role of emotion. She argues that no meaningful educational interaction can occur that is not in some ways 'emotional'.

Although work in these areas is relatively new, I argue that it is important. Previously, we have held to a rather intellectual and cognitive stance which accepted that learners will meaningfully engage in online interaction because it is available, suitably structured and valuable and useful to them, for 'academic' reasons. I would argue that they will interact meaningfully if they can do so easily and naturally, are stimulated to do so and receive some sort of 'reward'. They will also interact if they have a clear conception of their own and others' relative online identity, can observe and adopt the behaviour of others, and are sufficiently engaged and secure emotionally. A condition of the latter is that there must be sufficient levels of empathy, trust and respect within the educational community.

Discourse analysis and dialogue design

Given that theories of learning emphasise that dialogue is central to shaping conceptual development, there is a need to more closely examine the features that make educational dialogue effective in ways that inform the development and use of systems that support e-learning. Work investigating natural educational dialogues that aim to change student conceptualisations in a variety of situations, have produced some consensus as to the roles, strategies and speech acts (sets of moves) which are likely to be important. For example, using the DISCOUNT Discourse Analysis scheme (Pilkington 1999), which includes Exchange Structure, Move (Speech-Act) and Rhetorical analyses, it is possible to determine which participants are active in dialogue and how. DISCOUNT has been used to give insights into collaboration in natural and CMC dialogue contexts (De Vincente *et al.* 1999; Pilkington *et al.* 1999). From these and similar studies there is evidence that 'successful' exchanges are more likely to include clarifying, challenging, hinting and justification moves.

A more direct approach to linking discourse analysis to system design has been proposed by Ravenscroft and Pilkington (2000), who developed the methodology of *investigation by design* (hereafter IBD). This combines discourse analysis and dialogue game techniques (MacKenzie 1979; Walton 1984; Ravenscroft 2000) to specify formal dialogue models that can be implemented as intelligent and collaborative e-learning systems. A central method of this approach is to take some of the features of 'successful' dialogue (N.B. as yet, not fully proven to be effective) and actively design them into interaction scenarios aimed at supporting learning. Once these models have been developed, we can evaluate their effectiveness, and systematically vary the roles, strategies, tactics and moves adopted to further explore the utility of these features in guiding learners towards more systematic reasoning. Within this IBD scheme, we use the DISCOUNT (Pilkington 1999) method to develop dialogue models specified as dialogue games. A major advantage of the dialogue game approach is that it allows us to incorporate rules and constraints into the design of communicative interactions that are consequently structured and managed along the lines we prescribe. Therefore, these systems can act as powerful cognitive and mediational tools that guide the dialogue and lines of reasoning in ways that lead to improvements in individual or shared knowledge and understanding.

Research investigating and examining the suitability of this approach has been ongoing for the past ten years (see Ravenscroft 2001 for a review). It has shown that dialogue game theory can be used as a software design paradigm for types of computer-mediated and computer-based argumentation dialogue in educational contexts. Here, the notion of a game is used to characterise and specify discourse in terms of the goals of the interlocutors (for example, the elaboration of knowledge, the co-elaboration of knowledge, supporting or winning an argument), the relative roles of participants (for example, inquirer, critiquer, explainer) and the types of dialogue tactics and moves that are performed (for example, assert, challenge, withdraw). Rules govern the types of moves available to participants, the effect these have on commitment and beliefs, and issues of initiative and turn-taking. Note that, in focusing on pragmatic level knowledge, these projects have not needed to directly address issues of semantic and syntactic level natural language processing and generation that have been examined by Pilkington (1992) and Pilkington and Grierson (1996). Other research has demonstrated how dialogue game theory can represent a range of dialectical discourse genres (Maudet and Evrard 1998; Moore and Hobbs 1996), include multimedia features (Moore 2000) and be adapted to take account of multi-user polylogues (Maudet and Moore 2000).

System designs: cognitive tools and intelligent dialogue

Projects adopting the approach above have produced a number of successful designs. They have shown that a model of collaborative argumentation – a *facilitating* dialogue game – supports and stimulates conceptual change and development in science (Ravenscroft 2000; Ravenscroft and Matheson 2002). And a model of fair and reasonable debate – a DC dialogue game – can be used to teach generic reasoning skills for debating controversial subjects (Pilkington *et al.* 1992; Moore 1993). The former dialogue game has been implemented in the intelligent computer-based dialogue system called CoLLeGE and the latter model has been implemented in the DIALAB computer-mediated argumentation system which structures fair and reasonable debate. Another project called CLARISSA has used dialogue games to implement a computer modelling 'laboratory' for investigating collaboration (Burton *et al.* 2000).

However, as these dialogue games are evaluated and tested (Ravenscroft and Matheson 2002; McAlister 2001), the relevance of the broader, socio-cultural context is becoming increasingly apparent. To integrate these game approaches effectively within e-learning contexts, we need to better understand the appropriate 'conditions' for these systems and discourses, as we cannot hold a serious and engaging educational dialogue 'with anyone, about anything, at any time'. One current project is integrating a dialogue game for critical discussion, realised through a structured interface of sentence openers and preferred moves (McAlister *et al.* 2003), within a broader framework for educational conferencing and moderating devised by Salmon (2000). This links a cognitive tool with a framework that defines the local socio-cultural context in which it should be effective. However, preliminary findings from this project further emphasise the need to better conceptualise and design for the community and contexts in which educational discourses operate. In brief, we need to investigate, examine and, where possible, design, appropriate learning communities if we want to support effective e-learning discourse.

Towards a socio-cultural framework for cognitive change that is suitable for e-learning

I have argued, through a relatively comprehensive review of pedagogical theories and approaches (see also Ravenscroft 2004) that effective learning requires high-quality educational discourse, leading to, at least, improved knowledge, and, at best, conceptual development and improved understanding. This is possible, in the context of e-learning, if we adopt a sophisticated approach to dialogue development and design that accounts for necessary relationships between cognitive changes, dialogue processes and the communities, or contexts, for learning. Putting this another way, we need a socio-cultural framework for cognitive change that considers motivational and affective factors. In such a framework learning should be redefined as *the transformation and development of cognition, identities and communities.* Key features of this framework that arise out of this review include:

- *It should be based on relevant theory* A number of theories have been proposed that are sufficiently relevant and have attested pedigree in the context of developing dialogical approaches to learning and communication. In practice, we may require a blend of pedagogical approaches to address particular learning problems. Although some learning theorists may object to such marriages, arguing that they may involve reconciling conflicting epistemologies, we must remember that our focus is on producing high-quality interaction and e-learning designs, and remind ourselves that no theory of learning has yet become definitive.

- *It should be holistic and yet integrated* The framework needs to link the cognitive changes that represent learning to the dialogic processes that give rise to such conceptual development. Additionally these processes need to be placed in an appropriate community and cultural context, that will often involve the interplay of online and offline aspects. There needs to be a clear conjoining of socio-cognitive and socio-cultural aspects of the educative process.

- *It needs to reconcile more behavioural and motivational approaches with social constructivist perspectives* A particular problem with online dialogue, when compared with more naturalistic discourse, is that it needs to be carefully stimulated, fostered and cultivated as well as being managed and structured. In addition to addressing the need for structured activity along social constructivist lines, we need to adopt behavioural notions such as affordances (Gibson 1977; Kirschner 2002) that more closely couple perception to action, alongside motivation for, and value of, online behaviour. In many instances we will have to 'attract' and 'invite' people in to promote participation. As learners continue their participation and engage intellectually, one hopes they would achieve sufficient cognitive reward and development to continue their active involvement without further behavioural stimulation.

The state of development

Research over the past ten years has given us a reasonable idea of what counts as patterns of good educational discourse, and how we might design systems that employ favoured dialogue processes to achieve improved reasoning and dialectic processes (see Ravenscroft and Pilkington 2000 for a review). A significant current challenge is to examine how to design or develop the social conditions and communities – in online or blended situations – that give rise to, or accommodate, the dialogue models and discourse practices that are desired in e-learning contexts. A next step is to systematically compare different contexts and situations in e-learning communities, to develop a better conceptualisation of how and why they operate successfully, paying particular attention to motivational, empathic and social issues. This should then provide the basis either to harmonise the operation of desired dialogue genres within existing community practice or, more prescriptively, to develop communities that are aimed at supporting high-quality collaborative e-learning discourse. We need to better conceptualise the way learners behave in e-learning communities with flexibility in the adoption of theory. One example of this approach is represented in the ongoing work of Ravenscroft *et al.* (2002) who are integrating social learning theory (Bandura 1977) within a socio-cultural approach to cultivating online communities, articulated in their MOCCA framework (Maxims for developing Online Communities and Communication using Affordances). One way this is realised practically, is through devising animateurs or 'animator teams' (A-teams) who demonstrate and stimulate types of online behaviour, acting as *catalysts for interaction*. This involves planning and structuring authentic *exemplary interactions* that 'invite people in' and get them simply participating in the first instance. Once learners participate and engage intellectually, the assumption is that they will be achieving sufficient cognitive reward and development to continue their active involvement without animation, and so the animateur or A-team can 'fade out', allowing the community to grow organically.

Conclusion

This chapter has made an ambitious attempt to better understand what counts as effective educational dialogue and explore how it can be brought about using new media technology within carefully conceptualised contexts. The proposed framework is a starting point, or 'conceptual prototype', for improving our understanding and practice in this field. It is quite complex, requiring further testing and refinement, but holds, I would argue, timely and important ideas and pointers. Given the proliferation of work in this area and its importance in terms of individual, local and global intellectual development, it is essential that we devise thorough, integrated and sophisticated approaches. This will lead to a better understanding of our efforts to develop our minds within the emerging social and cultural labyrinths in which we now all practise, where, arguably more than ever before, 'no man is an island'.

Acknowledgement

This project has been carried out with the support of the European Community in the framework of the Socrates Programme. The content of this project does not necessarily reflect the position of the European Community, nor does it involve any responsibility on the part of the European Community.

Notes

1 In this chapter the term 'behavioural' does not denote a strict 'behaviourist' approach along the lines proposed by Skinner (e.g. 1954) and his followers. Instead it is used more loosely, and emphasises approaches that focus on the behaviour of learners and the way this relates to the environment in which they are placed, where the emphasis is given to activities that result from relatively direct perception–action couplings.
2 For brevity, henceforth, the word 'tutor' will be used in this chapter to refer to the person that is considered 'the more learned other', who may be a teacher, a more capable student or a mentor.

References

Anderson, J.R., Reder, L.M. and Simon, H.A. (1996) 'Situated learning and education', *Educational Researcher*, 25(4): 5–11.
Baker, M., Hansen, T., Joiner, R. and Traum, D. (1999) 'The role of grounding in collaborative learning tasks', in Dillenbourg, P. (ed.) *Collaborative Learning: Computational and Cognitive Approaches*, Amsterdam: Elsevier, pp. 31–63.
Bandura, A. (1977) *Social Learning Theory*, London: Prentice Hall.
Burton, M., Brna, P. and Pilkington, R. (2000) 'Clarissa: a laboratory for the modelling of collaboration', *International Journal of Artificial Intelligence in Education*, 11: 79–105.
Cooper, B. (2003) 'Care – making the affective leap: more than a concerned interest in a learner's cognitive abilities', *International Journal of Artificial Intelligence and Education*, 13(1): 3–9.
Damasio, A. (1999) *The Feeling of What Happens: Body, Emotion and the Making of Consciousness*, London: Vintage.
De Vincente, A., Bouwer, A. and Pain, H. (1999) 'Initial impressions on using the discount scheme', in Pilkington, R., McKendree, J., Pain, H. and Brna, P. (eds) *Proceedings of the Workshop on Analysing Educational Dialogue Interaction.*

Workshop at 9th International Conference on Artificial Intelligence in Education, 18th–19th July, 1999, Le Mans, France: University of Le Mans, 87–94.

Duffy, T.M., Jonassen, D.H. and Lowyck, J. (eds) (1993) *Designing Environments for Constructive Learning*, Berlin: Springer.

Engeström, Y. (1987) *Learning by Expanding: An Activity Theory Approach to Developmental Research*, Helsinki: Orienta-Konsultit.

Fosnot, C. (1996) *Constructivism: Theory, Perspectives and Practice*, New York: Teachers College Press.

Gibson, J.J. (1977) *The Ecological Approach to Visual Perception*, New York: Houghton Mifflin.

Issroff, K. and Scanlon, E. (2001) 'Case studies revisited: what can activity theory offer?' *Proceedings of International Conference on Computer Supported Collaborative Learning 2001 (Cscl 2001)*, Maastricht, Netherlands, 22–24 March, 316–323.

Jonassen, D.H., Mayes, T. and McAleese, R. (1993) 'A manifesto for a constructivist approach to technology in higher education', in Duffy, T.M., Jonassen, D.H. and Lowyck, J. (eds) *Designing Environments for Constructive Learning*, Berlin: Springer, pp. 231–247.

Kirschner, P.A. (2002) 'Can we support CSCL? Educational, social and technological affordances for learning,' in Kirschner, P.A. (ed.) *Three Worlds of CSCL: Can We Support CSCL?*, Nederland: Open Universitiet, pp. 7–47.

Knutti, K. (1996) 'Activity theory as a potential framework for human–computer interaction research', in Nardi, B. (ed.) *Context and Consciousness: Activity Theory and Human–Computer Interaction*, Cambridge, MA: MIT Press, pp. 17–44.

Lave, J. and Wenger, E. (1991) *Situated Learning: Legitimate Peripheral Participation*, Cambridge: Cambridge University Press.

Lewis, R. (1997) 'An activity theory framework to explore distributed communities', *Journal of Computer Assisted Learning*, 13: 210–218.

MacKenzie, J.D. (1979) 'Question-begging in non-cumulative systems', *Journal of Philosophical Logic*, 8: 117–133.

McAlister, S. (2001) *Argumentation and Design for Learning*, Dialogue and Design Research Group Technical Report DDRG-01-2, Institute of Educational Technology, Open University, Milton Keynes.

McAlister, S., Ravenscroft, A. and Scanlon, E. (2003) 'Combining interaction and context design to support collaborative argumentation in education', *Journal of Computer Assisted Learning: Special Issue: Developing Dialogue for Learning*, 20(3): 194–204.

McConnell, D. (2000) *Implementing Computer Supported Cooperative Learning*, London: Kogan Page.

Maudet, N. and Evrard, F. (1998) 'A generic framework for dialogue game implementation', in Hulstijn, J. and Nijholt, A. (eds) *Second Workshop on Formal Semantic and Pragmatics of Dialogue* (TWLT13), May 13–15, University of Twente, The Netherlands.

Maudet, N. and Moore, D.J. (2000) 'Dialogue games as dialogue models for interacting with, and via, computers', submitted to *Informal Logic*, 13(3).

Moore, D.J. (2000) 'A framework for using multimedia within argumentation systems', *Journal of Educational Multimedia and Hypermedia*, 9: 83–98.

Moore, D.J. (1993) *Dialogue Game Theory for Intelligent Tutoring Systems*, unpublished Ph.D. thesis, Computer Based Learning Unit, University of Leeds, UK.

Moore, D.J. and Hobbs, D.J. (1996) 'Computational use of philosophical dialogue theories', *Informal Logic*, 18: 131–163.

Nardi, B. (1996) *Context and Consciousness: Activity Theory and Human–Computer Interaction*, Cambridge, MA: MIT Press.

Norman, D.A. (1986) 'Cognitive engineering', in Norman, D.A. and Draper, S. (eds) *User-Centred Systems Design*, Hillsdale, NJ: Lawrence Erlbaum.

Pea, R. and Seely-Brown, J. (1993) in Chaiklin, S. and Lave, J. (eds) *Understanding Practice: Perspectives on Activity in Context*, Cambridge: Cambridge University Press, pp. vii–viii.

Pilkington, R.M. (1999) *Analysing Educational Discourse: The DISCOUNT Scheme*, Version 3, January, CBL Technical Report No. 99/2.

Pilkington, R.M. (1992) *Intelligent Help: Communicating with Knowledge Based Systems*, London: Paul Chapman.

Pilkington, R. and Grierson, A. (1996) 'Generating explanations in a simulation-based learning environment', *International Journal of Human–Computer Studies*, 45: 527–551.

Pilkington, R.M., Hartley, J.R., Hintze, D. and Moore, D. (1992) 'Learning to argue and arguing to learn: an interface for computer-based dialogue games', *International Journal of Artificial Intelligence in Education*, 3: 275–285.

Pilkington, R.M., Treasure-Jones, T. and Kneser, C. (1999) 'Educational chat: using exchange structure analysis to investigate communicative roles in CMC seminars', in Brna, P., Baker, M. and Stenning, K. (eds) *Roles of Communicative Interaction in Learning to Model in Mathematics and Science: Proceedings of C-LEMMAS TMR Conference*, 15–19 April, Ajaccio, Corsica, Computer Based Learning Unit, University of Leeds, UK.

Preece, J. (2000) *Online Communities: Designing Usability, Supporting Sociability*, John Wiley Ltd.

Ravenscroft, A. (2004) 'From conditioning to learning communities: implications of 50 years of research in e-learning interaction design', *Association for Learning Technology Journal*, 11(3): 4–18.

Ravenscroft, A. (2002) 'Communities, communication and cognitive change: social processes and designing engaging e-learning discourse', in Driscoll, M. and Reeves, T.C. (eds) *Proceedings of E-Learn 2002*, Norfolk, USA: Association for the Advancement of Computing in Education (AACE), pp. 792–797.

Ravenscroft, A. (2001) 'Designing e-learning interactions in 21C: revisiting and re-thinking the role of theory', *European Journal of Education: Special Edition on On-Line Learning*, 36(2): 133–156.

Ravenscroft, A. (2000) 'Designing argumentation for conceptual development', *Computers and Education*, 34: 241–255.

Ravenscroft, A. and Matheson, M.P. (2002) 'Developing and evaluating dialogue games for collaborative e-learning interaction', *Journal of Computer Assisted Learning, Special Issue: Context, Collaboration, Computers and Learning*, 18(1): 93–102.

Ravenscroft, A. and Pilkington, R.M. (2000) 'Investigation by design: developing dialogue models to support reasoning and conceptual change', *International Journal of Artificial Intelligence in Education*, 11: 273–298.

Ravenscroft, A., Hutchinson, A., Baur, E. and Bradley, C. (2002) 'Mocca framework: maxims for developing online communities and communication using affordances', *LTRI Technical Report – June 2002*, London: London Metropolitan University.

Salmon, G. (2000) *E-Moderating: The Key to Teaching and Learning Online*, London: Kogan Page.

Seely-Brown, J., Collins, A. and Duguid, P. (1989) 'Situated cognition and the culture of learning', *Educational Researcher*, January: 32–41.

Tolmie, A. and Boyle, J. (2000) 'Factors influencing the success of computer mediated communication (CMC) environments in university teaching: a review and case study', *Computers and Education*, 34: 119–140.

Vygotsky, L. (1978) *Mind in Society*, Cambridge, MA: Harvard University Press.

Walton, D. (1984) *Logical Dialogue-Games and Fallacies* (published thesis), Lanham, MD: University Press America.

Wenger, E. (1998) *Communities of Practice*, Cambridge: Cambridge University Press.

Wenger, E., McDermott, R. and Snyder, W.M. (2002) *Cultivating Communities of Practice*, Cambridge, MA: Harvard Business School.

Part 4
Subjects

10 Embodiment and risk in cyberspace education

Ray Land

Introduction

The counter-positioning of virtual learning environments with traditional face-to-face learning has given rise to comparisons in which cyberspace education is represented as somehow inauthentic, as a relatively impoverished experience located within a cold, even sterile medium. Recent commentaries (for example, Dreyfus 2001) have explored the notion that a compelling explanatory factor in this perceived lack of intensity might be the absence of risk, as experienced by both students and teachers. In this analysis, risk carries an affective intensity that is integral to embodiment, physical presence and the visibility of the teacher and the students. Moreover such intensity and authenticity are seen as crucial to the possibility of learner commitment, and other forms of social and ethical engagement. The absence, or diminished possibility, of such encounters in online environments renders what one does in cyberspace as having no 'real' consequences. This chapter will critically examine such claims and the extent to which online learning environments may be seen to minimise risk through mechanisms of control. Attributes of online environments, such as asynchronous time for reflection, relative anonymity, compartmentalisation of activity, controlled access through user-authentication, sophisticated surveillance and tracking tools would all seem to signal as much. Indeed it might be argued that online environments share certain properties with all simulacra or spectral phenomena – theme parks, televised sport, packaged holidays, computer gaming, etc. – in that they serve, apparently, to minimise risk and threat. The chapter will seek to problematise such notions and examine the possibility that learning in cyberspace, rather than being comparatively risk-free, contains risks and disquietudes that are qualitatively different. Similarly it will caution against what I have termed here the 'incorporeal fallacy' of assuming that cyberlearning is, indeed, disembodied. Rather it will argue the need to reconsider how notions of risk, the subjectivity of the learner and ideas of embodiment might all be differently constituted online.

Bodies and spaces

Consideration of such issues draws us to consider what characterises, and what is entailed by participation within, different learning spaces. We need to understand how knowledge and learning are reconfigured when they occur in radically different forms of space. The modernist project of education can be associated to a great extent with the notion of enclosed space that serves to order and regulate meaning and activity (Lankshear *et al.* 1996; Deleuze 1992). Within traditional higher education, since its medieval and Renaissance inceptions, such spaces of enclosure have been represented by the page, the book, the curriculum, the classroom, the discipline, the library and the university (Landow 1997; Bayne and Land 2000). The embodied learner and the embodied teacher might also each be represented (odd though it might seem initially to consider them in this fashion) as enclosed entities, insofar as they appear to be relatively clearly defined, with seemingly obvious physical boundaries. Cyberspace, on the other hand, complicates and disrupts such preconceptions and habituated practices. The hypertextual digital page is not confined by the boundaries of the printed page or book. The virtual university transgresses or ignores many of the privileges and access requirements of the familiar immured academy, and the web is no respecter of the boundaries of traditional disciplines. Moreover, as we shall see, the seemingly unified and centred subjectivity of the visible, embodied learner is rendered much more fluid within a digital environment (Turkle 1996). Cyberspace remains difficult to define as a learning space. Is it a space or what architects and designers might refer to as a 'non-space'? Usher and Edwards (2000) see it as 'neither here nor there but both here and there'. In their view it is:

> a (dis)location – something that is both positioned and not positioned, (dis)placed but not re-placed, a diaspora space of hybridity and flows where one and many locations are simultaneously possible.
>
> (3)

Their metaphor of dispersal is reflected in the metaphors of other commentators, many of which emphasise movement and fissure. Given this radical uncertainty within the cyberspace and its radical difference from traditional, more familiar environments, it is not surprising that anxiety emerges about the value and authenticity of the student's learning experience. One online learner describes it as a 'cold medium', pointing out that:

> Unlike face-to-face communication you get no instant feedback. You don't know how people responded to your comments; they just go out into silence. This feels isolating and unnerving. It is not warm and supportive.
>
> (Wegerif 1998: 1)

Accompanying the sense of anxiety here is a strong sense of loss – loss of contact ('feedback', 'silence'), loss of companionship and community ('isolating', 'it is not warm and supportive'), loss of confidence ('unnerving') and loss of certainty ('you don't know'). The metaphors of cold and silence suggest a sense of sterility – that what are missing are the warm bodies of fellow learners. The affective domain is highlighted here as an issue of importance and concern within the cyber environment. Tabbi (1997) also emphasises this seeming disembodiment, disembeddedness and decontextualisation of the cyber environment. It has no bodies, no history, no location. A further perceived loss is that of veracity. Feenberg (1989) raises the issue of physical presence as a supposed guarantor of veracity:

> In our culture the face-to-face encounter is the ideal paradigm of the meeting of minds. Communication seems most complete and successful where the person is physically present 'in' the message. This physical presence is supposed to be the guarantor of authenticity: you can look your interlocutor in the eye and search for tacit signs of truthfulness or falsehood, where context and tone permit a subtler interpretation of the spoken word.
>
> (22)

Veracity appears to depend on a notion of 'depth' wherein truth dwells. This would seem to be a preoccupation of modernism. We recall, for example, Freudian notions of the subconscious, the Marxist emphasis on base and superstructure, deep structures within Chomskyan transformative grammar, and, nearer to home, the privileging of 'deep' over 'surface' learning within phenomenographic representations of student learning. Conversely, experience of cyberspace environments has characteristically been associated with a sense of superficiality. Turkle (1996) talks of 'life on the screen', Johnson-Eilola (1998) of 'living on the surface'. This sense of a loss of veracity in cyber environments seems to arise from the fluidity and dispersal of identities which seem now to be relocated within language and text, where the online learner encounters 'a fluid, flowing space where users experiment with multiple subjectivities; where stories lose concrete beginnings, middles and ends; where the rules of games shift, are overwritten, and sometimes even disappear' (Johnson-Eilola 1998: 186). This leads to a sense of 'disquietude' in online environments (Bayne and Land 2001) which reflects that reported as a more general condition of postmodernity, such as 'boundariless anxiety' (Bergquist 1995) or 'ontological insecurity' (Giddens 1991).

The notion that the visibility of the learner or teacher serves as an anchor of truthfulness or veracity ('you can look your interlocutor in the eye') might lead one to conclude that authenticity is dependent upon physical embodiment. It would follow from this line of reasoning that lack of embodiment renders the cyberspace, which is unquestionably a simulated environment, a 'false' environment.

> One is no longer in front of the mirror; one is in the screen, which is entirely different. One finds oneself in a problematic universe, one hides in the network, that is, one is no longer anywhere.
>
> (Baudrillard, quoted in Thibault 1996: 3)

It would become, in this view, what Baudrillard has termed a simulacrum, consisting of signification only, without any meaningful reality. It is tempting to pursue this analogy and mischievously envisage cyberspace education, in a time of massification of higher education with its severely reduced resourcing and rapidly expanding student numbers, as the pedagogic equivalent of Baudrillard's Disneyland, that is, a representation of reality (ideology) which conceals the fact that the real is no longer real, and thus serves to save the reality principle.

> Disneyland exists in order to hide that it is the 'real' country, all of 'real' America that is Disneyland (a bit like prisons are there to hide that it is the social in its entirety, in its banal omnipresence, that is carceral). Disneyland is presented as imaginary in order to make us believe that the rest is real, whereas all of Los Angeles and the America that surrounds it are no longer real, but belong to the hyper-real order and to the order of simulation.
>
> (Baudrillard 1994: 6)

The world of Disney, argues Baudrillard, offers a form of childishness which serves to foster a sense that adulthood resides elsewhere, outside the walls of the theme park, in the 'real' world. In this way it occludes the recognition that childishness and sentimentality are, in Baudrillard's view, everywhere, and that by removing the walls of the theme park we would not discern any difference between the real and the simulated. In a similar way cyberspace education, in this view, becomes an 'antipedagogy', a phantom that serves as 'the proof of pedagogy' (Baudrillard, quoted in Thibault 1996: 19). The antipedagogy here reassures us that what is seen as a diminished experience on offer in the simulated world of online learning is unlike learning in the traditional 'real' world of higher education. It serves to conceal the impoverished, underfunded and under-resourced condition of learning in a majority of face-to-face higher education institutions.

The incorporeal fallacy

However, though we might engage to an extent with such notions, Baudrillard's assertions elsewhere (Baudrillard, quoted in Denzin 1991: 32–33), that within the simulacrum all bodies, through technological transformation, are destined eventually to undergo their own repetition, and that this will constitute the end of the body and its history, are not helpful in any serious discussion of embodiment and the experience of embodied learners in cyberspace. Indeed one can only conclude that the position of Baudrillard, and other commentators who envisage the death of the body within cyberspace and relegate it to 'meatspace' or similar, is a return to a position of cartesian dualism. It posits a dissociation of mind and body in which the learner's subjectivity in cyberspace will move out of the corporeal, and into a virtual, simulated realm, a state of immaterial being constituted entirely through image and the symbolic. Cyberspace, by this reckoning, comes to be seen as a disembodied space, a space in which the body is lost, abandoned or, as in the process grotesquely dramatised in E.M. Forster's famous science fiction short story *The Machine Stops*, becomes atrophied. A similar accusation might be levelled against post-structuralist analysis which, in its privileging of the textual, despite its ever vigilant wariness of marginalising oppositions, is perhaps in danger of setting up a new form of cartesian dualism in pitting the discursive against the material. It could be seen as reducing the body to a text, with language interpreted as something totally independent of embodiment (Burkitt 1999). Despite its often radical explanatory power in other contexts, post-structuralism, it would appear, offers no adequate account of embodiment. A more helpful direction would seem to be pointed up by Stone:

> It is important to remember that virtual community originates in, and must return to, the physical. No refigured virtual body, no matter how beautiful, will slow the death of a cyberpunk with AIDS. Even in the age of the technosocial subject, life is lived through bodies.
>
> (1991: 113)

The notion that we might experience learning within a cyberspace environment as an exercise of disembodied mind, as a form of subjectivity constituted entirely through text and discourse – attractive to contemplate as that might or might not be – is probably to indulge in what we might term the 'incorporeal fallacy'. From an anti-cartesian perspective Burkitt (1999: 147) has argued persuasively that there can be no such thing as the 'mind' considered as something separate from the body and its 'spatio-temporally located practices'. While we should remain wary of succumbing to any essentialist view or any form of corporeal determinism, it does seem difficult to contemplate any form of knowledge that is not both embodied and socially and historically situated. As Burkitt has pointed out 'a disembodied view of the world is a view from nowhere and is therefore impossible for humans to attain' (Burkitt 1999: 74). Human beings, he argues, are never able to understand the world from 'some passive and disinterested spot' but only ever from within 'an active and related perspective'. Such a perspective will involve the interaction of subjects with other subjects, objects, artefacts and symbols, and this can only ever be achieved through bodily agency. Even in cyberspace environments, as Stone (1991:117) has famously remarked, there is always 'a body attached'. Cyberspace could well be a non-space, but the subjects who inhabit it always remain embodied.

The phenomenologist Merleau-Ponty argues that as embodied beings we have a need more basic even than that of safety, which is to get some kind of optimal 'grip' on the world. When we look at something we tend unconsciously to find the optimal position from which to perceive both the totality of the object and its component parts (Merleau-Ponty, cited in Dreyfus 2001: 56). Similarly when we take hold of something we seek, in grasping it, to obtain the best grip. He speaks of the idea of 'sentience' in order to convey the body's sensitive and responsive relation to the environment in which it finds itself. It entails a constant readiness to cope with things in general that goes beyond our readiness to cope with any specific thing and it makes the world directly present to us. In effect our sense of self is based on the 'feel' we have of our own bodies and the ways they position us in the world (Merleau-Ponty 1979: 250).

An important dimension of Merleau-Ponty's anti-cartesian stance is, according to Burkitt (1999: 76) its implication that thought is not structured by any form of 'mind' that remains dissociated from the body, 'whether this is a set of cognitive structures or categories, or innate ideas'. Instead, suggests Burkitt, it is 'acquired bodily actions' or habits that make thought possible, such as learning to become proficient in playing a musical instrument, learning to drive a car or compose text on a computer. This notion of learned predispositions is similar to the habituated embodied practices which constitute Bourdieu's 'habitus' (Bourdieu 1977) or what Hayles refers to as 'incorporated practices' (Hayles 1999).

Learning, embodiment and risk

In his book on Internet learning Dreyfus (2001) draws on the reasoning of Merleau-Ponty to make somewhat large claims about presence and stability. He claims that our embodied experience gives us a sense of 'the direct presence of things' and a sense of the stable organisation of the world. Hayles (1999: 201) draws attention to what she sees as significant aspects of Dreyfus' notion of embodied learning. 'For Dreyfus,' she argues, 'embodiment means that humans have available to them a mode of learning, and hence of intellection, different from that deriving from cogitation alone.' Hayles is interested in the way that embodiment emphasises the importance of context to human cognition, thus reversing 'the decontextualisation that information underwent when it lost its body' in cartesian dualism. As regards education in cyberspace, however, Dreyfus asserts conversely that in 'telepresence', to understand the world sufficiently well for sophisticated learning to take place, 'one would not only have to be able to get a grip on things at a distance; one would need to have a sense of the context as soliciting a constant readiness to get a grip on whatever comes along' (Dreyfus 2001: 57). This conclusion follows his earlier argument that:

> perception is motivated by the indeterminacy of experience and our perceptual skills serve to make determinable objects sufficiently determinate for us to get an optimal grip on them. Moreover, we wouldn't want to evolve beyond the tendency of our bodies to move so as to get a grip on the world since this tendency is what leads us to organize our experience into the experience of stable objects in the first place. Without our constant sense of the uncertainty and instability of our world and our constant moving to overcome it, we would have no stable world at all.
>
> (56)

In the light of this sense of the uncertainty and instability of the world, Dreyfus draws attention to the importance of risk and vulnerability in the learning and teaching process. This gives the learning and teaching transaction an authenticity. He argues that in face-to-face environments 'there is the possibility of taking the risk of proposing and defending an idea and finding out whether it fails or flies. If each student is at home in front of his or her terminal, there is no place for such risky involvement' (39). What is required for this authenticating risk-function to operate are the visible and present bodies of teachers and learners. Otherwise there is no opportunity for vulnerability. 'There is no class before which the student can shine and also risk making a fool of himself' (39).

A feature, and probably part of the allure, of simulacra such as theme parks, computerised games, packaged holidays, televised sport, fast-food restaurants, is their apparent minimisation of risk through standardised, routinised and predictable procedures. Considered from this perspective there is an extent to which online learning environments might be seen to minimise risk through mechanisms of control. Such environments offer asynchronous time for reflection, obviating the need for instant responses or decisions. They provide the possibility of relative anonymity, minimising visible traces of representation relating to ethnicity, gender, age, disability, culture, appearance and style. There is an apparent absence of the requirement for the teacher to provide a charismatic 'performance' (possibly accounting for why some teachers are rated by students more highly in online environments than in face-to-face environments). There is controlled access to the space through user-authentication and the option of utilising sophisticated surveillance and tracking tools. There is the compartmentalisation of activity to render the potential boundarilessness of the cyber environment less threatening, more familiar and ordered.

In Dreyfus' analysis, risk carries an affective intensity which is integral to embodiment and *presence*. 'The professor's approving or disapproving response might carry some emotional weight,' adds Dreyfus, 'but it would be much less intimidating to offer a comment and get a reaction from the professor if one had never met the professor and was not in her presence' (39). Online learning's 'limitations where embodiment is concerned', contends Dreyfus (namely the absence of face-to-face learning), can lead to a stunting of students' learning, curtailing their development to a stage merely of 'competence', as opposed to 'proficiency' or 'expertise'. Online learning might be useful in supplying the facts and rules, as well as the drill and practice required for the novice, but to acquire expertise necessarily requires 'the involvement and risk that come from making interpretations that can be mistaken and learning from one's mistakes' (91). Such involvement is not available 'if one is just sitting alone in front of one's computer screen looking at a lecture downloaded from the Web' (91). Bodily presence and immersion in context are deemed essential to the acquisition of proficiency in many areas of human agency – 'distance-apprenticeship is an oxymoron' (69). Embodiment, including our emotions, plays a crucial role for Dreyfus in 'our being able to make sense of things so as to see what is relevant, our ability to let things matter to us and so to acquire skills, our sense of the reality of things, our trust in other people' (90).

Only in a classroom where the teacher and learner sense that they are taking risks in each other's presence, and each can count on criticism from the other, are the conditions present that promote acquiring proficiency, and only by acting in the real world can one acquire expertise. As for the apprenticeship necessary to becoming a master, it is only possible where the learner sees the day-to-day responses of a master and learns to imitate her style (91).

Perhaps most important for Dreyfus is the capacity that embodiment gives us for making 'the unconditional commitments that give meaning to our lives':

> It would be a serious mistake to think we could do without these embodied capacities – to rejoice that the World Wide Web offers us the chance to become more and more disembodied, detached ubiquitous minds leaving our situated, vulnerable bodies behind.
>
> (90)

In this Dreyfus is influenced by Kierkegaardian philosophy. Applying Kierkegaard's earlier critique of the press media of his day, he maintains that, while the Internet does not prohibit 'unconditional commitments', it actually undermines them by re-presenting life as a risk-free game, or, in Kierkegaard's words, 'it transforms the task itself into a an unreal feat of artifice and reality into a theatre' (Kierkegaard, quoted in Dreyfus 2001: 88). No doubt our imaginations can be engaged, as they are in playing electronic games or watching cinema, and our responses might be sharpened for real-world encounters. But for Dreyfus this does not constitute an alternative form of embodiment. For him cyber activity cannot simulate serious commitments in the real world. Discussing Rheingold's work on virtual communities (Rheingold 2000) he concludes that involvement in virtual communities is not a threat to political or civic engagement in one's real community but 'it becomes harmful if, as is often the case, its risk-free nature makes it more attractive than the dangerous real world' (Dreyfus 2001: 105). 'Like a simulator,' he suggests, 'the Net manages to capture everything but the risk' (88). In Kierkegaardian terms cyberlearning becomes categorised as an essentially 'aesthetic sphere,' with its risk-free mimicry of serious matters within the physical world. This minimises ethical engagement and the possibility of commitment insofar as what one does in cyberspace has no real or long-term consequences. The risks are only imaginary, unlike what Kierkegaard terms 'the danger and life's stern judgment' (cited in Dreyfus 2001: 88).

What is puzzling about Dreyfus' analysis is how it seems to take no cognisance of the many risks to identity, confidence, emotional security and esteem that are encountered on a daily basis by participants within online learning environments. Apart from the 'boundariless anxiety' and 'disquietude' mentioned earlier, one thinks immediately (particularly if one has been on the receiving end of it) of the disconcerting and often humiliating effects of 'flaming' behaviours. Dreyfus, as we have seen, advocates the value in face-to-face environments of 'taking the risk of proposing and defending an idea and finding out whether it fails or flies'. In his view the student 'at home in front of his or her terminal' has no opportunity for 'such risky involvement' (39). Any user of an online environment, even experienced and battle-hardened academics, surely could sympathise with the trepidation of a new, possibly shy student, being required to post up their response to a (possibly international) discussion group, in the knowledge, moreover, that their tentative contribution is likely to remain there, with all its feared inadequacies, for a considerable period, unlike the ephemeral and evanescent tutorial remark that is likely to be forgotten and beyond recall even before the students leave the room.

There is, too, the uncertainty of others' behaviour in an environment where bodies are not visible, and where the nuanced meanings normally derived from mannerisms, gestures, expressions and other visual and auditory cues are not available and the potential for misunderstandings or misreadings of others' responses makes participation difficult, if not hazardous, on occasion. This potential for increased apprehension applies not just to online learners but also to their teachers who have to establish a sense of presence (and often authority) in an environment where their own identity and that of their students has to be established and interpreted entirely through language, through a written medium. The role of online moderator entails a quite different activity system from that of the traditional classroom tutor. Whereas the engagement of a 'silent' or shy student in a face-to-face environment might be accomplished through a repertoire of subtle interventions, most of these are likely to draw on embodied practices involving physical movement, facial expression, vocal emphasis or intonation, none of which are available to the online modera-tor. Coping with the online equivalent – the lurker – becomes a quite differ-ent issue to address, which may, if not sensitively handled, lead to quite clumsy or heavy-handed interventions. The issues that arise from the prac-tice of online moderation, and the re-aligned, often levelled, power rela-tions between teacher and learners, point to a radically reconstituted form of intersubjectivity online. There is too, a re-adjustment of the sense of how one is positioned in relation to artefacts and spaces in the ways that online learners must orient themselves towards, and navigate through, the complex labyrinth of information, materials and communities which consti-tute the hypertextual world of cyberspace, separating, as they go, pattern from randomness (Hayles 1999). As Jameson has warned, language itself can become a threat when it ceases to be a tool for action and its rapid pro-liferation leads to stultification and the failure to discriminate meaning from noise. 'No society', he points out, 'has ever been quite so mystified in quite so many ways as our own, saturated as it is with messages and information, the very vehicle of mystification' (Jameson 1981: 60–61).

We should not forget either, the simple but dramatic risk of the com-plete failure of a network. In cyberspace education of course, when the network goes down, the university disappears. Imagine the consequences of this, for both teacher and learners, when the network fails during formal examinations using online assessment. This has been an unfortunate occurrence in more than one university in which I have worked.

On the other hand, the capacity of online environments to counter or minimise risk yields manifold learning benefits which Dreyfus does not acknowledge. Indeed, for some, exposing oneself to the possibility of face-to-face risk in order to gain trust and authenticity might be deemed a priv-ileged indulgence (Burbules 2002: 391). As du Preez (1999), writing from within a South African context, points out, certain groups of learners might feel vulnerable enough in physical environments to welcome the comparative safety that is on offer through the anonymity of cyberspace.

> If learners are restricted by their gender roles in real life, it may well be that they would gain from the possibility to enter into a group discussion as another gender. I am particularly thinking of rural women and women of colour. They may find it valuable to enter discussion forums as white men for instance, not that the gender constructions of white men are in all cases advantageous or emancipatory. In some cases one would obvi-ously prefer to speak from your real-life gender.
>
> (du Preez 1999: 6)

The comparative freedom that online learning offers from the judge-mental gaze of others would also be available for students with specific disabilities, not to mention the increased access to learning that the technology provides for such groups. Moreover, newly emerging class-room communication systems (CRS) such as 'Discourse' technology, and hand-held personal response systems (PRS) such as 'eInstruction', intro-duce the possibility of online anonymity within traditional face-to-face learning environments. Such systems are bi-directional, operate between people that are linked within a face-to-face environment, and allow them to ask questions, including open-ended questions, anonymously and 'on the fly' (McCabe and Lucas 2003). Users report the significant advantages of students feeling permission to reveal their lack of knowledge or anxiety without penalty or humiliation. Teachers also comment on the invaluable diagnostic feedback this can produce in terms of student understanding, allowing them to adjust the pace of the lesson or pause and revisit issues already covered if real-time online student feedback suggests that this is necessary. In certain instances such online anonymity has proved crucially important, revealing, for example, dangerous misconceptions on the part of medical students in relation to potentially lethal interventions involving adrenalin injections. Such erroneous knowledge seems far less likely to be revealed in face-to-face environments. For Dreyfus (2001: 69) 'distance-apprenticeship' may well remain 'an oxymoron'. Not so, it would appear, for medical apprenticeship, where the risk of humiliation and loss of face in traditional environments is sometimes deemed too high.

It is difficult not to conclude that Dreyfus, too, succumbs to the incor-poreal fallacy. The fallacy, with its central implication that reality or true knowledge resides in embodied presence, might be explained in Der-ridean terms as a logocentric practice that privileges speech over the essentially 'written' nature of cyberspace. Seen in this way, in terms of what Derrida (1988) refers to as 'the metaphysics of presence', live speech (as opposed to synthesised speech) appears to emanate directly from its 'author', and to be self-evidently dependent upon the latter's embodied presence. Furthermore, *presence*, in the sense of physical pres-ence, requires synchronicity. Writing, by definition asynchronous in nature, is traditionally seen as being a step removed from the 'author' in a way that speech is not. From a logocentric perspective asynchronous activity, which characterises much of cyberspace education, undermines such residing 'truth' at a glance. Moreover most communication across cyber-environments tends to be heavily mediated through both written communication and computer technology, though this is masked through metaphors of chatting, cafés and forums, suggesting presence. Face-to-face communication, in comparison, appears deceptively to be unmedi-ated. 'It is of course no such thing, and is as mediated, though by no means as self-evidently, through linguistic signs and signifiers that are as independent of the self and as dependent on a linguistic system and inter-pretation as any written text' (Land and Bayne 1999: 739). Nonetheless, it is not difficult to see how asynchronous text-based conferencing can become identified in the minds of learners with inauthenticity.

As a counter-argument to stances that rest on the incorporeal fallacy, du Preez (1999) reminds us that cyberbodies not only remain vulnerable in cyberspace environments but that they remain legally constituted:

> the fact that cases of Net rape have occurred has interesting implications for the debate on the state of the bio-body on the Internet. Firstly it indicates that our bodies form part of the equation in cyberspace and secondly it indicates that cyberspace also has legal implications, because we still constitute bodies while in cyberspace. Legal implications have physical implications.
>
> (6)

Finally, it is worth pondering how the emergent technologies mentioned earlier, such as personal response systems (PRS) and classroom communication systems (CCS) like 'Discourse', will complicate and disrupt current understandings of presence, visibility and embodiment. By allowing physically 'present', embodied learners to interact with the teacher and other learners anonymously if they so wish, the boundaries between face-to-face and virtual become blurred. Learners are simultaneously visible and invisible, physically embodied and virtually embodied, identified and anonymous. While the teacher is talking learners may be simultaneously communicating with each other in a separate space to pass opinions on the teacher's ideas – a phenomenon coming to be known as 'backchannelling' – or posting up responses or questions to the screen as she talks. The modernist spaces of enclosure, with their seemingly stable boundaries between subjects, bodies and reality, become, in this instance, less stable and more permeable.

Conclusion – towards a relational understanding of embodiment

Hayles (1999: 196) makes a helpful distinction for our purposes between the normative physical body and the notion of embodiment. The latter can be seen as specific articulations of the body with 'place, time, physiology and culture' (196) permitting what Poster (2001a: 111) has called 'new assemblages of self-constitution'. Burkitt (1999), drawing on Ilyenkov's earlier dialectical notions of 'radical realism' (Ilyenkov 1977), advocates what he calls 'a relational approach' to embodiment. This stresses the ways in which we become constituted within and reconstituted by forms of embodiment and the various articulations they involve with other subjects, objects and artefacts, much in the way that users of language are constituted through the language but also change the language by using it. We are constituted by pre-existing forms of embodiment but our creation and subsequent use of new artefacts *through* our existing embodiment in turn transform that embodiment and reconstitute our identity, which always remains embodied. This relational view would seem to share many of the characteristics of actor-network theory. From such a perspective we can see how new technologies and artefacts (which would include language itself) have always reconstituted the embodiment of learners. We can see how the development of written culture created, for example, dyslexic learners, or the way that online environments created the 'lurkers' mentioned earlier. du Preez (1999) has commented on the ways in which hypertextual environments may well encourage new forms of literacy in which learners make intuitive connective 'jumps' to other ideas or information, permitting 'radical interactive and nonlinear possibilities'. She indicates how this reflects the differently embodied nature of learners online:

> When constructing an online course, the nature of hypertext has to be accounted for. The fact that its results are immediate and that it requires a 'new literacy' so to speak, will also have to be kept in mind. Hypertext leads to different embodiment styles online. The immediacy of hypertext will be reflected through a different embodiment style. The fact that hypertext mimics human thinking patterns could indicate that learners find it easier to learn and make associations because hypertext works the same way as our minds apparently do.
>
> (7)

There is perhaps a hint of essentialist thinking or cognitive determinism in the final sentence, but the point that different technological contextualisations lead to our being differently embodied is well made. Citing the work of Heim (1993) she draws attention to the quite different forms of embodiment that are involved when we are writing on a page, holding a pen, and when we are composing on screen, directing the mouse in a 'cut and paste' mindset. These differences go well beyond bodily actions. Writing 'on screen' entails a sense, which is not replicable offline, of the virtual desktop, of texts sliding over each other in a cyberspace or being deposited and recovered from deeper within the electronic space. Heim (1993) prefers to differentiate between writing on paper and 'compiling' on screen:

> Digital writing is almost frictionless. You formulate thoughts directly on screen. . . . But the honeymoon fades, and the dark side of computing descends upon you. The romance with computers shows its pathological aspects: mindless productivity and increased stress. . . . You no longer formulate thoughts carefully before beginning to write. You think on the screen. You edit more aggressively as you write. . . . Possible changes occur to you rapidly and frequently, so that a leaning tower of printouts stretches from the wastebasket to the heights of perfection – almost.
>
> (5)

We might also contrast the differently embodied experiences of online and offline readers. We have already touched on the potentially 'saturated' online reader skipping and clicking down the endless garden of forking paths encountering ever-accumulating sources of information, skimming the surface of many different texts and probably not engaging in the reading of substantial blocks of texts, which seem to belong to a different activity system. How different from the embodied state of the offline reader holding the bound book. Birkets (1995), a renowned antagonist of the digital age, in celebrating the sensuousness of the physical book implies more or less that it is the actual form of embodiment involved in book reading that is of most significance when he asserts that 'I value the state a book puts me in more than I value the specific contents' (Birkets 1995: 15). In this we see a clear example of what Burkitt (1999) emphasises as the relational nature between embodiment, artefact, practice and subjectivity.

Finally, there remains an ethical issue in terms of transfigured personal relations in cyberspace environments. Where bodies are no longer visibly present, do such differently embodied forms of online experience, such 'assemblages of self-constitution', entail a loss of *veracity*, insofar as one appears to be able to re-invent and re-present oneself as one likes? The most candid response to this issue seems to be that of Poster (2001b), who argues that such fluidity only serves to raise the question of veracity in any social encounter. Perhaps we should conclude with recognition of what he advocates, that in a reconfigured world, reconfigured rules will inevitably apply.

> It brings into question the fact that there is always a question of veracity in personal relations, that we never really know in truth about the other – perhaps not even about ourselves – but that in the practice of communication on the Internet relations are established and continued and within the terms of those relations there is a different kind of veracity and unveracity, there is a different kind of responsibility and irresponsibility, a different kind of truth about oneself and untruth about oneself from that that is encountered in face-to-face interactions.
>
> (Poster 2001b: 148)

References

Baudrillard, J. (1994) *Simulcra and Simulation*, Ann Arbor, MI: The University of Michigan Press.

Bayne, S. and Land, R. (2000) 'Learning in the labyrinth: hypertext and new roles for the instructor and learner', in Bourdeau, J. and Heller, R. (eds) *Ed-MEDIA 2000: Proceedings of 12th Annual World Conference on Educational Multimedia, Hypermedia and Telecommunications*, Virginia: Association for the Advancement of Computing in Education.

Bayne, S. and Land, R. (2001) 'A strange sense of disquietude: understanding student resistance to learning technologies,' in Chambers, J.A. (ed.) *Selected Papers from the Twelfth International Conference on College Teaching and*

Learning, Jacksonville, Florida: Center for the Advancement of Teaching and Learning.

Bergquist, W.H. (1995) *Quality Through Access, Access with Quality: The New Imperative for Higher Education*, San Francisco, CA: Jossey-Bass.

Birkets, S. (1995) *The Gutenberg Elegies: The Fate of Reading in an Electronic Age*, Winchester: Faber and Faber.

Bourdieu, P. (1977) *Outline of a Theory of Practice* (trans. Nice, R.), Cambridge: Cambridge University Press.

Burbules, N.C. (2002) 'Like a version: playing with online identities', *Educational Philosophy and Theory*, 34(4): 387–393.

Burkitt, I. (1999) *Bodies of Thought: Embodiment, Identity and Modernity*, London: Sage.

Deleuze, G. (1992) 'Postscript on the societies of control', *October*, 59: 3–7.

Denzin, N.K. (1991) *Images of Postmodern Society: Social Theory and Contemporary Cinema*, London: Sage.

Derrida, J. (1988) 'Structure, sign and play in the discourse of the human sciences', in Lodge, D. (ed.) *Modern Criticism and Theory*, London: Longman.

Dreyfus, H.L. (2001) *On the Internet*, London: Routledge.

du Preez, A. (1999) 'Learner embodiment in cyberspace: morphing towards cyber-learners', *Progressio: Journal of the Bureau for University Teaching*, 21(2), http://www.unisa.ac.za/Default.asp?Cmd=ViewContent&ContentID=13435 (date of access: 21 February 2004).

Feenberg, A. (1989) 'The written world: on the theory and practice of computer conferencing', in Mason, R. and Kaye, A. (eds) *Mindweave: Communication, Computers and Distance Education*, Elmsford, New York: Pergamon Press.

Giddens, A. (1991) *Modernity and Self-Identity: Self and Society in the Late Modern Age*, Cambridge: Polity Press.

Hayles, N.K. (1999) *How We Became Posthuman: Virtual Bodies in Cybernetics, Literature, and Informatics*, Chicago: University of Chicago Press.

Heim, M. (1993) *The Metaphysics of Virtual Reality*, New York and Oxford: Oxford University Press.

Ilyenkov, E.V. (1977) 'Dialectical logic: essays in its history and theory' (trans. Creighton, H.C.), Moscow: Progress Publishers.

Jameson, F. (1981) *The Political Unconscious*, Ithaca: Cornell University Press.

Johnson-Eilola, J. (1998), 'Living on the surface: learning in the age of global communication networks', in Snyder, I. (ed.) *Page to Screen: Taking Literacy into the Electronic Era*, London: Routledge.

Land, R. and Bayne, S. (1999) 'Computer-mediated learning, synchronicity and the metaphysics of presence', in Collis, B. and Oliver, R. (eds) *ED-MEDIA: Proceedings of 11th Annual World Conference on Educational Multimedia, Hypermedia and Telecommunications*, Virginia: Association for the Advancement of Computing in Education.

Landow, G. (1997) *Hypertext 2.0: The Convergence of Contemporary Theory and Technology*, Baltimore: Johns Hopkins University Press.

Lankshear, C., Peters, M. and Knobel, M. (1996) 'Critical pedagogy and cyberspace', in Giroux, H.A., Lankshear, C., McLaren, P. and Peters, M. (eds) *Counternarratives*, London: Routledge.

McCabe, M. and Lucas, I. (2003) *Teaching with CAA in an Interactive Classroom*, Loughborough: CAA Conference Proceedings, Loughborough University.

Merleau-Ponty, M. (1979) *Phenomenology of Perception* (trans. Smith, C.), London: Routledge and Kegan Paul.

Poster, M. (2001a) 'Cyberdemocracy: the Internet and the public sphere', in Poster, M. (ed.) *The Information Subject*, Amsterdam: G + B Arts International.

Poster, M. (2001b) 'Communication and the constitution of the self: an interview with Mark Poster 14.8.1995', in Poster, M. (ed.) *The Information Subject*, Amsterdam: G + B Arts International.

Rheingold, H. (2000) *The Virtual Community: Homesteading on the Electronic Frontier* (revised edition), Cambridge, MA: MIT Press.

Stone, A.R. (1991) 'Will the real body please stand up? Boundary stories about virtual cultures', in Benedikt, M. (ed.) *Cyberspace: First Steps*, Cambridge, MA: MIT Press.

Tabbi, J. (1997) 'Reading, writing, hypertext: democratic politics in the virtual classroom', in Porter, D. (ed.) *Internet Culture*, London: Routledge.

Thibault, C. (1996) 'Baudrillard on the New Technologies', *An Interview with Claude Thibaut, Cybersphere 9: Philosophy*, http://www.uta.edu/english/apt/collab/texts/newtech.html (date of access: 21 February 2004).

Turkle, S. (1996) *Life on the Screen: Identity in the Age of the Internet*, London: Phoenix.

Usher, R. and Edwards, R. (2000) 'Lost and found: "cyberspace" and the (dis)location of teaching, learning and research,' *Research, Teaching and Learning: Making Connections in the Education of Adults*, Papers from the 28th Annual SCUTREA Conference, UK.

Wegerif, R. (1998) 'The social dimension of asynchronous learning environments', *Journal of Asynchronous Learning Networks*, 2(1), http://www.sloan-c.org/publications/jaln/v2n1/v2n1_wegerif.asp (date of access: 21 February 2004).

11 Screen or monitor?

Issues of surveillance and disciplinary power in online learning environments

Ray Land and Siân Bayne

Introduction

This chapter considers a little-discussed aspect of online learning – the surveillance or 'student tracking' capabilities of virtual learning environments (VLEs). In, at least, the two main commercially available VLEs – Blackboard and WebCT – sophisticated, powerful, easy-to-use means of collecting data on students' activities within the learning space are built in as part of its pedagogical functioning. Where such surveillance tools are often promoted, and accepted, as useful ways of evaluating course effectiveness through helping us to understand student usage of the online facility, we wish in this chapter to probe a little deeper and think about some of the broader cultural and pedagogical implications of using these tracking devices.

The chapter uses a theoretical framework drawn from the work of Foucault and from Poster's more recent approach to the 'database as discourse'. It begins by giving a brief overview of the kinds of surveillance tools which we have access to in WebCT and Blackboard, moving on to the application of Foucault's panopticon metaphor to such facilities, and finally examining the implications of their use for educational practice.

The unifying theme of our discussion relates to the way in which the individuality of our learners is affected by the use of cyberspace as a learning environment. We believe that the learning environments we use work to develop certain kinds of learners, thus the subjectivity of the online learner is our central concern.

Tracking students in virtual learning environments

Murray Goldberg, WebCT developer, asks in his online newsletter, 'It's 10pm, do you know where your students are?'(Goldberg 2000). He goes on to describe how the rationale for the development of the student tracking tools in WebCT grew out of his own experience of teaching online. The tools he refers to are, indeed, extensive. WebCT allows tutors to track the date and time of students' first and last logins, which pages each individual student has accessed and when, the total number of times the student has accessed the system, and for every section of the course to track the number of discussion board articles each student has opened and the number and date of each student's own discussion board contributions. At the same time, class records can be generated allowing tutors to organise their students according to frequency of accesses to the course, by date of first or last access, or by the number of discussion board items opened or posted.

WebCT's main out-of-the-box virtual learning environment rival, Blackboard, has a similar suite of surveillance tools, enabling records to be generated showing for each individual user the total number of accesses to the course as a whole, the total number of accesses to each individual area and page of content, number of accesses over time, accesses per day of the week and by hour of the day. With both VLEs the tutor can also, of course, keep permanent records of the more obviously 'visible' activities undertaken by the student – the number, time and quality of contributions to discussion boards, emails exchanged between tutor and student, and results from online quizzes (those intended for self- or formative assessment as well as those which are summative).

These tools are far more than the electronic equivalent of the attendance sheet. As in so many arenas, computers have enabled us to do things that were previously impossible or very difficult. VLE surveillance tools record every move a student makes within the learning space, and provide intimate details of every student's working hours and patterns of study. Where such a virtual learning environment (VLE) is integrated with wider institutional information systems, anyone wishing to generate a student record walks through an even richer information landscape. Similarly, system administrators may extract information at a similar level of detail from almost any networked activity, whether undertaken by students or staff. However, where previously to track activity within a web-based learning environment would have involved the deliberate, rather complex analysis of log files and server statistics (something for which the majority of teachers would be likely to have neither the time nor the inclination), within VLEs surveillance is a casual act – sophisticated and detailed reports on individual students can be obtained with a couple of mouse clicks. Further, such tracking tools are included in learning environments as an integral element of their *pedagogical* functioning. Goldberg, for example, describes how by enabling continual evaluation, such tools simply help him to be a better online educator, providing higher quality web-based courses:

> [the] benefit is all in the name of continually trying to improve my course offering, not only in response to direct student comments, but also in response to the way students are interacting with the course. Without this activity tracking I would be in the dark.
>
> (Goldberg 2000)

The aim of this chapter is not to deny the usefulness to tutors of such facilities, and we wish to avoid succumbing to the techno-paranoia which sometimes accompanies explorations of the impact of 'dataveillance' (Clarke 1991). Rather we wish to render strange an element of online learning which – much like the metadata described by Oliver in Chapter 5 – risks becoming banal, a matter of 'common sense', and to explore what we see as some important cultural and pedagogical implications of using such tools. From this we attempt, in the second part of the chapter, to hazard some tentative recommendations for practice. As McLuhan has argued, technology is not neutral: 'technological environments are not merely passive containers of people but are active processes that reshape people and other technologies alike' (McLuhan 1962: iv). The wish to avoid accusations of technological determinism should not prevent us from looking closely at how our technologies change the way we work and the way we experience ourselves and others. As Foucault has said, the point 'is not that everything is bad, but that everything is dangerous, which is not exactly the same as bad. If everything is dangerous, then we always have something to do' (Foucault 1983: 231–232).

The panopticon

The imagery of the panopticon is regularly drawn on in discussions of cyber-surveillance (see, for example, Bowers 1988; Zuboff 1988; Provenzo 1992; Lyon 1993; Spears and Lea 1994; Gandy 1996; Poster 1996) and does indeed provide a powerful metaphor for thinking about the way in which power relations are constructed in online environments.

In 1791, Bentham conceived of the architectural innovation of the panopticon as a way of achieving conformity and order within a 'humane' prison system (see Bentham 1962). The panopticon is a circular building, in which the cells of the prisoners occupy the circumference. The cells are divided from each other in such a way as to prevent any communication between prisoners. At the centre is the 'inspector's lodge' or observation tower from within which prison guards can see into every cell, without themselves being visible. The goal is the achievement of control through both isolation and the possibility of constant (invisible) surveillance.

For Foucault (1979) the panopticon encapsulates in its form the shift in the nature of power relations which took place during the seventeenth and eighteenth centuries. Where previously what Foucault refers to as sovereign power had exercised dominion through punishment of the physical body (physical torture, public execution), during this time a different, less visible, power mechanism emerged which Foucault calls disciplinary power. Disciplinary power is exercised over individual and collective bodies 'through surveillance and via a grid or network of material coercions which effected an efficient and controlled increase (minimum expenditure, maximum return) in the utility of the subjected body' (Smart 1985: 80).

The panopticon, as one of the 'technologies of power' of this regime, functions less through the imposition of physical force than through its ability to bring about conformity through self-regulation. As subordinates are never sure when they are being observed, they have no alternative than to assume an unwavering surveillance and hence internalise the 'normalising regime'.

> He who is subjected to a field of visibility, and who knows it, assumes responsibility for the constraints of power; he makes them play spontaneously upon himself; he inscribes in himself the power relation in which he simultaneously plays both roles; he becomes the principle of his own subjection.
>
> (Foucault 1979: 203)

Disciplinary power is not only manifested in the workings of penal institutions. For Foucault it is identified with the power–knowledge nexus which is inherent in the workings of institutions throughout the social sphere, including educational institutions. It is important to note, however, that power is not, for Foucault, simply a matter of repression or domination, the property of a particular individual, or group, or class. Rather it is a constituent element of contemporary society – it circulates throughout social relations like an energy. Power, like surveillance, is not necessarily 'bad' – as Ball points out, for example, 'Education works not only to render its students as subjects of power, it also constitutes them, or some of them, as powerful subjects' (Ball 1990: 5).

It is not surprising that those theorising the place of privacy in the information society have seized on Foucault's analysis and the panopticon metaphor, seeing in computerised and video surveillance a full realisation of the principles of the panopticon. Computerised student tracking systems like the ones described above do appear to represent the perfect disciplinary apparatus, the single gaze that constantly observes everything.

Surveillance for Foucault is an element of the hierarchical observation which is a key instrument of disciplinary power. Hierarchical observation binds the concepts of visibility and power. There is an unequal power relationship between the seer and the seen – the visibility of the seen enables the seer to 'know' them, to alter them. Access to this knowledge, to this power, is of course unevenly distributed.

We have to bear in mind that in the everyday functioning of the virtual learning environment, the tutor, or 'course designer', has access to extensive surveillance tools, and the student does not.[1] Whatever truth there may be in claims that computer-mediated communication has the potential to do away with many of the cues through which hierarchical relationships and status differentials are inscribed, the relation between teacher and learner is still – perhaps inevitably – a hierarchical one, not least where the teacher is also the assessor. How comfortable should we be, however, with such ready, casual access to tools which so starkly represent the 'power of mind over mind' (Foucault 1979a)?

The subject

Hierarchical observation is only one of the instruments through which disciplinary power exercises itself. The two main others – normalising judgement and examination – are also well known to educators. Their collective effect is one of classification and division, rendering the subject 'knowable' through the collection of data relating to them. For Foucault, the file, the document and the record are powerful tools representative of the exercise of disciplinary power. It is partly through these that the individual is constituted, the subject objectified. The power to classify, to collect data relating to students, is hardly new in education, yet in the use of online surveillance tools we see it reaching a new level of depth and detail, representing a further extension of what Foucault calls the 'progressive objectification and the ever more subtle partitioning of individual behaviour' (Foucault 1979: 178). As Provenzo points out, 'this desire to partition individual student behaviour into ever more subtle units – to systematically collect data – is built into the structure of many computer education programs' (Provenzo 1992: 185).

Foucault writes against the idea of the sovereign subject, seeing subjectivity as being formed by the exercise of power. Hence, within the panopticon, individuals are made to internalise the gaze of power, to adopt its values as their own, to conform. They are thus formed by power – rather than seeing it as an external force being applied to a pre-existing, stable subject, it is power which makes us who we are. Disciplinary power is an element of what Foucault calls discourse, in which individual subjectivity is seen not as the possession of the conscious self, but as something which is dispersed throughout a network of external structures and practices:

> discourse is not the majestically unfolding manifestation of a thinking, knowing, speaking subject, but, on the contrary, a totality, in which the dispersion of the subject and his discontinuity with himself may be determined. It is a space of exteriority in which a network of distinct sites is deployed.
>
> (Foucault 1966: 55)

It follows that discourse and practice are inseparable. Discourses are 'practices that systematically form the objects of which they speak' (Foucault 1974: 49) – in other words, the discourses of pedagogy create both the teacher and the taught; the discourse/practice of technology-assisted learning creates both the online learner and the teacher or facilitator of online learning.

In this scheme we can see disciplinary apparatuses or 'technologies of power' (of which the virtual learning environment is an example) as being about creating a *certain type of subject*; in using these technologies we are therefore also involved in creating a certain type of subject, a certain type of learner. For Lyotard, predicting back in 1979 the impact of technology on education, the kind of learner being produced would be one who, in the name of enhanced performativity, would be an efficient, skilled user of information (Lyotard 1979: 51). In the current discourse of learning technology we would be more likely to describe the kind of learner we are trying to produce as one who is 'active', 'independent', 'lifelong', 'flexible'. Applying the Foucauldian approach in any case problematises the notion that it is possible to place 'the learner' at the centre of the learning process. Instead, it would see the subjectivity of the learner as constituted through and by the learning environment and the discourses/practices located within it.

The 'superpanopticon'

Theory building on the work of Foucault highlights the way in which the virtual environment works to constitute the subjectivity of its users, restructuring the nature of individuality in the process. Poster (1996) analyses the particular impact on subjectivity of electronic databases, characterising the surveillance function of such technologies as a 'superpanopticon' (Poster 1996). The superpanopticon constitutes individual 'subjectivities' according to its own rules. For example, within interlinked electronic databases, the fields and records containing an individual's details (name, age, sex, etc.), highly limited by the determinations of the technology, actually become the 'retrievable identity' of that individual. In other words, the data held on an individual become a 'simulacrum' of that individual – a copy which, as far as the imperative of the technology is concerned, has no original. For Poster therefore, computerised databases are 'nothing but performative machines, engines for producing retrievable identities' (186). What is more, the individual has no control over – or possibly even awareness of – this 'other identity' which is circulating throughout the electronic network:

> Now, through the database alone, the subject has been multiplied and decentered, capable of being acted upon by computers at many social locations without the least awareness by the individual concerned yet just as surely as if the individual were present somehow inside the computer.
>
> (Poster 1996: 184)

The data represented in the discourse of the database comes to stand for the subject in 'a highly caricatured yet immediately available form':

> To the database, Jim Jones is the sum of the information in the fields of the record that applies to that name. So the person Jim Jones now has a new form of presence, a new subject position that defines him for all those agencies and individuals who have access to the database.
>
> (188)

Lyon (1994) characterises these representations as 'complementary selves' who are 'the sum, as it were, of their transactions':

> New individuals are created who bear the same names but who are digitally shorn of their human ambiguities and whose personalities are built artificially from matched data. Artificial they may be, but these computer 'selves' have a part to play in determining the life-chances of their human namesakes. Thus are subjects constituted and deviants defined within the Superpanopticon.
>
> (71)

We should perhaps not underestimate the extent to which this power to constitute and disperse the subject can be applied in virtual learning environments. While humanist ways of knowing might resist the idea that identity formation can take place outside the skin of the individual, we need to consider the possibility that the online student may be starkly objectified in her virtual construction, that 'the learner' may be, as far as our systems are concerned, to some extent constituted by records of her first login, last login, frequency of login, number of discussion board submissions, pattern of page visitation across the site, and so on. Such an identity might exist not only beyond the control of the individual learner, but its very existence – and the possibility of 'judgement' being applied to it either wittingly or not – might remain unknown to them. The literature is full of claims to the emancipatory potential of online communication in educational and other contexts, particularly in the way it enables us to reformulate ourselves and experiment with new identities. In our focus on the way in which we are able to 'make ourselves' in cyberspace, however, we should not neglect the ways in which cyberspace technologies may also make us.

Implications for educational practice

Paradigmatic contradiction

The ethos of the virtual learning environment can be viewed in many ways as managerialist. It is about order, efficiency, identified outcomes and control. The attraction of databases to the organiser of the VLE is not just their retrieval speed but their relational abilities and totalising nature. In its concern for control and managerial efficiency the VLE reveals the assumption of an individualised, rational and stable learner. The cultural technologies on which it is predicated, however (web-based learning environments, relational databases), give rise to discourses/practices which constitute the subject in a decidedly different fashion, as multi-faceted, heterogeneous and dispersed.

Despite such heterogeneity and multiplicity, however, the archival permanence promised by VLE databases militates in the opposite direction. Within such archival fixity and retrievability students can never escape their past. There is a loss of redemptive possibility from the digital database which, according to Poster, is 'perfectly transferable in space, indefinitely preservable in time' and 'may last forever everywhere' (Poster 1996: 182). There is here no Whitmanesque notion of the subject as a perpetually reinventing 'self', who is self-redeeming. 'Do I contradict myself? Very well then I contradict myself (I am large, I contain multitudes)' (Whitman 1975: 123).

Within a managerialist paradigm the learner may be individualised, a unified subject, but is not the Romantic self. What is offered, rather, is a disempowering and constraining constitution of the subject. And yet the poststructuralist interpretation of these technologies, as interpellating the subject within a primarily linguistic environment (in which even the databases themselves are a form of writing) offers a multiplicity, fragmentation and re-signification of the subject which, in its uncertainty and instability is the antithesis of the certainty and permanence that managerialism endeavours to achieve.

Insouciance

Perhaps because our current theories of learning are inadequate to explain and analyse the discursive practices that are now emerging within new technologies there appears to be a lack of critique or even a certain insouciance in regard to the (often occluded) effects of these rapidly developing new practices. We are reminded of President Richard Nixon's confident assertion at the onset of Watergate that, 'The country doesn't give much of a shit about bugging ... most people around the country think it's probably routine, everybody's trying to bug everybody else, it's politics' (cited in Marx 1996: 193). Though the American public were later to demonstrate their concern about his political mendacity, his observation about the public perception of surveillance may not have been inaccurate. Provenzo, for example, suggests that:

> students learn that surveillance is part of their education. Mastering the new computer literacy implies the acceptance that information will be automatically collected and that in turn control will be exercised.
>
> (1992: 186)

He cites Bowers, who argues that this kind of student experience might be deemed 'essential to the development of the socially responsible citizen, and thus it could be expected to view it as a normal, even necessary, aspect of adult life' (Bowers 1988: 19). Our own interviews with practitioners in UK higher education reveal a similar outlook:

> Now students don't mind. We speak to students. They don't care. They expect ... they know they're being logged. They're quite astonished to find they're being logged as little as they are. There seems to be, at least with them, an idea that it's acceptable to be logged through their educational activities. There are other activities where they wouldn't, which are more social or more exploratory. But they expect, for every crossed knees and twitch they make, that we try and log that.
>
> (Interview respondent)

We are reminded too of Poster's characterisation of such responses as 'a complicated configuration of unconsciousness, indirection, automation, and absentmindedness both on the part of the producer of the database and on the part of the individual subject being constituted by it' (Poster 1996: 187).

Insouciance notwithstanding, it is important to bear in mind that UK universities have a responsibility to comply with the Data Protection Act of 1998, which raises the interesting issue of whether certain undisclosed tracking activities within VLEs are actually legal under current European legislation. Discussions with university Data Protection Officers lead one to conclude that the, as yet, mainly untested application of this law to university practice still remains a grey area, pending further government guidance.

> The whole environment in which we're working is dynamically locking down on our responsibilities, on what we can and cannot do ... I have my doubts at three o'clock in the morning that we potentially could have a problem under the Data Protection Act because we don't have a full disclosure. We are very concerned about it. We keep ourselves as informed about it as possible.
>
> (Interview respondent)

Policies of acceptable use

The requirements of the Act, not to mention professional and ethical obligations, give rise to questions of what constitutes acceptable use of such technologies. Any code of practice, we suggest, would need to address a range of issues, principally:

- to adhere to the principle of informed consent;

- to specify which activities are tracked and for what purpose;
- to grant students and staff the right to see their own database;
- to grant third parties (for example, in the UK, external examiners?) the right to check usage of data (more inspection!);
- to issue a clear statement/policy of how long databases would be kept (for example, for appeal purposes only? for three months after resits?);
- to reach agreement on who 'owns' the database and to which other parties it might be made available (for example, would Quality Assurance Agency or similar inspectors/externals have a right to view it? – and which parts?) and with which other databases it might be made 'relational';
- to address the legal implications of operating franchises and other web-based activities outside European boundaries.

However, these measures, if implemented, probably have limited value. Such ethical responses tend to represent a liberal desire to democratise information, assuming a relatively unblurred demarcation between private and public spheres, and a separation of knowledge from power in the process. They posit the existence within these environments of learners who are autonomous actors for whom rationality is equated with freedom or political emancipation. However, from an alternative perspective, databases preclude such agency. There is no direct relation between increased access to data, increased knowledge and increased power.

> Postmodern culture configures multiple, dispersed subject positions whose domination no longer is effected by alienated power but by entirely new articulations of technologies of power. The cultural function of databases is not so much the institution of dominant power structures against the individual as it is the restructuring of the nature of the individual ... the viewpoint that I am proposing posits a different relation of knowledge and power, one in which knowledge itself is a form of linguistic power, the culturally formative power of subject constitution.
>
> (Poster 1996: 190)

Interpretation of tracking data

Interviews with practitioners provide salutary reminders that the interpretation of surveillance data in online learning environments can often be misleading. What does the pattern of logging activity actually mean? What does the data really signify? Using the classifications and divisions provided by VLE tracking activity to make judgements of student performance, or intention, appears fraught with dangers of misreading, misinterpretation and assumption.

The reporting is more important than the actual raw data. It's not terribly useful for us and I really question whether it's particularly useful for Blackboard or WebCT because what you're actually capturing is not what's actually going on. You're capturing what you *think*'s going on. The student may actually just look at a page, print it off, take it away or they can print off three copies for their friends or their friend is sitting next to them or they accidentally go to some pages or they do a quick flick through the pages to make sure they've covered all the things, the questions that they know there might be teaching about. You're not actually capturing what you think you're capturing. What you're capturing is only that that page has at any time been looked at by that student. That can be exceptionally misleading.

(Interview respondent)

The need to minimise the degree of interpretability of data assumes particular importance when it is used as the basis of assessment or other formative judgements. Caution and active inhibition would appear to be the operative watchwords:

Anybody you interview who's using WebCT or Blackboard, slap them round the face and say 'Do you know what you're doing?' – because I bet they don't! *(laughs)*.

(Interview respondent)

The role of the tutor

A final consideration is the way in which the subjectivity of the tutor becomes constituted through the discourses and practices of online learning environments. Though the discourse of flexible or student-centred learning might position or interpellate the tutor as 'moderator' or 'facilitator', the forms of agency inherent in practice within an online environment might include more problematic roles of monitoring, recording, interpreting and forwarding online data. Tutors, of course, are 'seers' of their students, but are also 'seen' by managers:

although surveillance rests on the individual, its functioning is that of a network of relations from top to bottom ... and laterally this network holds the whole together and traverses it in its entirety with effects of power that derive from one another: supervisor perpetually supervised.

(Foucault 1979: 177)

Another interview respondent described a situation in which the use by study advisers of management information systems (MIS) revealed which tutors were registered to make use of new university databases to advise their students. One tutor was identified as having never registered as a user or accessed the database and was deemed by managers to be potentially unsuitable to remain within the role, though such deliberations went on unknown to the tutor concerned. This reconstitution of the subject, through the *absence* of a data record, has a peculiarly postmodern complexion. There are problems too when the tutor is aware that his or her practice, or teaching material, is under surveillance. More than one vice-chancellor has been heard to argue that rendering the work and practice of teaching colleagues *visible*, through subjecting staff to the rigorous discipline of having to put previously 'invisible' content and class interaction online, has had radical effects in terms of improving quality standards. Exposure of one's work to the gaze of one's peers, managers and competitors is, it can probably be surmised, likely to produce compliance with a quality assurance standard. What is probably also likely as an unintended consequence is an increased unwillingness on the part of teachers to take risks with their teaching, engage in pedagogical experiment or any innovation which might now be deemed high profile. Such activities might also be construed as an important factor inherent in quality *enhancement.*

Academic staff also need to be aware of both the changes in authority and the more diverse forms of agency that can arise in online learning environments.

> There's a major underlying factor which I don't think they'd even admit to but they're afraid of losing their power. By introducing the [name of VLE] system we have introduced into the power equation issues of who controls, who monitors, who watches the [name of degree] progress. We've suddenly got developers in there, we've suddenly got the learning technology section in there who by holding on to, creating and capturing this information are suddenly incredibly powerful because that's the node to where everything goes. So in that respect there are major concerns about whether we should be there at all, about whether the power should be devolved. From personal positions of being threatened, of losing power, of losing influence and control of what's going on, both from their own personal point of view about advancement, responsibility and respect as well as professionally about 'Should we lose this power?'. So there's a fundamental point about when you introduce a VLE (you are going to change power balances; you can't help doing that in quite a fundamental and significant way) that the power structures will change.
>
> (Interview respondent)

Conclusion

The preceding discussion gives rise to a more fundamental concern in relation to learning within virtual learning environments. This concern relates to tendencies within currently dominant theories of learning in higher education to posit learners primarily as unified and stable subjects. Such analyses tend to emphasise and privilege notions of interior processing (the 'deeper' the learning the better) and cognitive restructuring. Transformation is sought to a more *reflective*, i.e. more fully interiorised, individualised and unified subject. Currently available learning theory appears increasingly inadequate to deal with the complexities of agency, discursive practice, identity and subjectivity within virtual learning environments. We suggest, therefore, that we need to identify and understand forms of agency and learning appropriate to the dispersed, multiple subject of virtual learning environments.

We may view with disquietude the way in which new technologies appear to represent an extreme manifestation of how a technology of power can achieve control by the total and thoroughly disempowering constitution of the subject, yet our chances of developing effective pedagogies for online learning will be greatly enhanced if we are prepared to recognise, and engage with, the new modes of identity formation and new articulations of power/knowledge which cyberspace technologies represent.

Note

1 An interesting exception is the – no longer widely used – conferencing software FirstClass, in which the hardly extensive, but functional, 'message history' tool is equally available to both. 'Message history' allows users to track who has read any given message, and when.

References

Ball, S.J. (1990) 'Introducing Monsieur Foucault', in Ball, S.J. (ed.) *Foucault and Education: Disciplines and Knowledge*, London: Routledge, pp. 1–7.

Bentham, J. (1962) 'Panopticon; or the inspection-house', in Bowring, J. (ed.) *The Works of Jeremy Bentham*, New York: Russell and Russell.

Bowers, C.A. (1988) *The Cultural Dimensions of Educational Computing: Understanding the Non-Neutrality of Technology*, New York: Teachers College Press.

Clarke, R. (1991) 'Information technology and dataveillance', in Dunlop, C. and Kling, R. (eds) *Controversies in Computing*, New York: Academic Press.

Foucault, M. (1966) *The Order of Things: An Archaeology of the Human Sciences*, New York: Pantheon.

Foucault, M. (1974) *The Archaeology of Knowledge*, London: Tavistock.

Foucault, M. (1979) *Discipline and Punish: The Birth of the Prison*, Harmondsworth: Penguin.

Foucault, M. (1983) 'On the genealogy of ethics', by Dreyfus, H.L. and Rabinow, P. (eds) *Michel Foucault: Beyond Structuralism and Hermeneutics*, Chicago: University of Chicago Press.

Gandy, O.H. (1996) 'Coming to terms with the panoptic sort', in Lyon, D. and Zureik, E. (eds) *Computers, Surveillance, and Privacy*, Minneapolis: University of Minnesota Press, pp. 132–155.

Goldberg, M. (2000) 'Message from Murray: student activity tracking', *OTL Newsletter*, http://webct.com/service/viewcontentframe?contentID=2339320 (date of Access: 20 February 2004).

Lyon, D. (1993) 'An electronic panopticon? A sociological critique of surveillance theory', *Sociological Review*, 41: 653–678.

Lyon, D. (1994) 'From big brother to electronic panopticon', in Lyon, D. (ed.) *The Electronic Eye: The Rise of Surveillance Society*, Minneapolis: University of Minnesota Press, pp. 57–80.

Lyotard, J.-F. (1979) *The Postmodern Condition: A Report on Knowledge*, Manchester: Manchester University Press.

Marx, G. (1996) 'Electric eye in the sky: some reflections on the new surveillance and popular culture', in Lyon, D. and Zureik, E. (eds) *Computers, Surveillance, and Privacy*, Minneapolis: University of Minnesota Press, pp. 193–208.

McLuhan, M. (1962) *The Gutenberg Galaxy*, Toronto: The University of Toronto Press.

Poster, M. (1996) 'Databases as discourse; or, electronic interpellations', in Lyon, D. and Zureik, E. (eds) *Computers, Surveillance, and Privacy*, Minneapolis: University of Minnesota Press, pp. 175–192.

Provenzo, E.F.J. (1992) 'The electronic panopticon: censorship, control, and indoctrination in post-typographic culture', in Tuman, M.C. (ed.) *Literacy Online: The Promise (and Peril) of Reading and Writing with Computers*, Pittsburgh: University of Pittsburgh Press, pp. 167–188.

Smart, B. (1985) *Michel Foucault*, London: Tavistock.

Spears, R. and Lea, M. (1994) 'Panacea or panopticon? The hidden power in computer-mediated communication', *Communication Research*, 21(4): 427–459.

Whitman, W. (1975) '"Song of Myself" from "Leaves of Grass"', in Murphy, E. (ed.) *The Complete Poems of Walt Whitman*, Harmondsworth: Penguin.

Zuboff, S. (1988) *In the Age of the Smart Machine: the future of work and power*, New York: Basic Books.

Index

Note: Page numbers followed by '*n*' refer to notes

academic autonomy 15, 24
academic legitimacy 3
academics: curricula design 75
access 13; widening 17
Acropolis (Athens) 26
activity theory 132–3
actor network theory 109, 161
addressivity: and audience 91–104; in
    conventional HE writing 92–3
Adobe: pdf format 59
American Historical Association 58
American Historical Review 62
Anagnostopoulou, K.: and Hayne, M.
    122
Anderson, J.R.: *et al* 136
Anderson, T.: and Garrison, D.R. 123
anonymity 29–30; benefits 158–9
anthropology 61
antipedagogy 152
Arachne: myth 2, 26
archaeology 62
archives: digital 60–3
Ariès, P. 57
Armada (Mattingly) 49
Ars Memoria 117, 118
Ashwin, P.: and Trigwell, K. 114
Athene (Greek goddess) 26
audience: and addressivity 91–104; issue
    96–9; limitless web audience 101;
    multiple and unknowable 101–2; in
    online environments 94–5; virtual
    4–5; web-based documents 101
authenticity 3, 149, 155; of online
    history 58–9
autonomy: academic 24; human 21;
    individual 24

Baker, M.: *et al* 133
Bakhtin, M. 1, 5, 92, 94, 96, 99;
    dialogism model 22; super addressee
    notion 101–2
Ball, S.J. 168
Bandura, A.: social learning theory
    136–7
Barnett, R. 11, 13, 14, 17; ideological
    institution 23
Baudrillard, J. 152, 153
Baym, N. 67
Bayne, S. 2; and Land, R. 159
Beazleigh, H.: and Foster-Jones, J. 73,
    74–5, 82, 85
Becker, C. 64
behavioural learning approach 136–7
Benedict, M.L. 69*n*
Benjamin, W. 69*n*
Bentham, J. 167
Bergquist, W.H. 151
binarism 124
Birkets, S. 162
Blackboard: VLE surveillance 165–6,
    175
Bolter, J.: and Grusin, G. 69
books: printed 12
Bourdieu, P. 154
Bowers, C.A. 173
brainstorming 118
British Joint Information and Science
    Council 121
British University Film and Video
    Council 52
Brown, J.S.: and Duguid, P. 108
Burkitt, I. 153, 154, 160
Burnett, K. 122, 126, 127
Burroughs, W. 124

canonical texts 126
capitalism 14
capitalist consensus 22
Castells, M. 13, 15
Center for History and New Media:
  George Mason University 63
certification: Internet as threat to 64
Chandler, D. 101
chat room: Internet 40*n*, 65, 67
children's learning 120
Chomsky, N. 151
citizenship 11, 19, 21, 23
Civil War (US) 59
Clark, R.: and Ivanic, R. 93
Clarke, R. 167
classroom communication systems
  (CC) 158–60
cognition: distributed 107
collaborative discourse 133–5
communities: e-learning 6, 130–45
Community-Centred Development
  (CCD) 133
Computer Supported Collaborative
  Learning (CSCL) 133, 134
computing: campus provision 113
Conole, G. 123; and Oliver, M. 79
control, deceit and desire 26–41
Cooper, B. 137
copyright law 59
cosmopolitan project 20–1
cosmopolitanism 127
Cousin, G. 6
creativity 17
critique 23
Crook, C. 113
Cuban, L. 12, 110, 111, 113
cultural imperialism 82
culture: educational versus metadata
  72–89; fragmentation 20;
  transmission 12
cultures 2–3
curriculum design: complexity 77

Daniel, J.S. 80; mega university 19–20,
  22
Data Protection Act (UK 1978) 173–4
dataveillance 167
de Masio, A. 137
Dearing Report (1997) 73, 74, 75, 80, 81
deceit: desire and control 26–41
Delanty, G. 11; cosmopolitan project
  20–1
Deleuze, G. 6; and Guattari, F. 124,
  125, 126

Denzin, N.K. 152
Derrida, J. 1, 56, 61
designers: e-learning 134
desire: control and deceit 26–41
deterritorialisation 126
dialogic discourse 5
dialogical cognitive tools 133
dialogism: Bakhtinian model 22
dialogue 23; design 137–9; processes
  and cognitive change 131–2
digital archives: history 60–3
digital cameras 52
digital disciplines 55–6
digital media 46–8
Digital Millennium Copyright law
  (DMC) 59
digital writing 161
digitisation 3
disciplinary power and surveillance
  165–78
discourse analysis 137–9; DISCOUNT
  scheme 138
discourses: of cyberspace 3–4
discussion board: dialogic nature 100
Disneyland 152
disquietitude 151
distance learning 12, 67
Distributed National Electronic
  Resource (JISC-DNER) 110, 111,
  114
Downes, S. 74, 78, 79, 81
Dreyfus, H. 6, 154–9
du Preez, A. 158, 160, 161
Duffy, T.M.: *et al* 136
Duguid, P.: and Brown, J.S. 108
Dutton, W.H. 17

e-mail 64, 94, 113; corporate footers 95;
  positioning 96–9; reader-response
  theory 96; self-regulation 96, 98, 99;
  To, Cc or Bc 96–9
e-University 17
Earle, A. 77
economy 23
education: consumerist 18;
  technological determinism 109–11
educational culture: versus metadata
  72–89
educational diversity 72
educational technology 11–12
Edwards, R.: and Usher, R. 150
elites 15
elitism: systems 21; traditions 14
embodiment 30; and risk 149–62

employability 19
Engeström, Y. 106
entrepreneurialism 13
environmental learning approach 136–7
epistemology: of modernity 18
Ernst, W. 62
ethics: of transfigured personal relations 162
exchange: non-instrumental 23
Extensible Markup Language (XML) 78

Feenberg, A. 151
feminism 24
Forster, E.R. 153
Fosnot, C. 136
Foster-Jones, J.: and Beazleigh, H. 73, 74–5, 82, 85
Foucault, M. 1, 7, 19–20, 57, 58, 79, 98, 165, 167–70, 175
Fox, S. 109
Freire, P. 79
French Historical Studies 62
Freud, S. 151
Friesen, N. 78–9, 82, 84; community-based metadata 83

Galbraith, J.K. 53
Garrison, D.R.: and Anderson, T. 123
Gibbons, M.: *et al* 11
Giddens, A. 151
globalisation 2, 11, 17, 18, 20, 22, 24, 82, 110; and university 13–16
Goldberg, M. 165–6
Goodchild, P. 125
Goodyear, R.: and Jones, C. 110, 111
Grierson, A.: and Pilkington, R.M. 139
Grusin, G.: and Bolter, J. 69
Guattari, F. 6; and Deleuze, G. 124, 125, 126

habitus 154
Haraway, D. 28, 39, 40
Hardy, C.: and Portelli, A. 49
Hawisher, G.: and Moran, C. 94, 95, 98
Hawking, S. 53
Hayles, N.K. 28, 154
Haynes, M.: and Anagnostopoulou, K. 122
Heim, M. 161
Herodotus 57
Higher Education Funding Council for England (HEFCE) 117
higher education (HE): design 111–14;

as market 81, 84; policy 109–11; resistance to change 110
history: cultural 57; digital archives 60–3; in digital domain 55–71; disciplining the discipline 56–8; epistemological rules 56–7; ethnography of internet use 65–7; historians online 63–4; historical data 58–60; life online 64–5; as media history 68–9; methodology 65; nature of historical truth 57–8; online history and authenticity 58–9; online journals 63; oral 62; qualification as 57; social 60, 62; teaching with digital technology 67–8; theory 65
Hotmail 119
Howard, T.W. 99–100, 102
human autonomy 21
human capital 15
Hutton Inquiry (2003) 103*n*
hypertext 5, 16–17, 64

Ideas in Cyberspace Education symposium (ICE) 1
identity 2; construction 26; contradictory identities 35; cyberspace 26–41; formation 2, 28, 29, 31, 35; of learners and teachers in cyberspace 26–41; metamorphosis 26; multiplicity 29; social formation 34; teacher 26–41
Ilyenkov, E.V. 160
incorporeal fallacy 152–4
individual autonomy 24
individuals: creation of artificial 171
informational economy 15
Ingraham, B. 3
insouciance 172
Institute of Electrical and Electronics Engineers (IEEE): Learning Technology Standards 73; Learning Technology Support Architecture 77, 78
instruction: components 73
Instructional Design Theory 73
Instructional Management Systems Learning Design Specification 73, 76, 77
Intelligent Tutoring Systems 73
internet: anonymity 105; cafes 65; learning context 105–16; as metaphorical rhizome 124–7
Issroff, K.: and Scanlon, C. 133
Ivanic, R. 93; and Clark, R. 93

Jacoby, R. 124
Jameson, F. 158
JISC (Joint Information Systems
  Committee) 110
Johnson-Eilola, J. 151
Jonassen, D.H.: *et al* 136
Jones, C. 5; and Goodyear, R. 110, 111
Joyce, J. 124
JSTOR (Scholarly Journal Archive) 59,
  60

Kierkegaard, S. 156–7
Kirschner, P.A. 135, 137
knowledge: commodification 76;
  contexts 18; democratisation 18, 23;
  mercantilisation 17; privileging 76;
  social distribution 17–18;
  transmission 22
Knutti, K. 132
Kress, G. 94–5

La Capra, D. 69*n*
Lacan, J. 35; psychoanalysis 58; thought
  29
Lancaster University 106
Land, R. 6; and Bayne, S. 159
Landow, G.: Dickens database 63–4
language: construction 79; oppression
  80
Laurillard, D. 17, 20; *et al* 49, 53
Lave, J.: and Wenger, E. 107, 134
learner/teacher visibility 151
learners: identity 26–41
learning: communities 130–45; failure
  108; from cyberspace 117–29;
  legitimate peripheral participation
  108; motivational approaches 137;
  nests 113; objectives 17; real world
  context 108; relationship with
  learning objects 75–7; situated 135–6;
  social aspect 107; spaces 150–2;
  theories 107–9; warranting and
  credentialing as central university
  function 108
learning materials 4; reusable 82–3
Learning and Teaching Support
  Network (LTSN) 52, 118, 119
lecturers: as material developers 74
lecturing: definition 79
Lewis, C.S. 106–7
Lewis, R. 133
Library of Congress: National Digital
  Library Program (NDLP) 58
Lillis, T. 93

literary criticism 61
Los Angeles 152
Lotus Notes 113
Lyon, D. 171
Lyotard, J.F. 76, 170

McConnell, D. 135
McKenna, C. 4–5
McKie, J. 21
McLuhan, M. 1, 118, 119, 167
Maginot Line 58
managerialism 13
market forces 21
marketisation 21
Marx, G. 172
Marx, K. 151
Marxism 56
Mattingly, G. 49
Mega Universities (Daniel) 19–20
memory 61–2
Merleau-Ponty, M. 154
Merrill, M. 73, 75, 80
metadata 4; automated systems 73;
  claims about 73–4; classification 83;
  community-based 83; cultural
  diversity 78; culturally sensitive 85;
  definition 72–3; feasibility of re-use
  77–8; implications for practice 82–4;
  learning objects 72–3; lecturers' roles
  74–5, 80, 82; marginalisation of
  academics' role 82–4; neutrality 77–8;
  and power 80–2; reconstruction of
  roles 74–5, 80; semantics 84;
  standardisation versus diversity
  78–80; subjectivity of descriptions 83;
  versus educational culture 72–89
Metamorphoses (Ovid) 2–3
Meyrowitz, J. 20
Microsoft PowerPoint 118
Miller, D.: and Slater, D. 65–7
MOCCA framework 141
modernism 151
modernity 28
Monroe, B. 29, 30
MOOs (Multi-User Domain: Object-
  Oriented) 30
Moran, C.: and Hawisher, G. 94, 95, 98
Morris, E. 110
motivational learning approach 136–7
multiculturalism 23
multimedia: costs 52–3
multinational corporations 20
Murphy, D.: *et al* 117
museums 61

mutability 27; of online subject 29–31
mutation 27
MyWashingtonPost.com 47

Nardi, B. 132
nation state: decline 14–15
Neanderthals 51
Neptune 26
net rape 160
network: failure 158; society 13
networked learning 5–6; context 105–16
networked technologies 12
new media 12–13, 22; and pedagogy
    16–18
new technologies: new identities 11–25;
    role and definition 18–22
Nilsson, M.: *et al* 83
Nixon, R. (President) 172
Noble, D. 75, 80–1
non-linearity 16, 17
Norman, D.A. 133

Oliver, M. 4; and Conole, G. 79
online classroom 30
online communication: audience and
    addressivity 91–104
online conferencing 99–100, 102
online learning 28; constructed self 32;
    constructing the *teacher* 36–8;
    dangers 31–3; deceit and perversion
    33–6; internet as metaphorical
    rhizome 124–7; loss of control 32;
    personality split 33; students' self-
    betrayal 31; students'
    metamorphosis 31–5; teachers'
    perspective 36–8
ontology: and technology 118–20
Open University (UK) 15, 19, 80
opportunities: equalizing 19
Oxford University 113, 120, 122

Palmer, R.R. 58
panopticon 19; in surveillance 167–9
part-time workers 17
Pea, R.: and Seely-Brown, J. 135–6
Pearce, L. 96, 102
pedagogical principles 6
pedagogy: and new media theory 16–18;
    Sausurrean 21–2; and technology
    dialectics 117–18
Pelletier, C. 2
performativity 17
Perseus Digital Library 63
Peterson, T.E. 22

Pilkington, R.M. 139; and Grierson, A.
    139; and Ravenscroft, R.M. 138
plagiarism 63, 67
Plato 55
pluralism 21
policy initiatives 5–6
political consciousness 15, 24
Portelli, A.: and Hardy, C. 49
post-colonial world 17
post-modernism 2, 11
post-structuralism 153
Poster, M. 3, 7, 12, 22, 24, 39, 160, 162,
    165, 170, 172, 173
postmodernity 29
Preece, J. 133
presence 155–9
private sphere 20
productivity 18
property rights: extension to
    intellectual matters 17
Prosser, M.: and Trigwell, K. 112
Provenzo, E.F.J. 169, 172
public domain 20, 21
public sphere 20–1

Ranke, L. von 60–1
Ravenscroft, A. 6; and Pilkington, R.M.
    138
RBL (Resource-Based Learning) 74
Readings, B.: university of dissensus
    21–2
reductive functionalism 18
relational approach 112–14
remediation 69
Rheingold, H.R. 156
risk 15, 17, 149–59
Rius-Rui, M. 118
Rosenzweig, R. 58

Salmon, G. 139
Scanlon, C.: and Issroff, K. 133
Schlesinger, A.M. 57: 69*n*
Schwartz, V. 69*n*
Scott, P. 11
Seely-Brown, J.: and Pea, R. 135–6
Sennett, R. 14, 17
sentience 154
shape-shifting 28–9
Shulman, L.S. 127
situated learning 135–6
Slater, D.: and Miller, D. 65–7
Smith, B. 60–1
social distribution: of knowledge 17–18
social learning theory 136–7

society: conflict 23
socio-cultural framework: for cognitive change 140–1
space: reconstitution 15–16
Steiner, P. 105
Stephenson, N. 56
Stone, A.R. 30–1, 153, 154
students: choice of material 75; collaboration 30; distance 113; learning relational theories 107; needs 19; tasks interpretation 113–14; tracking 7, 165–78
superpanopticon 170
surveillance 7; and disciplinary power 7, 165–78; for educational practice 171–2; tutor role 175–6
system designs 139

Tabbi, J. 151
Tapscott, D.: net generation 119, 120
teacher: charisma 155; as gatekeeper 111; identity 26–41; presence 157–8
teacher–student relationship 27
teaching: control 37; self-centred 36–8
technology: as enhancement tool 120; and ontology 118–20; and pedagogy dialectics 117–18
technological determinism 167
technophobia 20
Teesside University 47
television: digital satellite 50; interactive 46; violence 66
Thibault, C. 152
Thicydides 57
Thompson, E.P. 57
Thorpe, M. 76–7
Trigwell, K.: and Ashwin, P. 114; and Prosser, M. 112
Trinidad: internet use ethnography 65–7
truth systems: analogue 56; digital 56–8
Turkle, S. 29, 98–9, 151

uncertainty 17
United Kingdom (UK): Association of Learning Technologies 53; eUniversity 53

university: dissensus 21–2; identity 18; politics 22–4; virtual 20
Usenet: participation 67
Usher, R.: and Edwards, R. 35, 150

veracity 151, 162
Virginia, University of: Center for Digital History 68
virtual audience 4–5
Virtual Jamestown 68
virtual learning environments (VLEs) 5–7, 91, 117, 171; looking backwards with 120–4; managerial efficiency 171–2; student-centred approach 123; student-tracking capabilities 165–7; as transitional objects 128; and web-based writing 99–101
virtual universities 20
visibility 149
Vygotsky, L. 1; dialogue processes to cognitive change 131–2

Walking with Beasts (BBC) 3; critique as academic work 45–54
web-based writing: and virtual learning environments (VLEs) 99–101
WebCT: VLE surveillance 65–6, 175
WebLearn: VLE 122
Wegerif, R. 150
Wenger, E. 76, 82, 83, 134, 135; and Lave, J. 107, 134
White, H. 57
Whitman, W. 171–2
Wieseler, W. 81
Wiley, D. 3, 72, 73
William Blake Archive 63
Wilson, S. 30
women 17, 60, 158
Woolley, B. 124, 126
working-class 60

Xanadu: global hypertext library 63

zone of proximal development (ZPD) 131–2